A COMMENTARY ON THE

Gospel

OF

John

D1316422

A COMMENTARY ON THE

Gospel

OF

John

Rev. Albert Kirk
Robert E. Obach

PAULIST PRESS
New York/Ramsey/Toronto

Nihil Obstat: Most Rev. Carroll T. Dozier, D.D.
       Bishop of Memphis

Imprimatur: Most Rev. Carroll T. Dozier, D.D.
       Bishop of Memphis

Date: January 31, 1979

The Publisher gratefully acknowledges:

Scripture text © copyright American Bible Society 1966, 1971, 1976 used with permission.

Scripture and art from *GOOD NEWS BIBLE FOR MODERN MAN,* American Bible Society, used with permission.

Library of Congress
Catalog Card Number: 80-84505

ISBN: 0-8091-2346-0

Published by Paulist Press
545 Island Road, Ramsey, N.J. 07446

Printed and bound in the
United States of America

Contents

SAMPLE SCHEDULES FOR
THE STUDY OF JOHN'S GOSPEL

WEEK	14 WEEK STUDY	11 WEEK STUDY	8 WEEK STUDY
1	John 1:1-51	John 1:1-51	John 1:1 - 2:25
2	John 2:1 - 3:36	John 2:1 - 3:36	John 3:1 - 5:29
3	John 4:1 - 5:30	John 4:1 - 5:30	John 5:30 - 7:52
4	John 5:31 - 6:71	John 5:31 - 6:71	John 8:1 - 10:42
5	John 7:1 - 8:59	John 7:1 - 8:59	John 11:1 - 13:30
6	John 9:1 - 10:21	John 9:1 - 10:42	John 13:31 - 16:33
7	John 10:22 - 11:57	John 11:1 - 12:50	John 17:1 - 19:42
8	John 12:1 - 13:30	John 13:1 - 14:31	John 20:1 - 21:25
9	John 13:31 - 14:31	John 15:1 - 17:26	
10	John 15:1 - 16:33	John 18:1 - 19:42	
11	John 17:1 - 18:27	John 20:1 - 21:25	
12	John 18:28 - 19:37		
13	John 19:38 - 20:21		
14	John 21:1-25		

Each of these suggested schedules can be modified in order to harmonize better with the liturgical calendar.

Preface

We are pleased to share our diocesan study of John with other believers in the United States. In gathering around the Word of God, we discovered anew the life that it promises. Many of us experienced a deeper relationship with one another and with Jesus, the Master Teacher.

Christians have always given the Fourth Gospel a special place in their faith and devotion. Inspired by God's spirit with a catechetical genius, John was given the title "The Theologian" by believers in the early centuries.

In John we encounter the most profound understanding of Christ contained in the Scriptures. This is, after all, what we seek as we reflect on the Gospel. It is not enough to be content with "the facts," with what Our Lord did and said. The Spirit has been given to us so that we may understand the significance of the words and deeds of Jesus. The same Spirit will kindle in us the desire both to know and to live the meaning of those same words and deeds.

When Clement of Alexandria, one of the Fathers of the Church, called John the "spiritual Gospel," it seems that he was referring to the ability of the Fourth Gospel to plumb the depths of meaning in the life, death and glorification of Jesus of Nazareth. John was the last of the evangelists to write. Thus he brings us the gift of a long period of reflection (his own and that of the Christian community) on the mystery of Christ.

John wrote in the last decade of the first century, A.D., probably around the year 100. How can it be that a document written some 70 years after the Ascension can put us so closely in touch with the person of Jesus? The Fourth Gospel contains the answer. Before his death Jesus promised to send the Spirit of Truth in order to bring to the minds of the disciples all that Jesus had said to them.

In the Fourth Gospel Jesus speaks, as it were, from a timeless perspective. He addresses his original disciples on the shores of the Sea of Galilee and while seated around the table of the Last Supper. He also addresses those who believe even though they have never seen or heard him during the years of his earthly ministry. Through the working of the Holy Spirit, Jesus addresses not only those Christians living at the end of the first century but also the disciples of every generation. John declares that what Jesus said and did during his public ministry are signs of present realities that are experienced now, in the Church. The Fourth Gospel is telling us this: "In your life as the disciples of Jesus, as you celebrate the liturgy and hear the Word of God and receive the sacraments, you walk with the Master along the same paths as the original disciples did. Your inability to see Jesus in the flesh is no loss at all; you 'see' him by faith and you 'know' him in the worship and sacraments of the Church. In fact, you are more privileged than the first disciples. They did not really understand Jesus until after the Resurrection of Jesus and the coming of the Spirit at Pentecost. The same Spirit who inspired them to proclaim Jesus as the Lord of all creation is now at work in your hearts as you prayerfully reflect on these pages."

The key, then, for the most rewarding use of this commentary is prayerful reflection on the text of the Gospel. It is there that the Word of God is given. The commentary material will serve as an aid and a guide to the text of the Fourth Gospel. The Commentary will be useful only to the extent that it enables you to appreciate the Gospel more deeply.

In many sections we have provided an Overview to the passage. This contains material which will help you in an initial reading of the passage. Then we suggest that you read the commentary pages. At this point you are prepared to study the passage. Thus, each Gospel passage will be read at least twice: after the overview, and during (or after) your reading of the commentary.

Such study is joyful, but it is also hard work. It is difficult to do if you are rushed or surrounded by a dozen distractions. Ask the Lord to help you find the time to devote to his Word each week. Then, when you arrive at your study group session, you will bring something unique to share with the other participants. In faith we know that Jesus is waiting for us to come to him through the Gospel. He has things to say to each of us, inspiring insights to give us. Some of these will be personal to you; some you will want to share with your group.

We have included a Reflection section after many of the passages. These were thoughts and applications which were suggested to us by the Word of God. These reflections may provide additional insights for your group sharing. However, as you interact with the Word of God, you will discover your own reflections, reflections built upon the things which the Lord speaks to your heart.

Regarding the time required, the program is flexible. Each group should decide how long it wishes to spend and then, consulting the table on page six, assign the necessary sections for each week. Each participant may wish to divide the weekly verses into a daily study program, or accomplish the task in one sitting. The Jewish tradition has always considered the evening hours as especially suited for the study of God's Word. Perhaps members of a group might agree to put aside an evening's television in order to prepare for the group session.

We are grateful to the American Bible Society for permission to use their text, drawings and maps. The text is from their Today's English Version Bible-Old Testament: copyright © American Bible Society 1976, New Testament: copyright © American Bible Society 1966, 1971, 1976. Unless otherwise noted, all quotations from the Scriptures are from this translation.

We have benefitted greatly from the loving scholarship of Father Raymond Brown, whose two volume commentary on the

Fourth Gospel (Anchor Bible) has been our *vade mecum,* and of Father Bruce Vawter, whose lectures and conversation during his February visit encouraged us.

We would like to express our gratitude to all of those whose prayers, encouragement and assistance have created this volume: Bishop Carroll Dozier; our co-workers, Sister Barbara Spencer and Sister Julienne Curry; our typist, Sandy Henderson; our layout artists, Rose Mary Obach and Anne Powell; and our proofreaders, Sister Helen Morrison, Rozanne Pera and Peggy Burdick.

Reverend Albert Kirk
Pastor, Religious Educator
Diocese of Memphis

Robert E. Obach
Coordinator, Adult Education

Chapter One

THE PROLOGUE

OVERVIEW. The prologue of the Gospel according to John has a privileged place in the biblical writings. It may well be the most beautiful, the most profound, the most beloved passage in the Christian Scriptures. The prayerful reflection of believers will never exhaust the power and meaning of these few verses. Many passages in John require that we linger over them, pondering their significance. This passage, above all, invites us to study it in depth, and to return to it often as we move through the Gospel.

Parts of the prologue, probably verses 1–5, 10–12, 14 and 16, take the form of a hymn. Some translations place these verses in poetic form. Ancient poetry does not rhyme but relies on rhythm for its beauty. Such poetry also links key words from line to line. (The *Good News* translation loses something of this flavor because it chose to bring out the meaning for contemporary readers rather than to translate the original Greek literally.) In the literal translation which follows, notice how the lines are linked by the underlined words.

In the beginning was the <u>Word</u>;
the <u>Word</u> *was in* <u>God's</u> *presence,*
and the <u>Word</u> *was* <u>God</u>.

He was present with <u>God</u> in the beginning.
Through him all <u>things</u> came into being,
and apart from him not a <u>thing</u> came to be.
That which had come to be in him was <u>life</u>,
and this <u>life</u> was the <u>light</u> of men.
The <u>light</u> shines on in the <u>darkness</u>,
for the <u>darkness</u> did not overcome it.

The hymn was probably already being sung in the Church's liturgy before it was incorporated into the Gospel. (Other examples of hymns which have been incorporated into the Christian Scriptures can be found in Philippians 2:6–11 and Colossians 1:15–20.) Most agree that the hymn was not composed by the evangelist himself; however it may well have emerged from the Christian community of which John was a part and for whom he wrote his account of the Good News. One indication of this is the number of themes touched upon in the prologue which will be developed in the body of the Gospel. Music lovers might view the prologue as an overture; it not only begins the work but prepares the reader for the themes to follow. It serves to whet our appetite and provides us with a brief summary of all that the evangelist wants to share with us.

It is interesting to compare John's beginning with that of the other evangelists. Mark's account of the Gospel begins with the public ministry of Jesus, when he was almost thirty years old. Luke and Matthew begin their accounts with the events immediately preceding the birth of Jesus. John greatly enlarges the time perspective. In fact, he takes us back to a point before time itself began. He speaks of the pre-existence of the Word with God, long before the Word took flesh in Jesus of Nazareth.

John speaks of the presence of the Word in creation and in human history. Yet, he affirms, the Word also transcends history. In knowing Jesus of Nazareth we begin to know something of the inner life, the Trinitarian life of God. In Luke's account of the annunciation to Mary we catch a glimpse of this Trinitarian life; John hands on to us a later and more mature stage of Christian reflection on the mystery of God's presence in Jesus Christ.

To appreciate the prologue most fully, we will need to read be-

tween the lines and notice the many references to the Jewish
Scriptures. In particular, the prologue draws our attention to the
epochal first chapters of Genesis. As we study the first eight
verses, we will want to hear the echoes of the creation of the
world, of the primal sin of humankind and of the gracious promise of redemption. The themes of verses 14–18 remind us of the
formative events of the book of Exodus, especially chapters 19–
40. Finally, the prologue (and the entire Gospel) has been influ-
enced by the Wisdom literature of Israel, which includes the
Psalms, the Proverbs, and the books of Job, Wisdom and Sirach.
Particularly we want to notice the picture of God's Wisdom
which these books present. Examine these texts:

"The Lord begot me, the first born of his ways,
  the forerunner of his prodigies of long ago;
From of old I was poured forth,
  at the first, before the earth.
When there were no depths I was brought forth,
  when there were no fountains or springs of water. . . .

When he established the heavens I was there . . .
When he set for the sea its limit . . .
Then was I beside him as his craftsman,
  and I was his delight day by day,
Playing before him all the while . . ." (Proverbs, 8:21–30, *New
American Bible*).

"For she is an aura of the might of God
  and a pure effusion of the glory of the Almighty;
  therefore nought that is sullied enters into her.
For she is the refulgence of eternal light,
  the spotless mirror of the power of God,
  the image of his goodness" (Wisdom, 7:25–26, *New American
Bible*).

These texts summarize the teaching of the Wisdom literature.
We hear of God's Wisdom existing in the beginning with God,
coming forth from him in creation, dwelling among the Chosen
People, blessing those who seek her. In some passages she is spo-

ken of more as a person than as a thing. While John does not specifically call Jesus the Wisdom of God, we cannot doubt that this biblical portrait of Wisdom helped shape the beautiful teaching of his prologue.

READ 1:1–18

COMMENTARY: We are accustomed to a more familiar translation of the opening words of the Fourth Gospel, "In the beginning was the Word." Such a translation brings to mind the opening words of Genesis, "In the beginning. . . . " The author thus alerts us to the new creation, to the new beginning that is possible in Jesus Christ. Our *Good News* translation skillfully reveals another aspect of the first verse. The Word did not come into being with the moment of creation; the Word already existed before anything created came to be.

Verse 1 uses the verb "to be" three times, each with a slightly different meaning. As the initial use speaks of the Word's preexistence, the second—"he was with God"—indicates relationship. The Greek here is dynamic; the Word dwells with God, is fully present with him. The Word is at home with God. In its final affirmation verse 1 describes the Word as "the same as God." The Greek text here proclaims the divinity of the Word, while avoiding any suggestion that there is a second God, or that the Word can be personally identified with the Father. When the author concludes his account with Thomas' cry of faith, "My Lord and my God!" (20:28), he probably intends to remind us of this initial verse. It is crucially important to him that believers have an accurate and complete understanding of the identity of Jesus of Nazareth.

The title "Word" (*logos* in Greek) is a familiar one to us, even though it is not used very often in the Christian Scriptures outside of this prologue. It would also have been very familiar to John's readers, whether Jewish or Greek. The Greek reader would have encountered *logos* frequently in philosophical and theological writings. Sometimes it meant the eternal principle of order in the universe; at other times it referred to that which gives meaning and plan to the universe, or to the intermediary between God and his creation.

For the Jewish reader, God's word was that by which he expressed himself. His word brings forth and sustains life.

The first two verses draw us into a timeless perspective. With verses 3–5 we arrive at the history of the creation. The Word is not called here the Creator. Yet, contrary to our usual separation of the works of the divine Persons (the Father creating, the Son redeeming and the Spirit sanctifying), the evangelist pictures the Word as very active in the work of creation. The text is very emphatic: "Through him God made all things; not one thing in all creation was made without him. The Word was the source of life . . . " (1:3–4). We might understand this in two ways. First, the Word effects God's purpose; he is God's agent in bringing all things into being. Here we catch a strong resonance of the Hebrew concept of God's creative word. The second dimension links us with Greek thought, where the *logos* was understood as the mind of God or the plan of the universe. The Word, John affirms, is the model or the example which the Father uses in his creative work. What a profound truth is communicated in these simple words of the prologue! God's purpose in creation is not an "it," an idea, but a living person. The result is this: we cannot understand the meaning and end of creation outside the Incarnation of God's Word, that is, separate from Jesus of Nazareth.

The "life" of verse 4 probably means more than simple existence. It indicates some kind of sharing in the being of God. The Word is the source not only of physical life but also of eternal life. In other words it is eternal life which has come-to-be especially in the Word; and "this life brought light to men" (1:4). While the Word imparts physical life to the entire creation, he shares eternal life with humankind.

Life and light are frequently paired in the Jewish Scriptures. A typical example can be found in Psalm 36:9:

> *You are the source of all life,*
> *and because of your light we see the light.*

If we remember that Psalm 119:105—"Your word is a lamp to guide me and a light for my path"—was understood by the rabbis to refer to the Torah, or Law of God, we can appreciate what the evangelist is telling us. In the Word is revealed God's purpose, his plan for human life. This light however "shines in the darkness" (1:5). Darkness is the enemy of this light. Darkness is John's symbolic way of describing that which is set in opposition to God and his plan. In the fall of humanity, the original sin, the darkness attempted to quench the light. Yet the light of the Word cannot be quenched, even by the most intense opposition of his creation. The early Church interpreted the text of Genesis 3:15 (the woman's offspring would someday crush the biting head of the snake with their heel) as the first promise of the redemption which would come in Christ. At the very moment of the entrance of darkness into human history, God promises a renewal of the light. The light shines on in the hope of redemption.

In verses 6-9 the evangelist interrupts the hymn to the Word in order to discuss the preparatory role of John the Baptist. The Synoptic evangelists (Matthew, Mark and Luke) also note the important role of the "man named John." He is sent by God himself, an intrinsic part of the divine plan. His role?—"to tell people about the light" (1:7, see also 1:8, 23, 29-34, 3:28-30). The Greek word here is *martyria*, witness or testimony. This is the root of our word "martyr," a fact which reminds us that witnessing to the light can be costly. While the Synoptic Gospels use martyria only twice, the fourth evangelist speaks of witness over thirty times.

The Baptist proclaims the light so that all might believe and come to share in the eternal life which the Word makes available (1:7 and 1:4). This is the same purpose for which the evangelist has composed his account of the Good News. So he tells us in his concluding words:

> *These have been written that you may believe that Jesus is the*
> *Messiah, the Son of God, and that through this faith you may*
> *have life in his name* (20:31).

In verse 8 we catch a glimpse of one of the many "audiences" of John's Gospel. As we will see, the evangelist dialogues not only with the faithful believers of his own community, but with other groups as well. One of these groups is a community of the Baptist's disciples who have not accepted Jesus. Perhaps they thought of the Baptist as himself the promised light. Both in this chapter and in chapter three the evangelist clearly teaches the subordinate and preparatory role of John.

In 5:35 Jesus explains that John was "like a lamp, burning and shining." Because God was with him, it is not surprising that some people mistook John for the light. (In 1:20 we have an indication that some were proclaiming John as the Messiah.) The author wants to make it clear to both his own community and to the followers of John the Baptist: the real light, the genuine light promised by God, is the Word.

The expectation of a messianic light is very strong in the writings of Isaiah. For example:

> *The people who walked in darkness*
> *have seen a great light.*
> *They lived in a land of shadows,*
> *but now light is shining on them (9:2).*

> *Arise, Jerusalem, and shine like the sun;*
> *The glory of the Lord is shining on you!*
> *Other nations will be covered by darkness,*
> *But on you the light of the Lord will shine;*
> *The brightness of his presence will be with you (60:1–2).*

The first text is familiar to us as the beginning lines of the beautiful prophecy about David's coming successor, the child who will be born for God's people, the one who will be called Wonderful Counselor, Mighty God, Eternal Father and Prince of Peace. In the second text we note three themes which link Isaiah's prophecy with John's prologue: (1) Isaiah places the arrival of the light in the context of the darkness of the world; (2) he links the light with the glory of the Lord, which we shall see in verse 14; and (3) he notes that the light is not for Israel alone. All nations will be drawn to Jerusalem, there to share in God's light. In the same way, John teaches us, the light is for all.

The author has now prepared us for the entrance of the Word into the world (1:10–14). (We might note that scholars differ in interpreting the precise point in which the prologue begins to speak of the Incarnation. Some place it at verses 4–5; others think that the author speaks only of the period before Christ until verse 14.) Throughout the Gospel John uses the word "world" in several senses, two of which are evident in verse 10. God has made the world (the creation; all things which had come to be) through the Word, yet the world (creation as hostile to God, as opposed to his plan) refused him the trust and love which he deserved.

In verse 11 John makes more specific the Word's claim on his creation. Thus, the Word came to "his own country," that is, to his heritage, Israel, to the Promised Land. His "own people," however, did not receive him. We have a poignant reminder of the words of Yahweh to Israel at Mount Sinai:

> *"Now, if you will obey me and keep my covenant, you will be my own people. The whole earth is mine, but you will be my chosen people, a people dedicated to me alone, and you will serve me as priests"* (Exodus 19:5–6).

Yet some did welcome the Word; these he empowered (a pure gift, neither deserved nor earned) to become God's children (1:12). John frequently approaches the work of creation/redemption from the point of view of the Word. Earlier in the prologue he spoke of the Word's role in the creation of all things. Now he proclaims the role of the Incarnate Word in our redemption. The same mystery can also be approached from the viewpoint of the Father. In the First Epistle of John, a companion work to the Gospel, John declares:

> *See how much the Father has loved us! His love is so great that we are called God's children—and so, in fact, we are. This is why the world does not know us: it has not known God* (1 John 3:1).

Verses 11 and 12 aptly summarize the entire Gospel. In the first twelve chapters (The Book of Signs) the author describes the coming of the Word to his own land and people. Gradually we see their resistance and hostility deepen, until the moment of that fateful Passover celebration in Jerusalem. Just as we saw a key turning point in Matthew 13:36, when Jesus turned away from the crowds and began to instruct the disciples, so also John opens the second half of his account (The Book of Glory) with a decisive verse:

> *It was now the day before the Feast of Passover. Jesus knew that his hour had come for him to leave this world and go to the Father. He had always loved those who were his own in the world, and he loved them to the very end* (13:1).

In the remainder of the Gospel Jesus will gather "his own" around him, those who were the first to receive the gift of becoming God's children, being "fathered" not by natural means (which could transmit earthly/natural life but not heavenly/eternal life) but by the Father himself.

At this point we arrive at the climactic moment of the prologue:

> *The Word became a human being and, full of grace and truth, lived among us. We saw his glory, the glory which he received as the Father's only Son* (1:14).

If verses 11 and 12 summarize the Fourth Gospel, verse 14 summarizes the entire history of salvation. The Word who dwelt from all eternity with the Father, through whom all creation came into being, the Word who had shone upon Israel through the gifts of the Torah and the prophets, this very Word now enters history in person, now becomes fully human. Notice the strong parallels with verse 1:

Verse 1	Verse 14
The Word existed	The Word became
The Word dwelt with God	The Word dwells with us
The Word was the same as God	The Word became what we are

John contrasts the eternal being of the Word at God's side with the temporal becoming of the Word in history. Let us examine the five affirmations which this verse makes.

1. The Word became fully human. John uses strongly realistic language in speaking of the Incarnation. For "human being" he chose the Greek word *sarx,* which describes human nature in its concrete, fallen state. The chief desire of Greek religious thinkers was to escape from the material world (which they identified with sinfulness) into a pure and heavenly world. There may have been teachers in John's day who were interpreting the Christian message in this erroneous way. Perhaps they were teaching that Jesus was just the *appearance* of God in human flesh.

The evangelist may have been replying to them when he teaches that the divine Word became "flesh." The author of the First Epistle of John also struggled with this kind of heresy:

> *This is how you can recognize God's Spirit: every spirit that acknowledges Jesus Christ come in the flesh [sarx] belongs to God, while every spirit that fails to acknowledge him does not belong to God* (1 John 4:2–3, *New American Bible*).

The doctrine that God has become a human being would not only have been shocking to the Greek mind. To use a contemporary expression, it would have also boggled the minds of Jew-

ish believers. The entire Jewish tradition untiringly described the
majesty of God as that which is totally different from human experience. The same may be said about the eternal nature of his
word.

No wonder that faithful Jewish people found it difficult to
comprehend what God was doing in Jesus of Nazareth! Even two
thousand years later the mystery of the Incarnation of the Word
defies human understanding. The Word became one with us in
everything except sin (see Hebrews 4:15). He is not just an instru-
ment of God's activity or a fleeting appearance of God in human
form. He has taken on our human nature, not the perfect human
nature of Eden's garden, but the fallen nature which knows pain
and sorrow and disappointment.

**2. The Word has become the new place where God meets
his people.** The innocent looking phrase "lived among us" is a
good example of "theological shorthand." For a Jewish reader the
Greek *skenoun,* "lived" or "dwelt" (literally, "pitched a tent"),
would immediately bring to mind those texts in Exodus which
describe the sacred Tent of God's presence. We will look at two
of these:

> *The Lord said to Moses . . . "The people must make a sacred
> Tent for me, so that I may live among them"* (Exodus 25:1–8).

> *Whenever the people of Israel set up camp, Moses would take the
> sacred Tent and put it up some distance outside the camp. It was
> called the Tent of the Lord's presence, and anyone who wanted to
> consult the Lord would go out to it* (Exodus 33:7).

Thus the Tent or the Tabernacle was the site, the localization
of God's presence with his people. We see often in the prophetic
writings a longing for a more perfect "tenting" of Yahweh with
Israel (see Joel 3:17–21 and Zechariah 2:10). John is affirming that
the humanity of Jesus Christ is the new sacred Tent, the new
meeting place of Yahweh with his people.

**3. The Word is the fulfillment of all God's Covenant prom-
ises.** In the phrase "full of grace and truth" we have another ex-

ample of theological shorthand. Grace and truth express the chief characteristics of the Covenant God of Israel. Grace proclaims God's loving kindness to Israel. He chose her without any merit on her part. He continually forgave her unfaithfulness. Grace speaks of God's love, his kindness, his unconditional mercy. Truth is also a Covenant characteristic. The opposite of biblical "truth" is not falsehood but unfaithfulness. In spite of Israel's sins, Yahweh is always faithful to his people. He never takes back his promises or denies his mercy. A beautiful passage in Exodus expresses all these things:

> *The Lord then passed in front of him [Moses] and called out, "I, the Lord, am a God who is full of compassion and pity, who is not easily angered and who shows great love and faithfulness"* (Exodus 34:6; see also Psalms 25:10 and 86:15).

John is proclaiming that Jesus makes present Yahweh's faithfulness and loving kindness. In sending his Son, God is fulfilling all his promises to Israel. In Jesus the Covenant relationship of Yahweh and Israel exceeds all human expectations.

In Hebrew the word "Amen" is related to God's truth/faithfulness. To say Amen is to say, "God is indeed faithful to his promises." In a passage in Second Corinthians, Paul shows that he too understands Jesus as the fulfillment of the Covenant:

> *As God keeps his word, I declare that my word to you is not "yes" one minute and "no" the next. Jesus Christ . . . was not alternately "yes" and "no"; he was never anything but "yes." Whatever promises God has made have been fulfilled in him; therefore it is through him that we address our Amen to God when we worship together* (1:18–20).

4. As we have seen, the striking newness of these affirmations must have astounded both Jewish and Greek peoples. Each group must have cried out, "How can you say these things?" The response of the apostolic community shapes the fourth affirmation of verse 14. The proof that these things are true is this: *in Jesus Christ we have seen God's own glory!* In the Hebrew Scriptures glory expresses the manifestation of God's presence. It is the way in which he becomes "visible." When Moses went up to meet the Lord on Mount Sinai, we are told that a cloud covered it. "The dazzling light [glory] of the Lord's presence came down on the mountain. To the Israelites the light looked like a fire burning on top of the mountain" (Exodus 24:16–17). There is a close connection of God's glory and the Tent of meeting. Let us examine yet another text from Exodus:

> *Then the cloud covered the Tent and the dazzling light [glory] of the Lord's presence filled it. Because of this, Moses could not go into the Tent. The Israelites moved their camp to another place only when the cloud lifted from the Tent. . . . During all their wanderings they could see the cloud of the Lord's presence over the Tent during the day and a fire burning above it during the night* (Exodus 40:34–40).

To Israel God made known his presence in a visible way, through a cloud, a dazzling light, a burning fire. Though his presence was awesome and sometimes forbidding—in Exodus 40:35 Moses was unable to enter the Tent—still, it was an act of his gracious love, a reminder of his desire to be close to his people. Now, John affirms, God's glory is not seen in a cloud or in a fire. It has become visible in the very person of Jesus!

Thus in John, the affirmation, "we saw his glory," refers to the entire life and ministry of the Incarnate Word. But the supreme event of Jesus' glory is the Paschal event—his death, resurrection and return to the Father. Seeing the glory of Jesus began with physical vision, but it required the gift of God. As John himself says in 6:44: "No one can come to me unless the Father who sent me draws him to me." In a parallel tradition, Paul gives witness to the glory of the Incarnate Word:

> *The God who said, "Out of darkness the light shall shine!" is the same God who made his light shine in our hearts, to bring us the knowledge of God's glory shining in the face of Christ"* (2 Corinthians 4:6).

5. Jesus is unique. The glory of the Incarnate Word is his due, his connatural possession, since he is "the Father's only Son." The Greek word which we translate into English as "only" literally means "one-of-a-kind." On several occasions the Hebrew Scriptures called an individual (e.g., the king or the faithful Israelite) a son of God. John affirms that Jesus is a Son of God of a different order. He is unique.

Many scholars consider verse 16 as part of the Christian hymn which the evangelist uses to begin his account. Verses 17 and 18 are then understood as explanatory comments of the evangelist. As the loving-kindness ("grace") of Yahweh was poured out upon his people, so the fullness of the grace of the Incarnate Word overflows to those who believe in him. From his superabundant grace we all (not only the apostolic witnesses but also the entire community of believers) have received, "one blessing after another" (1:16). This phrase can mean that Yahweh's Covenant-love, which was pledged to his Chosen People on Sinai, is now pledged to all by his Covenant-love in Jesus.

If we accept this meaning, then verse 17 simply repeats verse 16 in different words. God's love under the Sinai Covenant was expressed in the gift of the Law, which came through Moses. The supreme love of God is now expressed in the grace and truth (the loving-kindness and constant faithfulness of verse 14) present in Jesus Christ. Jesus is not merely another in a series of prophets and leaders. In him begins a new order which surpasses all that went before.

Verse 18 continues the contrast between Moses and Jesus. The text of Exodus 33:19–23 is clearly part of the background here. During a conversation with God, Moses asks to see the divine glory.

The Lord answered, "I will make all my splendor pass before you and in your presence I will pronounce my sacred name. I am the Lord, and I show compassion and pity on those I choose. I will not let you see my face, because no one can see me and stay alive, but here is a place beside me where you can stand on a rock. When the dazzling light of my presence passes by, I will put you in an opening in the rock and cover you with my hand until I

*have passed by. Then I will take my hand away, and you will
see my back, but not my face."*

Clearly the evangelist is contrasting Moses' inability to see God
with the intimate vision of the "only Son, who is the same as
God and is at the Father's side." The Son has not only seen the
Father; according to the literal meaning of the Greek text he "exists unto the bosom of the Father." (This is a good example of the
difficulty of translating one language into the grammar and
thought patterns of another. It helps us understand why there are
so many current translations of the Scriptures. For there is not
just one correct way in which a particular verse of the Scriptures
must be translated. To provide only the literal translation, as
above, could mislead many contemporary readers. To depart sig-
nificantly from the literal meaning risks allowing the translation
to become a paraphrase. For example, the *Revised Standard* translation remains very close to the original Greek; while the *New Testament in Modern English* and *The Living Bible* are paraphrases. *Today's
English Version,* which we have chosen for our study program,
strikes a good balance between the two approaches.)

The phrase "exists unto the bosom of the Father" conveys two
things: (1) the relationship of the Son with the Father is dynamic
and vital; and (2) it is a union of love and affection. While Moses,
standing at a distance, sees Yahweh's back, the only Son dwells
at his side.

The prologue is full of good news for believers. The Word, we
have been told, shines in the darkness of our world, empowers
believers to become children of God, dwells among us as the fulfillment of God's Covenant promises and blesses us far more
abundantly than the people of the Sinai Covenant were graced.
John concludes his prologue with a final piece of good news. The
intimate friendship of the Son with his Father is not something
removed from us, existing in a different world than our own. No,
the Son reveals the Father to those who believe in him. As the
Israelites benefitted from Moses' friendship with God (see Exodus, chapters 24 and 32–34), how much more do Christians benefit from the relationship of Jesus with God!

Although we do not "see" God in this life, the mystery of Jesus is this: in seeing him we see the Father (14:9). By choosing to open his Gospel with the title, "Word," John emphasizes that Jesus comes to reveal the Father. Jesus does not reveal the Father as Moses or Isaiah did, passing on a message from God to the people. Jesus embodies that revelation in his person; he *is* the revelation of the Father!

The Word does not take on a new "duty" at the moment of the Incarnation. No, the Word is with God from the beginning. Already at the beginning, the Word is God's self-expression. From the beginning, within the Trinitarian life, the role of the Word is to reveal the Father (1:1). When the Father "decides" to bring into being a universe, the Word is his artisan, the agent through which he expresses himself (1:3–4). When the original sin obscured the beauty of his gift, the Father's Word shone in the darkness, a light of hope and promise (1:4–5). Finally, and most wonderfully, the Father expressed himself in the gift of the Word made flesh (1:11–14). In his humanity Jesus of Nazareth made known the Father's glory, his loving-kindness, his faithfulness (1:14).

Without exaggeration it can be said that the rest of John's Gospel will simply make clear how the Father revealed himself in the ministry, death and glorification of Jesus. Little wonder that the prologue of the Gospel has been a font of Christian contemplation and theological reflection since its appearance. The prologue is brief, only 252 words in the Greek text. Yet it spans time and eternity. It illuminates for us both the eternal design of God and the history of his Covenant-love in Jesus Christ.

REFLECTION. If we compare the understanding of the Christian mystery in the Synoptic Gospels with that in John, it is easy to see a pattern of growth. The understanding of who Jesus Christ was and the comprehension of his message did not emerge fully developed on the day of the resurrection, nor even on the day of Pentecost. The apostolic community grew in its understanding of the ministry, death and resurrection of Christ, a growth which is evident in the biblical writings.

Christian belief often runs ahead of the ability to express that belief in human language. From the beginning the Church believed in the divinity of Jesus of Nazareth. But the ability to correlate this belief with the biblical assertion that there could not be two divine beings required a long process of development. The ability to express this "incredible" mystery in precise language (Church doctrine) came only at the end of this process.

When we read Scripture we tend to understand it in concepts and language which were developed sometimes centuries later. John often speaks about the mystery of the Trinity, for example; yet he uses the more poetic, figurative language of Scripture rather than the philosophical, abstract doctrinal language with which we are familiar. In the Commentary sections we will try to use a more biblical language. The reflection sections will provide us with the freedom to link the biblical teaching with the doctrinal language which developed later.

We do not intend to establish a dichotomy between biblical and doctrinal teaching. Each is useful, indeed essential to the mission of the Church. Scripture is the continuing source of our spiritual life. It arouses in us deep feeling and growing commitment to Jesus and to his will. Yet the language of Scripture, because it is metaphorical, can be misunderstood. Inaccurate interpretations arise (later branded heresies), and the community of believers must defend the traditional faith. Thus doctrinal language arises as a protection, as a safeguard against false understandings of Scripture. Key doctrines are gathered together into the great Creeds.

As an example of what we are saying, compare the Apostles' Creed, the Nicene Creed and the Athanasian Creed. As each grows longer than its predecessor, its language becomes more philosophical, more precise. Yet each grows more difficult to apply to daily life.

Thus we approach Scripture from the vantage point of the highly developed doctrinal language of the Church. This language is a gift of the Spirit no less than the Scripture itself. Yet we should approach Scripture not just to find there our favorite doctrines but especially to allow it to speak to us in a fresh way. For we, too, are part of the continuing growth in understanding. It is logical that we should understand the mystery of Christ even better than our ancestors, for we stand on their shoulders. We benefit from two thousand years of prayerful reflection on and study of God's Word. In the words of Vatican Council II:

> *This tradition which comes from the apostles develops in the Church with the help of the Holy Spirit. For there is a growth in the understanding of the realities and the words which have been handed down. This happens through the contemplation and study made by believers, who treasure these things in their hearts (cf. Luke 2:19,51), through the intimate understanding of spiritual things they experience, and through the preaching of those who have received through episcopal succession the sure gift of truth. For, as the centuries succeed one another, the Church constantly moves forward toward the fullness of divine truth until the words of God reach their complete fulfillment in her (Dogmatic Constitution on Divine Revelation, #8).*

THE WITNESS OF JOHN THE BAPTIST

OVERVIEW. Acknowledging that the Prologue (1:1–18) has been added after the major part of the Fourth Gospel was written, we can see that John opened his account of the Good News in the same way in which Mark began. Both Mark and John start with the activity of John the Baptist. But the reader soon notices many differences in how the Baptist is portrayed.

Mark presents the Baptist as a prophet possessing both his own role, that of preparing the people for God's final intervention in human history, and his own message. "Turn away from your sins and be baptized and God will forgive your sins" (Mark 1:4). John, however, relates nothing of the Baptist's message of repentance. The prophetic role of the Baptist is not mentioned. The author of the Fourth Gospel gives to the Baptist one purpose: bearing witness to Jesus.

As you read the text of 1:19–51 you will see that the author has divided this section into a series of four days. The first two days deal with the witness of John the Baptist. The third and fourth days deal with Jesus as he calls disciples to follow him. At first glance it seems that the Baptist is the focus of the first two days and Jesus is the focus of the last two days. Upon closer look, we see that Jesus is the focal point of everything that takes place. The Baptist claims no title for himself. He is not the Messiah; he is not Elijah; he is not "the prophet." He has a single task: to witness to Jesus. He even sends his own disciples to follow the "Lamb of God" (1:35).

Questions and answers play an important role in the Fourth Gospel. From the testimony of the Baptist, to the trial of Jesus, we will find interrogations, the calling of witnesses, references to judgment, and the language of prosecution and defense. The great trial is one of John's key themes. At times it seems as if the forces hostile toward Jesus were putting him on trial. However, according to John's view, the ultimate outcome of Jesus' coming is that all people are either saved or sentence themselves according to their acceptance or rejection of the truth Jesus speaks to the world.

READ 1:19–34

COMMENTARY. When the Jewish authorities ask the Baptist, "Who are you?" (1:19), the great trial of Jesus begins. The *Jerusalem Bible* translation, "This is how John appeared as a witness" (1:19), is a more accurate indication of the evangelist's intention to present the Baptist as the first witness called to testify. John willingly submits to the interrogation. The first words he speaks are a denial: "I am not the Messiah" (1:20). This is the first of three denials: the Baptist is neither Messiah, nor Elijah, nor the Prophet (1:20–21). By piecing together the information given in the Christian Scriptures, we can conclude that John the Baptist presented the first century believers with a dilemma. On the one hand, John had baptized Jesus. There was no denying that the Baptist had a place in God's plan of salvation. On the other hand, it was difficult for the early Church to give the Baptist a major role in salvation history because the major role belonged to Jesus and Jesus alone.

Furthermore, there were the followers of John the Baptist to contend with. A community of the Baptist's disciples continued to exist long after his death, perhaps even into the third century.

The people of Judea had acknowledged John the Baptist as a prophet. He died a martyr's death. It appears that some of his disciples thought of him as the Messiah. We catch glimpses of a certain degree of antagonism existing between the followers of the Baptist and the disciples of Jesus:

> *Some of John's disciples . . . went to John and told him,*
> *"Teacher, you remember the man who was with you on the east*
> *side of the Jordan, the one you spoke about? Well, he is baptizing*
> *now, and everyone is going to him"* (3:25–26).

The author of the Fourth Gospel wants to make it clear that the Baptist's role is a supporting role and no more. Matthew interprets the Baptist as Elijah (Matthew 11:7–14). In the Fourth Gospel, however, the Baptist denies the title of Elijah (1:21). This reminds us of the freedom with which the evangelists adapted the tradition they had received to meet the needs of their audiences.

The interrogators, frustrated by the Baptist's denials, ask him for a positive statement which they may carry back "to those who sent us" (1:22). In the one positive statement that the Baptist makes about himself, he claims to be the voice of one in the desert preparing the way for God. This claim is based on Isaiah 40:3, a text which speaks of God's agents (angels) being given the task of preparing a road through the desert from Babylon to Israel. On this road God's Chosen People would travel from their Babylonian captivity (587–539 B.C.) back to their homeland. But the Baptist adapts this passage so that he is the agent, not the angels. Rather than preparing a road for the Chosen People to travel, he comes to prepare the road for God. Thus, the Baptist is the herald of the salvation coming in Jesus.

In the context of this interrogation, the messengers of the Pharisees are puzzled because the Baptist makes no claims to any title associated with the end-time expectations of Israel (Messiah, Elijah, the Prophet). Yet the action of baptizing has many overtones concerning the last days, the end of the world, and the coming of God. It is very likely that the Baptist's answer is intended more for the Christian readers of the Gospel than it was meant to satisfy the emissaries from Jerusalem. Thus the Baptist's statement, "I baptize with water" (1:26), would not bring much understanding to the official emissaries. As Jews, they already associated cleansing water with the giving of God's Spirit:

> I will sprinkle clean water on you and make you clean. . . . I will put my spirit in you and will see to it that you follow my laws and keep all the commands I have given you (Ezekiel 36:25–27).

The distinction between baptizing with water in contrast to baptizing with water and the Spirit seems to be an insight of the Christian community. By this distinction the author of the Fourth Gospel is able to relate the Baptist with Jesus in the scheme of salvation history. Jesus will be the one who opens up the world's last era by baptizing his disciples with the Spirit (see 1:33; Joel 2:28–29). It is noteworthy that all four Gospel accounts refer to the Baptist's use of water alone in his baptizing role.

Note the reason given by the Baptist as an explanation for his baptizing activity: he comes to point out to the people someone they do not know. There seems to be a three-fold meaning here. On one level the statement refers to the Baptist's role of witnessing to the one who is to come. On another level the statement has overtones and accusations. There is an implication that the Jewish authorities do not know because they refuse to know. In the Semitic sense of the word, knowledge includes personal involvement and commitment. On yet a third level there is a reference to Israel's expectation of the hidden Messiah, the one who comes out of nowhere to lead the people to salvation. The one who is coming is of such high rank that the Baptizer himself is not worthy to do for him even the slave's task of untying the master's sandals (1:27). With this, the scene taking place on the first day is complete.

Jesus appears on the second "day" (not necessarily twenty-four hours later, but a period of time after the interrogation of the Baptist in 1:19–28). As one reads the Fourth Gospel it is helpful to keep in mind that several audiences are being addressed at the same time. There is the original audience who heard the words of the Baptist and of Jesus, and there is the audience John is writing for in the late first century. John's practice of addressing several audiences at one time is often difficult to follow. However, our effort to be aware of the different audiences will bring us a deeper and rewarding understanding of God's Word. In this second day episode the evangelist presents a summary of the Baptist's witness. Not only does this summary convey the Baptist's message spoken sometime around the year 28 A.D., but it also addresses those living in the 90's, both the members of the Johannine community as well as those who still called themselves disciples of the Baptist.

We have seen that the Baptist was reluctant to speak about himself. But in testifying to Jesus he becomes very articulate. In a few sentences the Baptist makes a whole series of weighty assertions about who Jesus is. Jesus is the "Lamb of God," the "preexistent one," the "person expected by Israel," "the one who baptizes with the Holy Spirit," and the "Son of God" (1:29–34). The multiple levels of meaning in these assertions are most clear in the Baptist's description of Jesus as " 'the Lamb of God'" (1:29). With the benefit of 60 years of doctrinal and theological development behind them, the Johannine community recognized Jesus as the Paschal Lamb, slaughtered during the celebration of Passover in remembrance of God's deliverance of his people from Egypt. They also recognized the image of the lamb who says not a word before its shearers, taken from the prophecy about God's Suffering Servant (Isaiah 53:7,12). However, it is unlikely that the Baptist had these images in mind when he spoke of Jesus as the Lamb of God. The Baptist died before the crucifixion of Jesus. Historically, the ministries of Jesus and the Baptist overlapped only for a brief period. Shortly after Jesus began his public teaching, John the Baptist was martyred. Thus, we can say that the Baptist did not fully understand Jesus or the precise purpose of Jesus' ministry. Recall that the Baptist sent his disciples to Jesus to ask, " ... are you the one John said was going to come, or should we expect someone else?" (Matthew 11:3).

What then was the original meaning of the Baptist's assertion that Jesus was the Lamb of God who takes away the sin of the world? In the days of the Baptist there was an expectation that God would come at the end of time in order to annihilate sin in all its forms. Jewish literature often used animal imagery to convey theological teachings. In one end-time description we find that God is depicted as sending a lamb against the apparently superior and stronger beasts that represented the power of evil. As God's warrior, the lamb tramples these more powerful beasts to death, thus destroying sin forever. It is interesting that this imagery accords with the judgment theme in the Baptist's message as reported by the Synoptic tradition:

> *"You snakes—who told you that you could escape from the*
> *punishment God is about to send!"* (Matthew 3:7).

It is likely that the evangelist wants his readers to envision not only the warrior lamb, but also the lamb who said nothing before its shearers. That Servant of God would usher in an age of justice (sinlessness) for the whole world:

> *"Here is my servant . . . the one I have chosen, with whom I am*
> *pleased. I have filled him with my spirit, and he will bring*
> *justice to every nation"* (Isaiah 42:1).

The lamb has come and with him, justice, i.e., right relationship with God and with one another. The great sinful condition of humankind is taken away. Although our individual and collective sins continue, sin itself is no longer our tyrannical master. Since the best commentary on Scripture is Scripture itself, note what John wrote in his first letter:

> *Now you know that he appeared in order to abolish sin, and that*
> *in him there is no sin . . . . My children, do not let anyone lead*
> *you astray: to live a holy life is to be holy just as he is holy; to*
> *lead a sinful life is to belong to the devil, since the devil was a*
> *sinner from the beginning. It was to undo all that the devil has*
> *done that the Son of God appeared* (1 John 3:5–8, *Jerusalem*
> *Bible*).

The Baptist's paradoxical reference to Jesus as the one "coming *after* me" who "existed *before* I was born" (1:30) is another instance of the Johannine method of combining several levels of meaning. The Baptist's original statement probably referred to a Jewish expectation that an Elijah figure would come back at the beginning of the messianic age. Since Elijah had "existed" some nine centuries before the Baptist was born, the Baptist could assert that even though Jesus appeared later than he did, nevertheless Jesus (as Elijah) existed first. Of course, the evangelist clearly intends that the Christian reader would understand the Baptist's testimony as a statement about the pre-existing eternal Word.

Luke states that Mary, the mother of Jesus, and Elizabeth, the mother of John the Baptist, are kinswomen. Luke thereby placed the Baptist in the family of Jesus. But the impression given by the Fourth Gospel is that the Baptist and Jesus are strangers until this moment of God's revelation (1:31,33). The picture we are thus given is one in which the Baptist is aware of a divinely-given mission to reveal to Israel a Messianic-type figure. Only after Jesus is baptized does the Baptist recognize that the figure he awaited was Jesus (1:32–33).

A comparison with the Synoptic tradition shows that there is no explicit mention of Jesus' baptism in the Fourth Gospel. The baptism of Jesus is implied. However, two elements are common to both the Synoptic accounts and the Fourth Gospel: the descent of the Spirit and the reference to the Son. The Baptist's assertion that "he is the Son of God" (1:34) is linked with the Synoptic tradition which reports that a heavenly voice proclaimed, "This is my own dear Son, with whom I am pleased" (Matthew 3:17 and parallels).

When the Baptist spoke of the Spirit he probably thought in terms of the power given to prophets, in terms of the outpouring of God's power that would come in the Messianic age. Ezekiel wrote:

> *"I will pour out my spirit on the people of Israel and never again turn away from them. I, the sovereign Lord, have spoken"*
> (Ezekiel 39:29).

The Baptist perceived the Spirit as God's cleansing power. But the theology of the Holy Spirit in the Fourth Gospel is far more developed. Here the Spirit is clearly a distinct, divine entity, the Paraclete, whom Jesus will send after his exaltation upon the cross. The evangelist points out that the Spirit "stays" or "abides" upon Jesus (1:33). Thus, Jesus has the Spirit permanently. In stating that Jesus is the one " 'who baptizes with the Holy Spirit' " (1:33), the evangelist sums up the Messiah's mission: To bring about the rebirth of humankind in the Spirit. Because Jesus possesses the Spirit within himself he is able to give this Spirit to others. Christian readers of the late first century would see many references to their own Baptism in these verses.

The following diagram of the great cycle of descent, ascent and sending forth, can summarize the basic outline of the Gospel according to John:

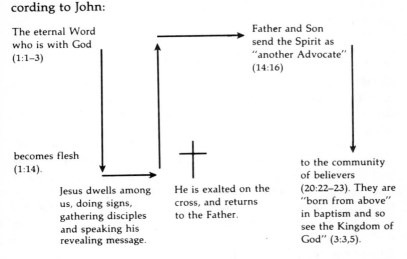

The eternal Word who is with God (1:1–3)

Father and Son send the Spirit as "another Advocate" (14:16)

becomes flesh (1:14).

Jesus dwells among us, doing signs, gathering disciples and speaking his revealing message.

He is exalted on the cross, and returns to the Father.

to the community of believers (20:22–23). They are "born from above" in baptism and so see the Kingdom of God" (3:3,5).

Verse 34 concludes the two days of the Baptist's witness. The *Jerusalem Bible* provides us with a better translation of 1:34, which makes evident the evangelist's desire to link this verse with 1:19:

> *"Yes, I have seen and I am the witness that he is the chosen one of God"* (1:34, *Jerusalem Bible*).

THE FIRST DISCIPLES OF JESUS

OVERVIEW. During the third and fourth days (1:35–51), the first disciples of Jesus acknowledge him by the key titles of "Messiah" (1:41), "Son of God" (1:49) and "King of Israel" (1:49). It is clear from the remainder of the Gospel that the disciples do not fully realize the implications of these Christological titles. Thus we note a special characteristic of the Fourth Gospel: Jesus is presented not so much as he was during his earthly life but as he is understood by the Johannine Church in the latter part of the first century. From the historical point of view, the identity of Jesus was originally revealed to his disciples only gradually, during the period of his earthly ministry and in the period after his resurrection. However, for the sake of the reader John has telescoped much of the gradual revelation of Jesus' identity into these first four days.

READ 1:35–51

COMMENTARY. The opening phrase of this section, "the next day" (1:35), links this passage with the early witness of the Baptist. "The next day" also indicates that the author is building toward a particular purpose in counting off this series of days.

After the Baptist points out the Lamb of God to his own disciples, two of them begin following Jesus (1:37). According to the author of the Fourth Gospel, "following Jesus" is the essence of discipleship. As Andrew and the unnamed disciple follow Jesus, the stage is set for the first words Jesus will speak in the Gospel According to John. They form a question: "What are you looking for?" (1:38). Here, as in much of the Gospel, the words have a double meaning. At first glance the question seems polite and ordinary, as if it meant, "What do you want?" or "Can I help you?" However, on the theological level, the question of Jesus refers to the fundamental need in the human person that urges each of us to turn to God. It is the most basic question of all, for it touches upon the quest for the meaning and purpose of human life. The two men then ask Jesus, "Where do you live?" On one level of meaning they are asking for his address; they want to go to his place, perhaps to learn more about the man whom their former teacher called "the Lamb of God." On a deeper level of meaning, the disciples' question symbolizes the longing of humankind to be with God. How does one cross the chasm between the divine and the human? The verb in their question, "Where do you live?" is the same verb found in 1:14, "The Word became a human being and . . . lived among us." Thus, on a theological level, the question asked by Andrew and the unnamed disciple is the question asked by all persons who are seeking God. It is as if they are asking Jesus, "Where does God dwell? We do not know how to find him by ourselves. How can we enter God's holy presence? Where can we encounter the One who can give full meaning to our lives?" Since God alone is capable of satisfying the hunger and thirst of the human heart, the question, "Where do you live?" is the question asked by every member of the human family.

The answer of Jesus, "Come and see" (1:39), answers the request of the two men following Jesus. On the obvious level of meaning, Jesus invites them to the place where he is staying so that they can talk. On the theological level of meaning, Jesus is saying, "If you are looking for God, then follow me. Believe in me." "Coming to Jesus" is John's description of faith. Without faith there is no way to bridge the infinite distance between God and humankind. Between the human and the divine exists a chasm which no one can cross. But the Good News is this: humankind does not have to cross the chasm! God has come to us in the event of the Word made flesh! The words of Jesus, "Come and see," are also addressed to the readers of the Fourth Gospel. The evangelist is saying, "Jesus invites you to believe. Come and share in the rest of the Gospel. Then you will find where God dwells and how to enter his holy presence." According to John, the alternative to dwelling with God is that of existing in the world. As the domain of Satan, the world is the place of darkness, the den of illusion and appearance. Because the world caters to those judging and living "according to the flesh," the world will never satisfy the human heart. Jesus alone is the true bread, the slaking of human thirst, and the giver of eternal life.

Accepting Jesus' invitation, these first disciples spend the day and perhaps the night with him. Although we do not know what was said, we can guess that the three discussed the Scriptures and conversed about the messianic hopes of Israel. Andrew's response is to announce to Peter, "We have found the Messiah" (1:41). When Peter arrives, Jesus displays his more than human knowledge of both the man and his future: "Your name is Simon . . . but you *will be called* Cephas" (1:42). The change of a person's name is a biblical way of indicating that the person is being called to play a new role in the history of salvation. (See Genesis 17:5 and 32:28 for the new names which Abram and Jacob receive.) The Johannine account does not elaborate on the significance of Peter's new name. However, the role that Peter will play in the Church after the death and resurrection of Jesus is implied already in this initial action of Jesus.

On the fourth "day" Jesus calls Philip to join himself, Andrew, Peter and the unnamed disciple (probably John) as they are about to leave for Galilee (1:43). Note Philip's response. Just as Andrew went out to find Peter in order to bring him to Jesus, so now Philip seeks out Nathanael. Whereas the Baptist had denied that he was "the Prophet" (1:21), Philip professes that the prophet spoken of by Moses is "Jesus, the son of Joseph, from Nazareth" (1:45).

But Nathanael knows the Scriptures: they say nothing significant about Nazareth (1:46). At this point the fourth evangelist introduces another theme which will carry through the entire Gospel: the debate about the origins of Jesus. Again and again Jesus will be judged in terms of his lowly origins. According to appearances, Jesus is from Nazareth or Galilee. But the reader of the Gospel knows that Jesus is from God. The real point at issue for the people who encounter Jesus is not his earthly birthplace, but whether they will accept his signs and his message. His deeds and his revealing message testify that he is "from God." Philip answers Nathanael's objection with the very same words Jesus addressed to Andrew and the other disciple: "Come and see" (1:39, 46). This is the invitation to faith. Nathanael accepts.

Jesus tells us why Nathanael is the kind of person who could overcome the deceiving appearances regarding unimportant Nazareth: "Here is a real Israelite; there is nothing false in him!"

(1:47). In the Hebrew Scriptures, being false was related to practicing idolatry. But Nathanael is described as an authentic Israelite, a man faithful to the Covenant. He is a man who is sincerely seeking to do God's will. "Doing the truth," was a Hebrew expression for keeping the faith. (See Genesis 24:49; Ezekiel 18:8.) Nathanael is able to come to faith, his priorities are in the right order. There is nothing "false" in him that blocks access to Jesus.

Nathanael, recognizing the accuracy of Jesus' description, half exclaims, half questions how Jesus could know so much. Jesus' answer, regarding Nathanael's presence under the fig tree, is difficult to interpret. It could refer to Nathanael's practice of reading Scripture, according to the custom of some rabbis, under the shelter of a tree. For us, however, the important aspect of this conversation is Nathanael's profession of faith in Jesus as "Son of God" and "King of Israel." Thus it belongs to Nathanael, "the true Israelite," to bring to a close the long list of messianic titles given to Jesus in the first chapter. Jesus stands in the midst of his disciples, known to them as "the Lamb of God" (1:29, 36), "the Messiah" (1:41), "the Prophet" (1:45), "the Son of God," "King of Israel!" (1:49)

But the faith of the chosen disciples is not complete. While the reader knows of the Word's eternal existence with God, Nathanael and the disciples do not. Although Nathanael confessed Jesus as "the Son of God," this is not an explicit recognition of his divinity. The climax of Nathanael's profession of faith is this: "you are the King of Israel!" (1:49). Thus Jesus is understood as the messianic King whom true Israelites await. Jesus tells Nathanael that his appreciation is only at the beginning: "You will see much greater things than this!" (1:50). The "much greater things" is a reference to the signs Jesus will give, the first of which will be given three days from now in Cana of Galilee. The faith of the disciples will only come to completion after the resurrection, as we will see in Thomas' profession of total Christian faith: "My Lord and my God!" (20:28).

Verse 51 interrupts the transition from the promise of Jesus that his disciples would see "much greater things" to the first great sign given at Cana (2:1–11). It is possible that this verse was inserted by an editor of the nearly-completed Gospel. Verse 51 links two symbols found in the Hebrew Scriptures: Jacob's ladder and Daniel's vision of the Son of Man. According to the book of Daniel, the writer has had a vision of a figure of heavenly origin, probably a symbol of a victorious Israel:

> *"I gazed into the visions of the night.*
> *And I saw, coming on the clouds of heaven,*
> *one like a son of man.*
> *He came to the one of great age*
> *and was led into his presence.*
> *On him was conferred sovereignty,*
> *glory and kingship,*
> *and men of all peoples, nations and languages became*
> *his servants"* (Daniel 7:13–14, *Jerusalem Bible*).

Jesus links the title, "Son of Man," with Jacob's vision of angels ascending to heaven and descending to earth on a ladder (see Genesis 28:10–17). In John, the Son of Man himself becomes the ladder upon which the angels (messengers of God) go up and come down. Perhaps it is the author's intention to express Jesus' role as the one who bridges the great chasm between the realm of God and the world of humankind. As we move through the Gospel we find that there are three passages in which the "Son of Man" title is related to Jesus' exaltation-glorification on the cross (3:14; 8:28 and 12:34). Other "Son of Man" passages refer to Jesus' future glory. Thus, in verse 51 we find allusions to heavenly origin, salvation for Israel, intimacy with God, the union of heaven and earth, crucifixion, return to the Father, and the simultaneous revelation of both God's glory and the glory of the Son of Man.

The culture in which the Gospel originated had its own method or logic of bringing people to the desired conclusion. This method would make a series of statements through the use of dialogue, titles, dramatic scenes, allusions to Scripture and repetition. At the center of all these would stand the subject, the focus of the drama, claims, titles, etc. Thus in John 1:19–51 we have a Semitic way of asserting the identity of Jesus:

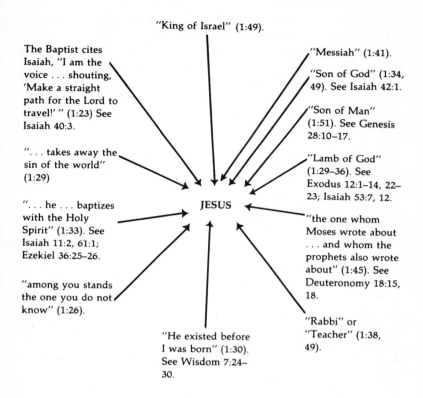

"King of Israel" (1:49).

The Baptist cites Isaiah, "I am the voice . . . shouting, 'Make a straight path for the Lord to travel!' " (1:23) See Isaiah 40:3.

". . . takes away the sin of the world" (1:29)

". . . he . . . baptizes with the Holy Spirit" (1:33). See Isaiah 11:2, 61:1; Ezekiel 36:25–26.

"among you stands the one you do not know" (1:26).

"Messiah" (1:41).

"Son of God" (1:34, 49). See Isaiah 42:1.

"Son of Man" (1:51). See Genesis 28:10–17.

"Lamb of God" (1:29–36). See Exodus 12:1–14, 22–23; Isaiah 53:7, 12.

"the one whom Moses wrote about . . . and whom the prophets also wrote about" (1:45). See Deuteronomy 18:15, 18.

"Rabbi" or "Teacher" (1:38, 49).

JESUS

"He existed before I was born" (1:30). See Wisdom 7:24–30.

By the end of the first chapter, the evangelist has woven into the tapestry of the narrative most of the Christological titles given to Jesus by the early Christian believers.

REFLECTION. The tools of biblical scholarship tell us that the Gospel according to John comes to us in its present completeness only after a process of about sixty years. That process included the disciples' experience of Jesus during his earthly ministry, their first preaching about Jesus risen from the dead, the later organization of that early preaching into memorized units, the handing on of these organized preaching units as traditions (first memorized and then written), and finally, the delicate structuring of some traditions into the Gospel format.

We have seen aspects of the developmental process operating in the composition of the Gospel according to John. We have caught glimpses of the recollections of John, who was probably among the first disciples called by Jesus. We have found evidence of the contributions of other writers, who, although not eyewitnesses, were thoroughly acquainted with John's preaching and theology. As we progress through the rest of the Gospel we will see other indications that there was probably an original body of material based on Johannine preaching and expanded by a redactor or editor belonging to the Johannine community. The addition of the prologue as preface to the Gospel account and the purposeful subordination of John the Baptist to Jesus are examples of editing by a hand other than that of John the Apostle. Nevertheless, behind the whole account of the Fourth Gospel there stands an ancient tradition of the sayings and deeds of Jesus. At the source of this ancient tradition stands the authority of John, son of Zebedee, one of the three disciples closest to Jesus.

As we carefully study the Fourth Gospel we will see that the ancient Johannine tradition is independent of the traditions underlying the Gospel accounts of Matthew, Mark and Luke. The Fourth Gospel, although it is the last account written, nevertheless contains some of the earliest memories of those who walked with Jesus. For example, John has told us that Jesus first called his disciples in Judea, not in Galilee as indicated by the Synoptic tradition. We have also learned that the disciples of Jesus were first the disciples of John the Baptist.

On the other hand, the Johannine portrait of Jesus is obviously a much later view of the significance of what Jesus said and did. We can see the difference when we compare the Jesus in the Fourth Gospel with, for example, the Jesus portrayed in Mark's account. The Johannine Jesus clearly displays knowledge that is beyond the scope of any human being. But Mark's portrayal of Jesus seems to be closer to the original experience of the disciples. For example, when the woman touches Jesus' cloak in order to be healed, Jesus doesn't know who it was who touched him (Mark 5:30–32).

STUDY GROUP QUESTIONS

1. "We saw his glory!" John proclaims (1:14). The subject of the sentence is John's community. "We" stands for the people who believe that Jesus is the Father's only Son" (1:14). How do you see yourself in relationship with the community for whom John speaks? Why is it that the words of this account of the Gospel can be addressed both to you as well as to those first-century believers?

2. How does the Fourth Gospel portray John the Baptist differently from the Synoptics (Matthew, Mark and Luke)? Why do you think the author does this?

3. Two disciples of the Baptist follow Jesus. He turns and asks them, "What are you looking for?" (1:38). What is the deeper significance of this question?

4. John portrays Jesus as the one who fulfills the messianic expectations of Israel (1:19–49). Still, Jesus promises that Nathanael, the true Israelite, will see "much greater things" (1:50). According to John, what else will be "seen" by those who believe completely?

Chapter Two

THE FIRST OF JESUS' SIGNS

OVERVIEW. John completes the account of the call of the disciples with the first of Jesus' signs, the changing of water into wine at the wedding feast in Cana. The "miracles" of the Synoptic Gospels become "signs" in the Fourth Gospel. In this way John asks his readers to move beyond a preoccupation with the miraculous and begin to see who Jesus really is. The signs point beyond themselves; they reveal the glory of Jesus (2:11). Thus they call forth the belief of those who have been called to be disciples.

This passage begins a section (chapters 2–4) in which the evangelist portrays Jesus as replacing the rituals and holy places of Judaism. The Jewish custom of washing before meals necessitates the presence of the large water jars at the banquet. In changing the water into wine, Jesus symbolically replaces this Jewish ritual with the "best wine" of his teaching and person.

READ 2:1–12

COMMENTARY. This passage richly deserves its place among the favorite texts for Christian reflection and prayer. In a few sentences it presents us with a wealth of insights into the early ministry of Jesus. It is another indication that in the fourth evangelist we encounter a master catechist.

By the phrase "two days later" John links this episode with the call of Philip and Nathanael in 1:43–51. Literally, the Greek text reads "on the third day." This might signal the desire of the author that we read this miracle of the choice wine in light of the Resurrection. Certainly he intends that the setting of the first sign carry deep meaning for us.

As the prophetic tradition developed, both wedding and banquet became well-known signs of the messianic days. Israel was understood as the spouse of Yahweh. She had been unfaithful, but in the days to come Yahweh would redeem and restore her. (See Isaiah 54:4–8 and Hosea, chapters 1–3.) The key banquet text can be found in Isaiah 25:6:

> *Here on Mount Zion the Lord Almighty will prepare a banquet*
> *for all the nations of the world—a banquet of the richest food and*
> *finest wine.*

In our study of Matthew 22:1–14 we saw how Jesus specifically compared the Kingdom of God to a wedding banquet. Throughout his account, John often points out that the Kingdom has already arrived in the ministry of Jesus.

The mother of Jesus is present at the Cana wedding. She may have been related to the bride or groom, which would explain her prominence at the banquet. Perhaps Jesus and his disciples have been invited because of her. John mentions Mary in four places (2:1 and 12; 6:42 and 19:25–27), never by name but always as the mother of Jesus.

Mary's request and Jesus' response present us with another example of theological shorthand. Unfortunately, the translation is inadequate in this case. It omits a key word in the Greek, *gynai*— "woman." A more adequate translation would be: "Woman, what has this concern of yours to do with me?" Jesus seems to refuse her request because his time or his hour has not yet come. "The hour" is a favorite theological word in John. It refers to his death and glorification.

The use of "woman" is closely connected with Jesus' hour. As

a form of address, "woman" was normal and polite. However, its use is highly unusual between a son and mother. John will introduce "woman" again in 19:25–27. That he intends a clear parallel between these two passages is evident from the use in both cases of "mother-woman-hour." This explains the enigmatic reply of Jesus to Mary. He is telling her that she does not have a role in salvation history until the time of the hour. At the foot of the cross she will receive her role: to welcome as mother the "children" of Christ's Passion.

A full understanding of this theology demands that we examine another "woman" passage in the Christian Scriptures, that of Revelation 12. It is important to read the text in light of Genesis 3:15, which pictures the lasting conflict between the woman (and her offspring) and the serpent.

> *Then a great and mysterious sight appeared in the sky. There*
> *was a woman, whose dress was the sun and who had the moon*
> *under her feet and a crown of twelve stars on her head. She was*

*soon to give birth, and the pains and suffering of childbirth made
her cry out.*

*Another mysterious sight appeared in the sky. There was a huge
red dragon with seven heads and ten horns. . . . He stood in front
of the woman, in order to eat her child as soon as it was born.
Then she gave birth to a son, who will rule over all nations with
an iron rod. But the child was snatched away and taken to God
and his throne* (Revelation 12:1–5).

The woman of this text is both the mother of the Messiah and
the mother of the New Israel, the Church. Genesis 3:20 explains
that Eve received her name because she was "mother of all the
living" (*New American Bible*). At the foot of the cross Mary becomes the New Eve, for she becomes the mother of all those who
are "the living"—the offspring of the cross of Christ.

Thus Mary's role begins in the hour of the great struggle between her offspring and the serpent, the hour which is also that
of Jesus' glory. Yet John clearly states that already at Cana "Jesus
revealed his glory" (2:11). This explains how Jesus can both refuse Mary's request and yet respond to it. The refusal is necessitated by the nature of Jesus' ministry. We find a similar
indication of this in the Synoptic tradition. After Mary and Joseph have found their young Son in the Temple, they hear these
strange words from Jesus' lips: "Why did you have to look for
me? Didn't you know that I had to be in my Father's house?"
And Luke adds, "But they did not understand his answer" (Luke
2:49–50). Another strange episode is recorded in Mark 3:32–35:

*A crowd was sitting around Jesus, and they said to him, "Look,
your mother and your brothers and sisters are outside, and they
want you."*

Jesus answered, "Who is my mother? Who are my brothers?"

*He looked at the people sitting around him and said, "Look! Here
are my mother and my brothers! Whoever does what God wants
him to do is my brother, my sister, my mother."*

We see that both in the Synoptic Gospels and at Cana Jesus insists that human kinship cannot affect the decisions he makes about his ministry. These are in the hands of the Father. To paraphrase John, Jesus is not free to initiate the hour whenever he chooses. The hour begins when the Father so chooses. Not even the petition of his mother can change that.

Yet Jesus has called his disciples. He has promised that they will see "much greater things" (1:50). The fullness of the messianic blessings will be poured out in the death and glorification of Jesus. But here at Cana, in anticipation of the "hour," Jesus reveals his glory. Thus, this first sign anticipates the messianic blessings symbolized by the vast abundance of the wine. (The six jars held between 120 and 150 gallons of water/wine!) Amos had foretold this abundance in a prophecy about the restoration of the kingdom of David:

> *"The days are coming," says the Lord,*
> *"when grain will grow faster than it can be harvested,*
> *and grapes will grow faster than the wine can be made.*
> *The mountains will drip with sweet wine,*
> *and the hills will flow with it"* (Amos 9:13).

The person in charge of the feast seems to chide the groom for his poor economy: "You have kept the best wine until now!" (2:10). The primary meaning of the wine is the gift of salvation which Jesus brings, that salvation promised for the messianic days which is anticipated here. The evangelist, however, probably intends his readers to think also of the Eucharist. Certainly the changing of water into wine would lead believers to recall the eucharistic wine. (An early Christian catacomb painting joins Cana with the multiplication of the loaves.) In addition John connects this first sign (2:13) and the account of the multiplication of the loaves (6:4) with Passover. The Christian reader would already know that the Passover festival was the time in which Jesus gave the Eucharist to his disciples. The perceptive reader might also contrast the water of Jewish purification with the wine of the cleansing blood of Christ.

REFLECTIONS. The Cana miracle is an ideal illustration of the way in which preaching and teaching often develop meanings which were not intended by the biblical author, or which were not his primary meaning. Thus most of us in the Roman Catholic tradition have learned to see this passage as if it spoke chiefly about Mary. Since the Middle Ages preachers have emphasized the role of Mary in the Cana event; she was the one who powerfully intervened on behalf of the bride and groom! But John meant this to be a Christological text. This event is the first moment in Jesus' ministry in which his glory was revealed; it is the first fulfillment of the "much greater things" Jesus promised to show his first disciples (1:50).

In our present age, when some professed Christians seem to be ambiguous about the divinity of Christ and his unique role in salvation, Catholics can rejoice that our witness to Christ has been clear and unambiguous. Likewise, our clear recognition that Mary has an important role in the history of salvation is a gift which we can offer to other Christian churches.

In honesty, however, we must ask ourselves if our devotion to the mother of the Lord has acted as a stumbling block to our Protestant brethren. Mary at Cana is the perfect example of obedience to her Son. She lived according to her words, "Do whatever he tells you." That is what she continues to remind us to do. Authentic devotion to Mary unfailingly leads us to a deeper love for her Son. Her absolute trust in his sovereign power and goodness becomes our model.

Thus Vatican II reminded us of a more ancient, a more "traditional" Marian theology. She is the New Eve, the mother of all Christians. She is also the model disciple, the first believer. By her obedience, trust and courageous love she shows us what we, the Church, should be. (See paragraphs 53, 65 and 68 of the *Dogmatic Constitution on the Church.*)

If our witness of devotion to Mary has "scandalized" other Christians, perhaps it is because our love for Mary did not always seem to lead us into a deeper love for Christ. It does not seem coincidental that devotion to Mary and the saints became pronounced in the Church in the centuries following the Arian heresy. In their zeal to protect the divinity of Christ, preachers and theologians began to proclaim his majesty, his awesomeness—and unfortunately, his distance from us. A visitor to Rome can still see the great mosaics in the basilicas, which go back to the fifth and sixth centuries. Christ is pictured as supremely powerful, the Creator of all things, the Judge. Gradually, Jesus became unapproachable. Sinful humanity was unworthy to approach his throne. Thus his mother and the saints were appealed to as intercessors. They would carry our prayers to him.

Without question, the Church maintained her belief that it was Jesus himself who answered the prayers. Neither Mary nor the saints had any saving power of their own. It may have been a diminishment, however, for the Church to grow weak in her experience of the closeness of her Lord and of his desire for a personal friendship with the community of believers. In a desire to renew this awareness, St. Francis of Assisi in the thirteenth century preached devotion to the Infant Jesus in the crib and to the crucified Jesus on the cross. For a similar reason, in the seventeenth century, St. Margaret Mary taught the world a renewed devotion to the Sacred Heart.

We do not "need" Mary because Jesus is unapproachable and remote from us. The Incarnation itself remains the chief proof that he is ever with us and available to us. On the other hand, Mary's role in salvation history is not something we can take or leave because of personal preference. *We* do not decide her place. That decision was God's. Both in Nazareth and at the foot of the cross Mary's role is important, even crucial. She allows the Incarnate Word to become flesh in her womb, and she, as Mother of the Church, receives those who have been renewed in the water and blood which flowed from the side of Christ (19:25–37).

THE CLEANSING OF THE TEMPLE

OVERVIEW. In this second episode following the call of the disciples, John continues his theme of replacement. At Cana the water of Jewish ritual is replaced by the wine of messianic blessings. In this passage John anticipates the replacement of the Temple, the center of Jewish worship, by the risen body of Jesus. Thus the cleansing of the Temple is also a kind of "sign." It too reveals the true significance of Jesus.

As the Cana sign looked toward his death—the "hour" of his death was anticipated—so this Jerusalem event also prefigures his death, together with the resurrection. The zeal for his Father's house, which prompts the expulsion of the merchants, will eventually consume ("burns in me," 2:17) his own life. (As we will see, the fourth evangelist realizes that all the other signs can be misunderstood. The death of Jesus is the truly adequate sign which reveals his glory.)

READ 2:13–25

COMMENTARY. The Synoptic Gospels are unanimous in locating the cleansing of the Temple at the end of Jesus' public life. (See Mark 11:15–17 and the parallel accounts.) The cleansing is a decisive moment in the ministry, and Mark 11:18 notes that afterward the Jewish leaders sought a way to kill him. How can we understand John's decision to place the cleansing at the beginning of the ministry?

Biblical scholars are in agreement that there were not two cleansings of the Temple. Nor is it a question that either John or the other evangelists were mistaken in dating this event in Jesus' life. The Synoptics recount only one Passover Festival and only one journey of Jesus to Jerusalem. John knows of at least three Passover celebrations during Jesus' ministry. (See also 6:4 and 13:1; it is John's account rather than that of the Synoptics which has provided Christian devotion with the tradition of a three-year public life.)

It is possible that the cleansing occurred early in the ministry. (Thus the Synoptics placed it near the Passion because they record only one visit to the Temple during the ministry.) More probably, the Synoptic dating is more accurate historically, and John has moved it to the first Passover for theological reasons. John wishes to link this event with both the witness of the Baptist and the first of the signs at Cana.

As the account begins, Jesus goes up to Jerusalem. Three times a year devout Israelites were called to make the pilgrimage up to

Jerusalem: for Passover, and the Feast of Weeks (spring festivals which correspond to the Christian feasts of Easter and Pentecost), and again for the Feast of Tabernacles (an autumn festival, also called Booths).

In a comparison of the cleansing with the Synoptic accounts, we notice two significant differences. In John's account, not only the merchants but also the animals are driven from the Temple. Secondly, in Mark and the parallels, Jesus quotes sayings from Isaiah and Jeremiah which place the emphasis on the dishonesty of the merchants: "You have turned it into a hideout for thieves!" (Mark 11:17). In John, however, Jesus' complaint is voiced in his own words and is directed not toward dishonesty—in reality the merchants and money changers provided a real service for the pilgrims—but against the profanation of the Temple. These two changes which the fourth evangelist introduces into the traditional account of the cleansing heighten the intensity of Jesus' protest against the Temple (which in 2:16 has become "my Father's house") and the profanation of Jewish worship.

Perceptive witnesses of this symbolic action would have understood it in light of a messianic theme. In the days to come, the prophets announced, the Lord himself will visit his Temple, in order to purify it. (See Malachi 3:1–5.) "When that time comes, there will no longer be any merchant in the Temple of the Lord Almighty" (Zechariah 14:21).

John notes that the disciples "remembered" a verse from Psalm

69. This probably refers to a deeper understanding of Jesus' act which the disciples reached after the Resurrection. It would be helpful here to read Luke's narrative of the encounter of Jesus and the two disciples on the road to Emmaus. According to Luke, only after the Resurrection did the disciples begin to understand the deeper meaning of what the Master had said and done. Note particularly Luke 24:25–27:

> *Then Jesus said to them, "How foolish you are, how slow you are to believe everything the prophets said! Was it not necessary for the Messiah to suffer these things and then to enter his glory?" And Jesus explained to them what was said about himself in all the Scriptures, beginning with the books of Moses and the writings of all the prophets.*

After the Resurrection, the apostolic community realized that Jesus' prophetic action fulfilled a verse of Psalm 69. (See the Reflection section for an explanation of why John composed his account in this way.)

Psalm 69 might be called the Prayer of the Righteous Sufferer. The early Church interpreted it as a messianic psalm, and it became one of the most frequently quoted passages from the Hebrew Scriptures. Unfortunately, our translation is not as helpful as it might be. Let us study a portion of the psalm from the *New American Bible.*

> *Since for your sake I bear insult,*
>   *and shame covers my face.*
> *I have become an outcast to my brothers,*
>   *a stranger to my mother's sons,*
> *Because zeal for your house consumes me,*
>   *and the insults of those who blaspheme you fall upon me*
> (Psalm 69:8–10).

When John uses this text, he puts the verb in the future tense. Thus the passage is more accurately translated in this way: "His disciples remembered that the Scripture says, 'Zeal for your house will consume me' " (2:17). In the Fourth Gospel the text is used as a prophecy. It looks forward to the Passion, when Jesus will literally be consumed because of his faithfulness to the Father's will.

Jesus' prophetic action is followed by a challenge to his authority from the Jewish leaders (2:18). In the Synoptic Gospels Jesus' response is recounted during the trial before the Sanhedrin. There Jesus is accused of threatening to destroy the Temple and then rebuild it. Mark 14:58 has: "We heard him declare, 'I will destroy this temple made by human hands' " (*New American Bible*).

Note the important shift which John makes. Jesus' response indicates that it is the Jewish leaders themselves who will destroy the Temple. They take Jesus' words in their literal sense, and scoff at the impossibility of replacing in three days what required forty-six years to construct.

From his later vantage point, John sees it clearly. Jesus was speaking about the temple of his body (2:21). Thus John changes the Greek verb which Mark used ("I will construct another," 14:58), substituting one ("I will build it"; literally, "I will raise it," 2:19) which is used in other Christian writings to speak of the Resurrection. The Jewish leaders would tear down this temple, but Jesus would raise it up again after three days. Again John notes the remembering of the disciples (2:22). The significance of Jesus' reply was not clear to them at the time. Probably, they were as astonished and incredulous as the Jewish leaders. After the Resurrection, however, they understood that both the Hebrew Scriptures and Jesus himself had foretold his death and resurrection.

Verses 23–25 are used as a transitional passage. They conclude the event of the cleansing and prepare the reader for Jesus' dialogue with Nicodemus in chapter three. In the Greek the words translated "believed in him" (2:23) and "did not trust himself" (2:24) are two forms of the same verb. We might then translate in this way: "Many believed in him. . . . But Jesus did not let himself be believed in by them." Jesus is suspicious of faith that concentrates on the miracles without recognizing that they point to the One whom the Father has sent. As John will often note, Jesus knows the human heart and mind. In this area he needs no teacher.

REFLECTIONS. In 2:17 we meet the first instance of Johannine "remembering." This word is a clue to the reader that the evangelist is introducing into his account a later understanding of the event being described. John writes with the greater comprehension that developed during the six decades since the Ascension. During those years the Holy Spirit was at work, in fulfillment of the promise of Jesus: "The Helper, the Holy Spirit, whom the Father will send in my name, will teach you everything and make you remember all that I have told you" (14:26). John chose to write a Gospel, a structured recounting of Jesus' words and deeds, rather than a letter (Thessalonians or Corinthians) or a theological essay (Hebrews). Yet the Gospel format, while it was based on the ministry of Jesus, was not intended to be a biography or history of Jesus.

John offers the Church a rich, new understanding of the life and person of Jesus, an understanding which emerges from the synthesis of his own theological-catechetical genius and the inspiration of the Helper-Spirit. Yet he does not choose a purely theological form for his contribution. He chooses to write a "gospel"—a type of literature in which the Church's faith in Jesus takes historical form. In the Gospel according to John then we hear a dialogue between history and theology. The theology does not transcend history, it is built upon it. Yet theology understands those historical events from the vantage point of the 90's.

Thus, John, writing in the 90's, has a vantage point, a perspective which enables him to see more deeply into the mystery of Christ than those who wrote before him. The difficulty, however, is this: he expresses that deeper insight in terms of the original historical events. We might say that he narrates what was taking place (history) in order to affirm what was going on (theology). The event of the cleansing of the Temple is an excellent example. John sees several things which were not clear to the original witnesses: (1) that the real meaning of Jesus' protest is that Jesus has replaced the Temple as the place of worship and encounter with God; (2) that Jesus' zeal for the house of his Father did consume him literally, that is, it did eventually lead to his death; and (3) that the Temple which Jesus promised to rebuild was that of his crucified body.

However, John does not separate, as we might do, the original event from the later interpretation. The richer understanding is expressed through the narration of the historical event. Another example might help. Suppose you decide at age fifty to write an account of the life of your mother, who died when you were fifteen. That account will be much different from the account you might have written several months after her death. At that time you probably would have listed in a literal fashion many events of her life. But after fifteen years your understanding of the real significance of her words and deeds would have been limited. After fifty years of life's experience your account would probably include fewer events; but those events will carry much more meaning. At fifty you will be much better able to express who your mother really was. In a similar way John is better able to express the mystery of who Jesus is than those who preceded him.

STUDY GROUP QUESTIONS

1. In 2:1–11 there are several levels of meaning. On the surface level, a newly married couple is spared the embarrassment of running out of wine at their wedding feast. John, however, seems to be more interested in the theological meaning. Share with the members of your group your understanding of the connection(s) between the water-turned-to-wine and the messianic hopes of Israel. What is the deeper significance of the words "mother," and "time" ("hour")?

2. Suppose you were asked to state whether the following statement is "true" or "false": "The Gospel of John is a biography or life of Jesus." In the light of the commentary on 2:13–22 and in light of the reflection on 2:17, what answer would you give? Share with your group why you chose to answer either "true" or "false."

Chapter Three

JESUS AND NICODEMUS

OVERVIEW. In this chapter we find some of the most memorable portions of the Christian Scriptures. We find here the dialogue with Nicodemus, the assertion that "God loved the world so much that he gave his only Son," and the final testimony of the Baptist, "he must increase while I must decrease". Verses 1–21 may contain the basic elements of an early baptismal instruction. All these themes converge on one reality: the meaning of faith in Jesus. Faith comes through the work of the Holy Spirit (3:3, 5). Faith brings eternal life to the believer (3:16, 18, 36). Refusal to have faith in Jesus brings a person to judgment in its most negative sense: separation from God (3:18, 19, 36).

From the point of view of the literary development of chapter 3, there are some problems. For example, it is difficult to tell exactly when the conversation of Jesus and Nicodemus ends and the reflections of the evangelist begin. In addition, verses 31–36 repeat the ideas in verses 13–21. It is the common opinion that the uneven sequence of the events and reflections of chapter three indicate a re-working process, done either by the original writer or by an editor.

READ 3:1-21

COMMENTARY. We are accustomed to viewing Nicodemus as a cautious Jewish official, prudently protecting his reputation by coming to see Jesus at night. Since the Fourth Gospel uses darkness as a symbol for evil, deceit or ignorance, the reference to Nicodemus' night visit may well convey John's idea that Nicodemus is moving from ignorance to the truth of Jesus.

However, there is another way of viewing the significance of the coming of the evening. It is a time of cessation from work, a time of relaxation, of rest, and a time for learning. The rabbinical tradition recommends the night as a good time for the profound study of the Torah (the Hebrew name for the first five books of the Bible). John does not give us much information about the original encounter between the two men who acknowledged each other as rabbi (3:2, 10). The conversation, which must have extended originally for hours, can be read aloud in a minute and a half. John is interested in the crux of Jesus' message: salvation comes not from man but from God. Judging from Jesus' opening statement, "I am telling you the truth: no one can see the Kingdom of God unless he is born again" (3:3), it is possible that Nicodemus came to Jesus to ask the most profound question of all: How can a human being make his or her way into the life-giving presence of God? Jesus tells the great teacher that no one can "see," that is, "experience" the Kingdom unless God raises that person to a new level of existence through the process of being "born again" (3:3, 5).

The Greek for "born again" also means "born from above." In Nicodemus' startled response (3:4) we note the use of the Johannine literary technique called "misunderstanding." The technique works like this: Jesus makes his point; the one addressed misunderstands Jesus; Jesus then explains the point more extensively. When Nicodemus cannot grasp the idea of spiritual rebirth, Jesus elaborates: one must be "born of water and the Spirit" (3:5). The words of Jesus thus form a link with the Baptist's testimony. It was the Baptist's mission to point out to Israel the man "who baptizes with the Holy Spirit" (1:34). This man now encounters Nicodemus. According to the Fourth Gospel Nicodemus represents the apex of Israel's leadership. As a rabbi, he is utterly serious about God's will as it is expressed in the Mosaic Law. As a member of the Sanhedrin, he has the responsibility of helping to order society in accordance with the will of God. As a keen observer of what is happening, Nicodemus is able to recognize that God is with Jesus (3:2).

To help Nicodemus understand, Jesus develops two analogies which explain the necessity of being born from above. Jesus points out that by natural birth we are human beings, but by spiritual birth we become the children of God (3:6). This spiritual birth is the only way a human being can traverse the infinite distance that separates the realm of God from the human condition. Only God can give the gift of eternal life. Jesus draws a second analogy. In Greek the same word can mean "wind" or "spirit." A person can experience the natural phenomenon of the wind, but much about the wind remains mysterious. Before the advent of meteorology, no one could tell where the wind came from, even though one could perceive its sound and feel its effects. Jesus points out that just as people hear the mysterious wind, some people will also hear the "sound," that is, the "voice" of the Holy Spirit (3:8).

While the reader of John's Gospel understands the catechesis on baptism contained in these lines, Nicodemus cannot: "How can this be?" (3:9). Jesus then rebukes the great teacher for his lack of understanding (3:10). It is likely that verses 11 and 12 reflect the frustration of the Johannine community in its lack of success in preaching to their fellow Israelites. Nicodemus (representing Judaism) is unable to understand the spiritual truths in the earthly analogies of parenting and of the activity of the wind. Jesus asks how, then, can he expect to understand the mysteries (the things of heaven) Jesus comes to reveal (3:12).

Jesus has spoken to Nicodemus about "the things of heaven," that is, the mysteries of God. In verse 13 Jesus offers confirmation of what he has said. The Son of Man has seen God (he alone has "gone up to heaven") and is thereby qualified to speak about the things of heaven. The "proof" that the Son of Man has seen God is found in the fact that he "came down from heaven" (3:13).

Having completed his brief sketch of the dialogue between Nicodemus and Jesus, John continues with his own reflections on the significance of "the Son of Man who came down from heaven" (3:13). An incident recounted in the book of Numbers serves as John's point of departure. God had commanded Moses to hang a figure of a snake upon a pole so that those bitten by snakes could be saved from death by looking upon the figure (Numbers 21:4–9). John uses this obscure incident to make three points. First, as the snake was lifted up, so must Jesus be lifted up on the cross. Second, God's salvific will is involved in both exaltations. Third, natural life was restored to those fatally-bitten Hebrews when they looked at the bronze snake; but eternal life is given to all those who come in faith to gaze upon Jesus hanging on the cross.

John is using typology. This is the technique of taking an incident or person from the Jewish Scriptures and using it as a type or prefigurement of a person or event recorded in the Christian Scriptures. Here, the hanging up of the serpent is used as an image that prefigures the crucifixion. Since the raising up of Jesus is part of God's plan of salvation, we have the Johannine version of the first prophecy of the Passion: the Son of Man "must be lifted up." Notice the similarity with the first mention of the Passion in the Gospel according to Mark:

"The Son of Man must suffer much. . . . He will be put to death, but three days later he will rise to life" (Mark 8:31).	". . . the Son of Man must be lifted up, so that everyone who believes in him may have eternal life" (John 3:14–15).

The action of "lifting up" refers to the interdependent aspects of the Paschal mystery: Jesus is hung on the cross, Jesus rises from the dead, Jesus is glorified, and Jesus ascends to the Father. John is asserting that the whole Paschal mystery (death, resurrection, and ascension of Jesus) is the means through which believers will "have eternal life" (3:15).

In verse 16 John seems to anticipate the reader's question,

"Why does God offer us the gift of eternal life?" The evangelist explains:

> *For God loved the world so much that he gave his only Son . . .*
> (3:16).

In this magnificent verse we find a summary of the entire Christian message of redemption: God's giving of his Son. First, the Father "gave" his Son in the Incarnation (1:14); secondly, the Father "gave" his Son in the crucifixion (3:14). Love is the one motive God had in acting. The best commentary on this verse is found in John's first letter:

> *And God showed his love for us by sending his only Son into the world, so that we might have life through him. This is what love is: it is not that we have loved God, but that he loved us and sent his Son to be the means by which our sins are forgiven. . . . God is love . . .* (1 John 4:9–16).

Although the Father sent the Son into the world not to be its judge but to be its Savior (3:17), the Son's coming brings the world to a point of crisis. Now humankind must choose between the light who is Jesus and the darkness which is both sin and sin's ultimate effect, the refusal to believe (3:19).

To grasp John's thought more accurately, remember that he uses the term "world" in two different ways. On the one hand, the world is the place where people live. We are born into the world, and at death we leave the world. God cares for the world as his creation (1:3, 10), and God loves the people in the world (3:16). On the other hand, the world is the sum total of the effects of sin. As the realm dominated by Satan, the world stands in opposition to all that is good, to all that is "of God." This negative sense of world serves as the context for John's teaching in 3:18–21. Although Jesus does not come to judge in the sense of condemnation, the very fact of his presence demands that people make a choice. According to John each person must decide either to believe in Jesus or to reject him. The first decision looks to salvation; the second choice leads to death. There are only two alternatives: faith or judgment.

In order better to appreciate John's brilliant theologizing, mention must be made of John's dualistic outlook. Dualism is a rigid division of reality into white and black. All is light or darkness, life or death, obedience or sin. No allowance is made for anything in between. There are no grey areas. Although dualism is basically an over-simplification of reality, it nevertheless serves John's purpose. He wants to state quickly and clearly what is ultimately at stake for his audience. In Jesus there is an urgency that confronts each of us. We are compelled to choose. Conversion cannot be put off to some future time. There are only two lifestyles and, depending on which is chosen, one has either accepted birth from above or one has chosen to bring judgment down upon oneself.

The act of sentencing oneself is called loving the darkness rather than the light (3:19). For John, loving the darkness means preferring darkness to light. Some people choose not to accept Jesus; they willfully reject the light shining in the darkness (1:5).

The author of the Fourth Gospel is a master in using contrasting images to make his point. In verses 18 to 21, John sketches the whole history of the interaction between God and humankind. To "prefer" or "love" darkness is the epitome of sin; it is the total disregard of God; it is the deliberate choice of creature instead of creator. In effect, it is humanity's denial of any reality beyond itself. Since sin and truth cannot co-exist, the one who judges according to the flesh commits herself or himself to a lifestyle of avoidance. Such a person must hide from the very light which would reveal his/her deeds for what they in fact are: evil. Having decided not to change, the sinful person finds himself imprisoned in the consequences of his decision: he hates the light, flees from the light, refuses to come to the light (3:20).

John's summary statement (3:21) confirms the believer in his or her decision to live as God wills. Like Nathanael, the true Israelite (1:46), such a person does the truth by living in accordance with God's priorities. Notice the similarity between verses 20 and 21 and the following statements found in the Dead Sea Scrolls: "According as a person's inheritance is in truth and righteousness, so that one hates evil. But insofar as the person's heritage is in the portion of wickedness and perversity within, so that one hates truth" (1 Qumran Scroll 4:24).

REFLECTION. In the wake of repenting Watergate sinners and the vocal evangelical activity of many Christian communities, let us view the phrase "born again" in its proper context. According to John's Gospel, the contemporary phrase, "born again Christian," is a misnomer. The phrase speaks as if there are two kinds of Christians, the "first born Christian" and the "born again Christian." The phrase, "born again Christian," is often used to indicate that a person has suddenly become very serious about Jesus.

While the Gospel is the pearl of great price, and while a certain zestful enthusiasm accompanies an appreciation of the gift of faith in Jesus, the term, "born again Christian," is not a suitable phrase for this conversion experience. The movement of a person from a position of merely taking Jesus for granted to a position of sincerely trying to live as God wills is, indeed, a gift for which we should pray. But the danger in referring to this conversion process as being "born again" is that it undermines the Johannine understanding of the sacrament of Baptism. When John writes about the necessity of being born again (3:3, 5), he is speaking of the movement from being merely children of human parents to becoming children of God. This "birth from above" is accomplished in baptism. Therefore, only the person who is an unbeliever can be "born again." Once a person becomes a child of God, he or she is always God's child. The Christian, by definition, is one who has already been "born again." It is as if God addressed each person baptized with these words, "You are now my child and nothing you can ever do will ever change this." While Charles Colson was committing the crimes he later repented of, he was doing them as a child of God; he had already been baptized. During the period of imprisonment, Colson experienced not rebirth but conversion. He turned back to God, reordered his priorities, wrote a book about the process and mistitled it *Born Again* instead of *Conversion*. We need to find a more appropriate expression than "born again Christian" to describe those of us who begin to take our faith more seriously than before.

JESUS, JOHN THE BAPTIST AND A SUMMARY
READ 3:22–36

COMMENTARY. Although the text makes a passing reference to the baptizing activity of Jesus and his disciples (3:22), later it is asserted that Jesus did not baptize, but only his disciples did (4:1–2). At this point it is still early in Jesus' ministry, for the Baptist has not yet been imprisoned. The baptizing activity of the disciples may indicate that Jesus was still in the process of gathering his disciples.

The precise issue in the argument dealing with ritual purification in verse 25 is not mentioned. The main concern of the evangelist is to teach the appropriate relationship between Jesus and the Baptist. Verse 26 indicates that tension exists between the disciples of the Baptist and the disciples of Jesus. The frustration of the Baptist's disciples occasions the Baptist's final testimony. The Baptist repeats the purpose for which he had come: to point out the Lamb of God, the one who will baptize with the Holy Spirit. As we have seen, the water changed to wine at Cana had a messianic significance; so does the Baptist's taking the role of the best man at the wedding. Just as the bridegroom's friend rejoices at the marriage ceremony, so the Baptist rejoices in the arrival of the messianic bridegroom. The Baptist's mission is finished. He declares that the recognition already given him will fade away in proportion to the increasing recognition of Jesus as the Messiah (3:30).

Just as John's account of the changing of water into wine at Cana contains references to the sacrament of the Eucharist, so also does the account of Jesus' conversation with Nicodemus contain references to the sacrament of Baptism. With the mention of the baptizing activity of Jesus' disciples (3:22 and 4:2), we may find ourselves asking, "Is this the occasion when Jesus instituted the sacrament of Baptism?" The answer to the question is this: the evangelist did not address himself to the question of the precise moment of the institution of any sacrament. When the

Fourth Gospel was being completed, the community had long been celebrating the baptismal and eucharistic liturgies. John's interest was in pointing out the connection between the liturgical rituals of the community and the words and deeds of Jesus. To accomplish this purpose John wove the threads of his sacramental theology into the whole cloth of the Gospel of Jesus.

Verses 31–36 repeat the themes found in 3:1–21. For example, when Jesus is described as "one who comes from above" (3:31), we are reminded of the necessity of "birth from above" (3:3). This assertion of the heavenly origins of Jesus has messianic overtones. He is God's revealing Word, envoy, ambassador and spokesman.

Verse 33 contains a sharp transition in perspective, moving from those who refuse to accept Jesus' testimony to the believing community. Because Jesus is the Father's envoy, Jesus speaks the message his Father gave him (3:34). The prophets were given God's Spirit for the accomplishment of a particular task; for example, speaking God's word to his people. Jesus, however, has received from God "the fullness of his Spirit" (3:34). The Spirit remains with Jesus always. In verse 35 the evangelist introduces two items which will be developed later in the Gospel: the Father's love for the Son and the Son's consequent authority over all things.

REFLECTION. William Golding's novel, *Lord of the Flies,* makes interesting supplemental reading. While Golding says nothing about God, his novel brilliantly depicts the situation of humanity without God. The novel depicts the struggle for order and hope among a group of English boys marooned on a Pacific island. Golding's theme is that for humankind there is no help, no rescue, no salvation. If John were able to review this novel, he would probably say that Golding is correct as far as he goes. We cannot save ourselves; God alone can.

STUDY GROUP QUESTIONS

1. Niels Bohr, the Nobel Prize winning physicist, once said, "When it comes to atoms, language must be used as it is in po-

etry. The poet is more concerned with creating images that convey meaning than he is concerned with describing facts." Bohr was referring to that which lies below the range of sight: atoms. The biblical author describes realities that lie beyond the realm of our senses. The biblical writer also has much in common with the poet—for both must rely on images to get the message across. In the images of water, wind, parenting, life and death, light and darkness, being born and being born from above (3:1–21), John strives to give his readers an understanding of the meaning of Jesus. Share with one another how well these images help you understand the meaning of Jesus. How does this understanding have an impact on the way you live your life?

2. The Gospel according to John addresses several different audiences. What does the message of 3:22–30 say to the followers of John the Baptist who were living when the Gospel was being circulated in the 90's?

3. When some people suddenly become serious about Jesus, they refer to themselves as "born again Christians." What would John say about this expression? What expression or word would you use to describe a person who wants to truly live according to the values and teachings of Jesus?

Chapter Four

JESUS AND THE SAMARITAN WOMAN

OVERVIEW. Jesus has spoken of birth from above in his dialogue with Nicodemus. In this chapter Jesus encounters a Samaritan woman and speaks with her of living water as a fountain springing up into eternal life (4:7–30). Then Jesus restores life to an official's dying son (4:46–54). Nicodemus is a Jew; the Samaritan woman is partly Jewish and partly Gentile; the official is probably a Gentile. While Jesus speaks of eternal life to both the rabbi and the Samaritan, his commanding words, "Go, your son will live!" (4:50), restore life to the dying boy. Like ripples expanding in the water, the words of Jesus spread out in concentric circles touching the people of Israel, the inhabitants of Samaria, and finally the Gentile world.

READ 4:1–30

COMMENTARY. The Pharisees, who had previously taken steps to interrogate the Baptist (1:24), now take a suspicious interest in Jesus (4:1). Noting their attention, Jesus leaves Jerusalem for Galilee (4:3). The writer of the Fourth Gospel does not give us enough information to understand clearly the relationship between the interest of the Pharisees and Jesus' departure from Judea. There were Pharisees in Galilee as well as in Judea, so we know that Jesus does not fear the Pharisees as a group. It is possible that Jesus left because the Judean (southern) Pharisees were hostile to him.

Verse six depicts a tired and thirsty Jesus resting near a deep well. Lacking vessel or skin with which to draw, the water is inaccessible to him. About the same time a lone woman leaves her dwelling. She has waited until noon for her daily trek to the well. It is unlikely that she will meet anyone there at this hot and uncomfortable hour. A loner and social outcast, she prefers the heat of the day to the scorn of the town's respectable women.

Arriving at Jacob's well, she ignores the presence of the Jewish man. Being a Samaritan, the woman had little in common with Jews from either Galilee to the north or Judea to the south. In fact, there is much enmity between Samaritan and Jew. The Jews looked upon the Samaritans as the paganized descendants of northern Israelites and Assyrian colonists. They were an "unclean" people in spite of the fact that they clung to the Mosaic Law expounded in the first five books of the Hebrew Scriptures. The second book of Kings relates the story of five Assyrian groups who brought their own gods and then combined their worship with the worship of Yahweh, the God of Abraham, Isaac and Jacob:

> *So they worshiped the Lord, but they also worshiped their own gods according to the customs of the countries from which they had come. They still carry on their old customs to this day*
> (2 Kings 17:33–34).

When Jesus not only speaks to her but even asks her for a drink of water (4:7), the woman is startled. She is not only a Samaritan, but also a woman. Furthermore, this Jew is asking for a drink from her drinking vessel, the very use of which would make him ritually unclean (4:9).

The response of Jesus moves the entire exchange to a deeper level of meaning (4:10). Surface appearances begin to give way to divine reality. It appears that Jesus is the one in need of water, and the woman has the tool for providing it. But at the deepest level of reality the truth is that the woman thirsts for the water

of intimacy with God, and Jesus is the revealer who comes to give this living water of his message to her.

The Johannine technique of "misunderstanding" is once again evident in the woman's uncomprehending response. She, like Nicodemus, understands only the literal meaning of Jesus' words. He appears to be offering her fresh running water. Nicodemus puzzled, "How can a grown man be born again?" (3:4). The woman asks, "Where would you get that life-giving water?" (4:11). Her question deals with the situation of every human person. Within each of us is a quest, a hunger, a thirst for understanding and union with God. In the Hebrew Scriptures, spring water symbolized both God (Jeremiah 2:13) and the gifts of the messianic age (Isaiah 55:1). The book of Proverbs speaks of "the teachings of the wise" as a "fountain of life" (Proverbs 13:14). The rabbis themselves frequently spoke of the Torah as the divine gift that satisfies one's thirst.

Without waiting for an answer, the woman refers to the well given by Jacob, the patriarchial ancestor of both Jew and Samaritan. Perhaps she is thinking that Jesus claimed to know the location of a nearby spring, a source of water other than Jacob's well. Thus, both the patriarch Jacob and this man would be benefactors to the people nearby. Since she is still thinking of water in its literal sense, and since Jacob's well is already such an excellent source of water, she wonders how could the new water given by this man Jesus be better. She asks, "You don't claim to be greater than Jacob, do you?" (4:12). Her question is an example of Johannine irony. While she speaks the truth (for he does indeed claim to be greater than Jacob), she does not realize (though the reader does) the deeper meaning of her words.

Addressing her misunderstanding, Jesus says that he is not referring to water of the sort found in either well or spring. That water provides only a temporary slaking of physical thirst (4:13). The water he comes to give will satisfy/fulfill the deepest yearnings of the human person. Perhaps this provides a richer understanding of the living water. The verb "drinks" in verse 14 is in the aorist tense, which means that the believer drinks only once (a reference to baptism?). One drink suffices, because the water becomes a fountain within the believer. This living water is the gift of God (4:10) which fulfills the prophecies of Isaiah (12:3 and 55:1) and Ezekiel (47:1). What in the Christian life corresponds to the description of the living water? Jesus is speaking both of his own teaching and of the Holy Spirit (14:26 shows that they are not separate realities). Jesus' teaching is not impersonal. It is the living word which abides in the believer (15:7) and becomes the beginning of eternal life. In the same way the Spirit/Truth dwells within the believer as a refreshing spring and a source of eternal life.

However, the woman continues to think of water in the literal sense. But she does understand that the new water Jesus offers will somehow make her independent of created things. She asks for this extraordinary water so that she will no longer have to trek to the well to relieve her physical thirst (4:15). She does not understand that the water symbolizes the revelation that will bring her into a new and deeper relationship with God.

In order to lead her beyond the realm of touch and taste, Jesus introduces the subject of her husband. When she denies that she has a husband, Jesus demonstrates his more than human knowledge by revealing much of her life story. Immediately, the dialogue between the Samaritan and the Jew moves to a deeper level. Recognizing that she has been talking with a man of God, she states, "I see you are a prophet . . ." (4:19). Lifting her eyes to Mount Gerizim, a few miles to the southwest, she asks the question that introduces the bitter Samaritan-Jewish controversy about the proper place to worship God. Yahweh had commanded this:

> *"You are not to offer your sacrifices wherever you choose; you must offer them only in the one place that the Lord will choose in the territory of one of your tribes. Only there are you to offer your sacrifices . . . and do all the other things I have commanded you"* (Deuteronomy 12:13–14).

While Jews believed that Jerusalem was that one place, the Samaritans worshiped on Mount Gerizim. The question of the Samaritan woman shows that she has finally begun to recognize that her encounter with Jesus involves religious issues. The customary view that her question was an attempt to avoid further discussion of the morality of her present life-style is incorrect. Jesus' reference to the six men in her life was intended to bring the woman to a deeper perception of his person and his words.

The woman's question about the place of sacrifice provides the perfect point of departure for what Jesus wants to teach: "the worship of the Father as he really is" (4:23).

The second theme of the discourse is introduced by this topic sentence:

> *". . .the time will come when people will not worship either on this mountain or in Jerusalem"* (4:21).

Jesus refers to a new era in which the encounter of God with his people will not be restricted to a particular place.

Jesus also asserts that "it is from the Jews that salvation comes" (4:22). It is not out of arrogance that Jesus tells the woman that the Jews know whom they worship whereas the Samaritans do not. Rather, Jesus is speaking to a non-Jew about the significance of the religious heritage of the Jewish people. Before Jesus can explain how it is that Jew as well as Samaritan will soon worship the Father in a radically new way, he must first establish the historical context of God's final revelation. The Jews are God's first chosen. God gave them his Law. God has sent them his prophets. In Jesus God gives his ultimate gift. God's own Son is born a Jew.

Jesus tells the Samaritan woman that the special time ("hour") "will come," "is coming," and "is already here" (4:21, 23). The different tenses reflect the different audiences being addressed. From the point of view of the dialogue between Jesus and the Samaritan woman, the hour of Jesus' crucifixion-exaltation and the giving of the Spirit is still in the future. But from the perspective of John's late first century audience, Jesus has already died, ascended to the Father, and sent the Spirit.

The true worship desired by the Father (4:23) is that worship offered by those who are in union with his Son (the Last Supper discourse will develop this theme). Jesus does not mean that Jewish believers were offering God a false worship, for he admits that they know whom they worship. They knew God as Yahweh, as I Am Who I Am (Exodus 3:14). In Jesus, however, God is doing a new thing. The Covenant relationship with Israel is being brought to a new perfection. From now on, Jesus says, only the person who knows the Father as I do will worship him as he is. Only the person who possesses the Spirit will truly worship him.

Jesus is the one who reveals his Father to those who believe. It is through the power of the Spirit that people are "born from above" (3:3–6). In that rebirth the believer has received a new identity. He or she has become the Father's son or daughter. Verse 24 is related to verse 23; the assertion that God is Spirit is not a definition but a description of his nature. One cannot be in intimate relationship with God if one remains on the "natural" level of existence. That is why Jesus taught: "A person is born physically of human parents, but he is born spiritually of the Spirit" (3:6). Because he or she is a follower of Jesus and a child of the Father, the believer can worship the Father "as he really is" (4:24).

But the woman does not comprehend his teaching about worshiping the Father as he really is. Once again she turns to the teachings of the Samaritan religion. Referring to the Samaritan

expectation of the Messiah, she tries to hold her own in her encounter with the Jewish prophet:

> *"I know that the Messiah will come, and when he comes, he will*
> *tell us everything"* (4:25).

The Samaritans had divided what we call "the Ten Commandments" (see Exodus 20:1–17; Deuteronomy 5:1–21) into nine sections to which they added a tenth. This last section ("tenth
commandment") had two parts, the first dealing with the sanctity
of Mount Gerizim, and the second dealing with the Samaritan
hope for a prophet-like-Moses (Deuteronomy 18:15, 18). Just as
Moses had brought God's will (the Law) to the Jews, so the future prophet-like-Moses (the Samaritan Messiah) would reveal
God's saving will to the whole world! These Samaritan expectations explain why the woman, not comprehending Jesus, takes
refuge in the hope for the Messiah who "will tell us everything"
(4:25).

The response of Jesus is without parallel in the Synoptic accounts of the Gospel. It is the most direct claim to messiahship
that is found in all the Christian Scriptures:

> *"I am he, I who am talking with you"* (4:26).

Verse 26 also introduces the "I am" expression, the first of
many that John will report on the lips of Jesus. For the reader familiar with the Hebrew Scriptures, "I am" is a reference to the divine name of God.

With this revelation of himself, the dialogue between Jesus and
the Samaritan woman reaches its climax. The disciples arrive
with provisions. They are astonished to perceive their rabbi
breaking racial, social and religious precedents by speaking with
a woman who is a Samaritan. Nevertheless, they dared not criti-
cize either the woman or their Master (4:27).

The woman leaves her water jar in order to race as fast as possible to the townspeople (4:28). She invites them to come to Jesus
with the same words Jesus had earlier addressed to the disciples

of the Baptist (1:39), and Philip had addressed to Nathanael (1:46): "Come and see . . ." (4:29).

She has been impressed to such a degree that she risks personal embarrassment in telling the townspeople about the man who had prophetic knowledge of her life story (4:28–29). However, she is cautious with regard to what Jesus has revealed to her in verse 26. Her tentative expression, "Could he be the Messiah?" is perhaps an indication that the townspeople must make their own decisions to believe in Jesus.

REFLECTION. If each one of us could come to a deeper appreciation of Jesus' teaching that God's presence is no longer restricted to Mount Gerizim or to the Jerusalem Temple, we would discover another way of doing what Brother Lawrence calls "practicing the presence of God." If we could thoroughly integrate this teaching into our daily lives, we would discover a new way of relating to each other, be we husband or wife, married or single, cleric or religious, relative or neighbor, friend or stranger.

The abiding or indwelling presence of Father, Son and Spirit within each member of the believing community is, as we shall see in chapter 13, the basis for Jesus' new commandment: "As I have loved you, so you must love one another." Jesus also told us the consequences of our obedience: if we so love one another, "then everyone will know that you are my disciples" (13:35).

JESUS, THE DISCIPLES, AND THE TOWNSPEOPLE

OVERVIEW. Between the woman's proclamation and the arrival of the townspeople at the well, John introduces a third theme into the chapter: the importance of missionary work (4:31–38). The fourth evangelist held the Samaritan community in high esteem. This is indicated by the fact that Jesus' "missionary discourse" is placed between the Samaritan woman's bringing her news about Jesus to the townspeople (4:29) and their subsequent acceptance of Jesus in faith (4:39–42). Nowhere else in the Fourth Gospel does John report such overwhelming success as Jesus has in Samaria.

READ 4:31–42

COMMENTARY. The disciples' offer of something to eat occasions Jesus' discourse. Using food as a metaphor, Jesus refers to another source of sustenance, food that his disciples "know nothing about" (4:32). Since the disciples misunderstand his meaning, Jesus explains that his food is obeying the will of the one who sent him; his food is finishing the work the Father has given him to do (4:34). The two actions are so united that they are in fact one; the two actions summarize his mission. The theme of obediently finishing the work his Father has given Jesus to do will recur throughout the Gospel (see 5:17–19; 6:38–40; 14:10). Jesus will climax his work of obedience on the cross: "It is finished!" (19:30).

In verse 35, Jesus refers to a proverb that deals with the interval between sowing and planting. We may visualize Jesus pointing to the crowd of approaching townspeople as he contrasts the proverb with the event taking place before the eyes of his disciples. The people of Samaria are the fields ready to be harvested. Note that Matthew places this saying of Jesus as an introduction to the missionary discourse (see Matthew 9:37–38). "Harvest," in the Hebrew Scriptures, often carried end-time associations, because the act of gathering in, followed by the separating process, was an apt symbol for judgment day. Verse 36 is most likely an application of Amos 9:13 or Psalm 126:5–6. In both of these passages the abundance of the messianic age is depicted. When that time comes, there will no longer be an interval between planting and reaping. Thus, sower and reaper rejoice together. The Samaritans are a sign of the final harvest; the seeds planted by Jesus have immediately become crops ready for harvesting.

With verse 37, probably another proverb, the time sequence and perspective shift. Whereas a moment before Jesus was speaking of harvest coming immediately after planting (4:35–36), now he implies that a long time has passed between sowing and reaping. He tells his disciples that they are reaping only because someone else labored before them (4:37–38).

In verses 39–42 we reach the climax of the narrative that began with the encounter between Jesus and the Samaritan woman. By means of her witness to Jesus, many townspeople believed in him (4:39). After Jesus accepts their invitation and stays with them for two days, "Many more believed <u>because of his message</u>" (4:41). These words have been underscored because they express John's "theology of faith." The Samaritans are models for those who come to faith in Jesus. They first display an openness to what the woman said about Jesus. Then they went out to meet Jesus. They manifested a readiness to hear his teaching. Finally, they did not need signs (miracles); Jesus' message is sufficient to lead them to belief. That is why they tell the woman that they no longer believe because of her testimony; they believe because "we ourselves have heard him . . ." (4:42). As a result of Jesus' word, they profess "we know that he really is the Savior of the world" (4:42).

The title, "Savior of the world," is the climax of a series of titles attributed to Jesus in this episode. He was first recognized as a prophet, then as Messiah, and then as the world's Savior. We have seen a similar progression of titles in chapter one. Jesus was there perceived as the Messiah (1:41), the prophet spoken of by Moses (1:45), and Son of God and King of Israel (1:49). These are patterns of faith for the fourth evangelist. The people who encounter Jesus in faith first see him as an ordinary man. Then Jesus reveals some aspect of himself. When the people respond, their understanding of Jesus becomes more penetrating, more intimate. In chapter one we saw the progression of faith from the perspective of the believing Israelites. They came to recognize Jesus as the "King of Israel." In chapter four the Samaritans come to recognize Jesus in accordance with their expectation of a messianic prophet who would reveal the will of God to the world just as Moses had done for the Jews. "Savior of the world" is a title that exceeds the expectations of the Jewish people. When the man born blind moves through this pattern of faith and comes to know Jesus as "Lord" (9:38), the expectations of the Samaritan people will be surpassed.

REFLECTION. Jesus said, "My food is to obey the will of the one who sent me and to finish the work he gave me to do" (4:34). We can refer to this statement as "the spirituality of Jesus." Since we are called to be his followers, should not the spirituality of Jesus be ours also? Jesus was thirsty and hungry. We can picture him drinking the water given by the Samaritan woman as he spoke with her of living water springing up into eternal life. We can visualize him eating the food offered to him by his disciples, even as he spoke of his desire to do always the Father's will.

We need to ask ourselves if living the spiritual life is a question of doing the one before the other—as if we should or could do God's will before we drank or ate! The fact of the matter is that it does not make a big difference whether we fast or we feast, as long as we are striving to do the Father's will in all we do. We do not have to choose between praying or making a living. To say that one must decide to do the ordinary human activities or decide to be a person of prayer is to offer a false choice. Jesus is our model. He was both a human being and a prayerful person. The fact that he needed to drink and eat did not mean he ceased to do the work his Father gave him to do. It is the same for us. The fact that one must hustle for the dollar, or prepare the family meal, or plow the south forty acres does not exclude one from the presence of God.

Perhaps the key to developing the interior life we are called to live is this: to realize that "whatever you do, whether you eat or drink, do it all for God's glory" (1 Corinthians 10:31). A believer can see all things and all activities bathed in the light of God's presence.

On the one hand we have been given a human nature. Thus we glorify God by being what we are, by being as authentically human as possible. All the "natural virtues" have a bearing on this right kind of human living—prudence, justice, fortitude and temperance. On the other hand, we have become children of God. We know the Father "as he really is," as our Father. Without diminishing that which is truly human in us, we are called to live with the same set of priorities that Jesus lived by. Each of us is called to do the Father's will; each of us has his or her own unique mission in life. Each of us is called to live in such a way that "now and at the hour of our death" we can pray, "Father, my food is to do your will. May I some day finish the work you have given me to do."

JESUS HEALS AN OFFICIAL'S SON
READ 4:43–54

COMMENTARY. Having spent two days with the Samaritans, Jesus arrives in Galilee. The saying about the lack of respect for a prophet in his own country (4:44) does not accord with the welcome Jesus receives from his Galilean countrymen (4:45). It is possible that the final editor of John's Gospel tucked the saying in here as a summary of Jesus' Galilean ministry, which, in fact, was largely unsuccessful.

A government official whose son is sick (4:46) seeks Jesus. There is a similar incident involving the son or servant of a Roman centurion recorded in Matthew 8:5–13. If the government official in John's account is the Roman centurion, then John is presenting a progression in the faith-response to Jesus. Nicodemus, the Jewish Pharisee listens openly, acknowledges Jesus as rabbi or teacher, but does not further commit himself. The half-pagan, half-Jewish Samaritan woman recognizes that Jesus is a prophet and perhaps the Messiah. She bears witness to Jesus, and her townspeople come to believe in him. Now the pagan official stands before Jesus, asking him to heal his son, "who was about to die" (4:47).

It seems as if Jesus rebukes the man interceding for his dying son:

> *"None of you will ever believe unless you see miracles and wonders"* (4:48).

However, these words are not addressed to the official alone. The "you" is plural; the rebuke is addressed to the whole crowd. We have here a miniature presentation of the Johannine theology of signs, i.e., miracles. The evangelist has stated that during the first Passover "many believed in him as they saw the miracles he performed" (2:23). When Jesus returned to Galilee, the people welcomed him because they had been at the same Passover and "had seen everything that he had done during the festival" (4:45). But, according to John, that which is crucial is the message of Jesus. To truly believe in Jesus is to accept his words. Everything short of this total adherence to Jesus and the words he speaks is not real faith. Jesus is the Word made flesh. His words reveal the Father. Acceptance of Jesus only on the basis of the signs he performs is not sufficient.

For John, belief in the person of Jesus and his word is the important thing. John is very much in the mainstream of the Jewish "theology" of miracles when he makes this affirmation. By themselves, signs and wonders are neutral. What counts is the power that stands behind the miracle-worker, and the direction the sign points out. The power may be good and it may be evil. The sign might lead to God or away from him. Thus the touchstone for the authenticity of a miracle is both the source and the destination of the sign. If the sign leads to God and if the sign confirms people in the traditional belief of the community, then it is good and the doer of the work is approved. On the other hand, if the worker of signs leads others away from the traditional belief, away from God, then that wonder-worker must be put to death (Dt. 13:2–6). We can see how well John's Jewish understanding of signs meshes with his understanding of Jesus. All that Jesus does he does because the Father so wills. The signs Jesus does are among the works the Father has given him to do. His works point to the Father because their purpose is the revelation of the Father. So, when people stop at the signs themselves, when the people do not see how they point to and authenticate Jesus who reveals the Father, their purpose is frustrated. That is why Jesus makes the exasperated accusation, "Unless you people see signs and wonders, you do not believe" (4:48, *New American Bible*).

A paraphrase of Jesus' complaint is this: "You people ought to believe in me first, but you do not. You wait around for a display of power, and, when it is given, you only commit yourself in proportion to the size of the miracle. Can't you understand that faith is not like that? Do you not know that believing always comes before receiving proof?"

But the preoccupied official misses the point of Jesus' rebuke: "Sir, come with me before my child dies" (4:49). Then Jesus puts the official to the test: "Go; your son will live!" (4:50). This is the invitation to authentic faith. If he leaves without Jesus, if he departs without seeing any sign, then he will have believed in Jesus on the strength of his word alone! John writes: "The man believed Jesus' words and went" (4:50). This is the moment of conversion; the official made the decision to believe without the assurance of signs and wonders. It was enough for him to have Jesus' word, "your son *will* live" (4:50).

On the way home, the official's servants bring the news, "Your boy is going to live!" (4:51). The boy's father then asks for the time of his son's recovery. He learns that the turning point happened at the very hour when Jesus had told him that his son would live (4:53). For John, this is the correct sequence regarding the signs of Jesus. First we are to believe in Jesus; after this comes the sign that confirms us in that faith commitment.

The account of the early Galilean ministry, which began at the wedding feast where Jesus performed the first of his revealing signs (2:11), now ends with the affirmation of Jesus by the official's family. With the mention of the second miracle Jesus performed in Galilee (4:54), John indicates to the reader that another section of his writing is complete (2:1 through 4:54).

REFLECTION. It is interesting to note how we turned John's theology of miracles upside down during the nineteenth and twentieth centuries. Thus we are accustomed to approach the unbelieving and the skeptical by first speaking of the miracles Jesus performed, as if by themselves they could convince another that Jesus is God and thereby bring that person to faith. But this progression is precisely what Jesus refuted. According to John, belief in Jesus had priority; signs were secondary. The earliest members of the Church believed in Jesus first. Then, because Jesus was perceived with the eyes of faith as the one sent from God, they "believed" in his miracles. It is the same for us. When we consider our own situation, we believe not because we have seen miracles, but because we have faith in Jesus.

The Johannine understanding of signs can help us to bring our own spiritual lives, our own "religious" practices, into a correct perspective. Just as the miracles mean little apart from faith in the person of Jesus, so also the supports of faith which the Church offers us are weak apart from our personal faith. We can have the most relevant liturgies, the most colorful religious education texts and well-staffed parish programs of every kind. Yet if our personal faith and commitment to Jesus Christ are weak, all these important and worthwhile accomplishments are built upon sand.

STUDY GROUP QUESTIONS

1. Between 4:7 and 4:29 the Samaritan woman changes from a stranger who is unconcerned about the thirsty Jewish man by the well to an enthusiastic missionary who invites her townspeople to "Come and see" the one who might be the Messiah. Share with one another how each perceives the course of her spiritual journey. Do you think that John could have made this incident less difficult to understand? If yes, how? Do you think it is worth the effort to study 4:7–29 in depth? Why or why not?

2. In narrating the meetings of Jesus with the Samaritans and the official, John emphasizes the primacy of faith over signs. Compare 4:39–42 with 4:43–54, and share with one another how your own view of miracles has or has not changed as a result of John's perspective.

Chapter Five

A SABBATH HEALING

OVERVIEW. With this chapter John introduces a long section (chapters 5 through 10) in which he compares Jesus with the major Jewish feasts. Chapter five is another example of John's creative use of the earlier tradition. It is important here to remember how John understands Jesus' miracles. They are not an end in themselves; as signs, they point beyond themselves to the real nature of Jesus. Thus John takes a miracle story from the tradition and uses it to introduce a long reflection on the person of Jesus: his work and his relationship to the Father (5:19–47). What was probably a minor part of the earlier tradition—that the healing took place on a Sabbath—becomes the focal point of the Johannine narrative. John wants to compare Jesus with the Sabbath. Jesus is above the Sabbath, and a co-worker with the Father.

READ 5:1–18

COMMENTARY. For the second time Jesus makes the pilgrimage from Galilee to Jerusalem (see 2:12–13), in order to participate in the Temple celebrations. John does not tell us what feast it was, possibly because he wants to emphasize the Sabbath as a continuing feast throughout the year. Close to the Temple area there was a pool at which the sick would gather in hope of healing. (The remains of the pool have been discovered recently by archeologists. It lies beneath the Church of St. Anne in Jerusalem.) Why does the evangelist give us the Hebrew name for the pool? It may be that he wants to highlight the healing power of Jesus by contrasting it with the failure of the "Jewish waters" to heal the sick man. Does he also want us to remember the water of purification (chapter 2) and the water of Jacob's well (chapter 4)?

Jesus knows the duration of the man's illness (5:6) and takes the initiative without a request being made. The healing is effected by Jesus' powerful word. Immediately the man's strength returns and he begins to walk. It is interesting to compare two healing accounts in Mark, each of which shares some similarity with this event. In Mark 2:1–12 a paralyzed man is healed by a similar command of Jesus to get up, pick up his mat and go home. In Mark's third chapter, Jesus takes the initiative to heal a crippled man on a Sabbath day. Afterward, Mark notes, the Jewish leaders began making plans to kill Jesus (Mark 3:1–6).

In the last part of verse 9 John notes: "The day this happened was a Sabbath." For the Jewish people the Sabbath was a day sacred in the eyes of Yahweh. The Lord himself had commanded its observance:

> *The Lord said to me, "Jeremiah, go and announce my message at the People's Gate. . . . Tell them that if they love their lives, they must not carry any load on the Sabbath; they must not carry anything in through the gates of Jerusalem or carry anything out of their houses on the Sabbath. They must not work on the Sabbath; they must observe it as a sacred day, as I commanded their ancestors* (Jeremiah 17:19–22).

The rabbis specifically forbade carrying one's bed on the Sabbath. Thus the healed man's obedience to Jesus' command brings him into conflict with the Jewish leaders. The man must have known this. His response to their accusation implies that the one who healed him must have the authority to countermand the Law. The leaders completely ignore the sign of God's power and are only concerned about the disruption of the Sabbath (5:12).

Surprisingly, the man does not know who healed him; in explanation John notes how crowded the pool area had been. On their
subsequent meeting in the Temple, Jesus warns the man that the
gift he has received must lead to a conversion of heart. If not, the
judgment of God ("something worse") would fall heavily on him.

In the command to stop sinning there may be an indication that
the healing involved more than physical health. Jesus is presented
in the discourse as one who gives eternal life (5:21–29). John may
intend his readers to understand that the man has received this
gift as well. At the beginning of chapter four there was a hint of
the hostility of some Pharisees toward Jesus (4:1–3). Now, upon
hearing that it was Jesus who healed the crippled man, the Jewish
authorities "began to persecute Jesus" (5:16). Thus John agrees
with the Synoptic tradition (Mark 3:6) that the opposition of the
Jewish leaders to Jesus began very early in his ministry.

Note that in the Synoptic Gospels Jesus justifies his Sabbath
healings on humanitarian grounds: God's intent was not to prevent people in need from being helped and healed. But in John's
account, Jesus' justification is startling:

"My Father is always working, and I too must work!" (5:17).

The author of Genesis had taught that God stopped working
when he had finished his creative task (Genesis 2:2–4). In reflecting on this, the rabbis linked man's Sabbath observance with
God's great Sabbath rest. They realized, however, that God could
not rest from all work. Even on the Sabbath God continued to
give life (for were not children born on the Sabbath?), and likewise he continued to exercise his function as judge (for did not
people die on the Sabbath?). In this light we can better understand the violent reaction of the Jewish leaders:

*This saying made the Jewish authorities all the more determined
to kill him; not only had he broken the Sabbath law, but he had
said that God was his own Father, and in this way had made
himself equal with God* (5:18).

Verses 16–18 might be considered an introduction to the discourse as well as the conclusion of the healing narrative. They clarify what is really important in the narrative. Not only is Jesus greater than the Sabbath (Mark 2:28); he does the same works that the Father does! The Jewish leaders are not slow in detecting Jesus' claim to divinity in his statement, "I too must work." They saw the claim as blasphemy. Certainly the protection of God's honor and uniqueness had been a driving force throughout Israel's entire history. Perhaps in a world in which emperors were claiming divine honors the Jewish leaders felt a special need to be vigilant. Their implied accusation (5:18) reminds us of texts in which Adam and Eve (Genesis 3:4–7) and the king of Babylon (Isaiah 14:12–21) desire to make themselves like God.

A DISCOURSE ON THE WORK OF THE SON
READ 5:19–47

COMMENTARY. This discourse is one of the most powerful and profound in the Gospel. Because his authority to act has been called into question, Jesus answers his critics by equating his actions with the actions of God. The entire discourse is steeped in the style of rabbinic theological argument. (We have already noticed how the introductory section in verses 16–18 rests on the rabbinic understanding that God continues to work even on the Sabbath.) The discourse can be divided into two halves: 5:19–30 and 5:31–47.

Jesus' claim to work even as the Father does has drawn the bitter criticism of the Jewish leaders (5:16–18). Now, in the first half of the discourse Jesus defends his claim. The rabbis had spoken of the rebellious son as one who made himself equal to the father; that is, one who no longer recognized the authority of his father. In verse 19 Jesus firmly refutes that accusation: he is not a rebellious son. Indeed, "the Son can do nothing on his own: he does only what he sees his Father doing" (5:19). Only the beloved Son has seen the Father (1:18). It is this vision of the Father, this intimacy with him which authenticates the actions of the Son.

Far from being rebellious, the Son is in complete unity with the

Father's will. Thus every act of the Son is an act of the Father. The intimacy of Father and Son is one of love. As proof of this, Jesus affirms that the Father hides nothing from him but shows him "all that he himself is doing" (5:20). (We will again meet this linking of love and knowledge in 15:15, in a description of the friendship of Jesus and his disciples.) Jesus is the complete revelation of the Father. So far the Jewish leaders have seen the power of God in the physical healing of a sick person. How much greater will be their amazement when they recognize that the Son also shares God's power to give eternal life!

In verses 21 and 22 Jesus claims to do the works which God does not cease even on the Sabbath—the works which are most "proper" to God. According to Jewish teaching, God would raise the dead to life and judge them on the last day, the Day of the Lord. Jesus is saying, "The last day is already here! It is the Son who now bestows eternal life! It is the Son who now judges!"

The Son gives life "to those he wants to" (5:21). We meet here one of the key themes of the Fourth Gospel: salvation or eternal life is a gift. This is clearly shown in the healing narrative which precedes the discourse. There were many sick people crowding the pool with five porches. Yet Jesus singled out only one. A similar teaching, expressed from the Father's perspective, is found in 6:44: "No one can come to me unless the Father who sent me draws him to me; and I will raise him to life on the last day."

The second work of the last day is that of judgment. We have already seen in 3:17–21 that the Son has come as savior rather than judge. By his very coming, however, the Son creates a crisis. (It is interesting that the Greek word which in the Gospel is translated "judge" is the root of our English word "crisis.") Unless one responds to the light, one remains in darkness and thus comes to judgment.

Raising to life and judging, then, are two sides of the same coin. The role of the Father as Judge does not wait for the last day. It happens now in the very activity of the Son's giving life. If that life is accepted, there is a judgment unto eternal life, a judgment of vindication. If the life which the Son offers is refused, there occurs a judgment unto condemnation. Yet it is not the Son who condemns. He has come as Savior. The individual condemns himself/herself. Because the Son gives life and has the right to judge, he must be honored in the same way that the Father is honored. "Whoever does not honor the Son does not honor the Father who sent him" (5:23).

Verses 24 and 25 clarify the teaching already given. The key to life is found in hearing the words of Jesus (verse 24) or hearing his voice (verse 25). The spiritually dead can come to eternal life now. They undergo the test of the day of judgment even in the present moment.

A careful study of 5:26–30 shows that these verses match the first part of the discourse (5:19–25). Notice these parallels:

5:19–25		5:26–30
verse 21	As the Father gives life/is source of life, so also the Son gives life/is source of life.	verse 26
verse 22	The Father has given the Son the full right to judge.	verse 27
verse 20	Response of amazement/surprise.	verse 28
verse 25	The time is coming (has already come) when the dead will hear the voice of the Son, and those who hear it (who have done good) will live.	verse 28 verse 29
verse 19	The Son does nothing on his own; he does what he sees the Father doing/what the Father tells him.	verse 30

The important themes in the first passage are repeated in the second. The passages differ, however, in their understanding of the end-time. In 5:19–25 the end-time is viewed as already present. Those who believe in the Son do not have to wait until the end to be judged and raised to life. They already have eternal life. Thus "the dead" in verse 25 should be understood as the spiritually dead. The voice of the Son is summoning them to rise from their spiritual death.

Verses 26–30 have a different conception of the end-time. Here the end-time is a *future* event, in which the Son of Man *will come* to judge the dead. (The "dead" in verse 28, then, are the physically dead.) In this section the Son is given the title Son of Man

(5:27), which links us with a passage in the book of Daniel. In a series of visions Daniel sees thrones set up and the Ancient One taking his place for judgment. Then he sees:

> *One like a son of man coming, on the clouds of heaven;*
> *When he reached the Ancient One and was presented before him,*
> *He received dominion, glory, and kingship;*
> *   nations and peoples of every language serve him.*
> *His dominion is an everlasting dominion*
> *   that shall not be taken away,*
> *   his kingship shall not be destroyed* (Daniel 7:13–14, *New American Bible*).

We might note here that the title "Son of Man" was the one which Jesus most frequently used of himself. However, it was not generally adopted by the early Church; titles such as "Christ" (that is, Messiah or Anointed One) and "Lord" were preferred and became more familiar. Possibly, the reason why the title, "Son of Man," was not widely used in the Church was this: this title clearly portrays its bearer as taking possession of his Kingdom (and the right to judge) at the end of time. As Christians reflected, under the inspiration of the Holy Spirit, on the life and exaltation of Jesus, they came to see that he was already king and judge.

In this first half of the discourse Jesus answers his critics. He acts as he does precisely because he is the Father's Son. He is not rebellious but obedient. He does only what the Father does; he also does all that the Father does. The section ends with a preview of Jesus' greatest sign. Mention of the dead in their graves who will hear the voice of the Son and rise (5:29) anticipates the raising of Lazarus in chapter 11.

The Jewish leaders, however, do not "see" the signs. They are unable, or refuse, to see in them a testimony to Jesus' true identity. Although not stated in the text, their demands for additional evidence for his claims is presumed in interpreting 5:31–47. The section might be entitled "The Witnesses to Jesus." Witness or *martyria* is an important theme in the Fourth Gospel. We have already seen it in chapters 1 and 3. According to rabbinical practice, a person's witness to himself was not valid. The evidence of at least one other person was required. Jesus affirms that there is another who testifies for him (5:32). This "someone else" is the Father himself, and his witness is true. His witness is the only one that really counts. Using a rabbinic style of argument, Jesus shows that there are four witnesses to his claims. These four are all aspects of the Father's own testimony.

The first witness was John the Baptist. In chapter 1 the evangelist carefully distinguished him from the light who is Christ himself. "John was like a lamp, burning and shining" (5:25). The author may be thinking of a verse in Sirach describing the prophet Elijah: "Then the prophet Elijah arose like a fire, his word flaring like a torch" (48:1, *Jerusalem Bible*). Popular Jewish tradition expected that Elijah would return in the last days. According to Matthew 17:10–13, the early Church interpreted the Baptist as fulfilling the expectation of Elijah's return. The fourth evangelist agrees with this tradition in describing the Baptist's ministry with Sirach's praise of Elijah.

The second witness which Jesus offers is the evidence of his deeds. The Jewish authorities would have understood Jesus' deeds as his works of healing. These provide clear evidence that God backs up his claims. As Nicodemus had said: "Rabbi, we know that you are a teacher sent by God. No one could perform the miracles you are doing unless God were with him" (3:2). The Christian reader sees a further meaning in Jesus' words. Evidence for his claim is provided not only by his miracles but also by the fact that he grants eternal life and has the authority to judge. These also are the "deeds" of the Son.

The first two witnesses provide external testimony. The third witness is interior. The Father himself bears witness to his Son (5:37). This refers to the voice of the Father speaking in the hearts of his people. Yet his voice finds no home in the hearts of Jesus' opponents.

The final witness to Jesus is that of the Scriptures. For the Jewish people the Torah was the prime font of life. One of the rabbinic writings states that the person "who has acquired the words of the Law has acquired for himself the life of the world to come." The Jewish leaders are diligent in studying the Torah. Yet they miss the very life which it contains, for the Scriptures speak of Christ (5:39). Their failure does not stem from a lack of intelligence but from a deliberate refusal to recognize in Jesus the source of life; 5:40 contains an accusation similar to that which we saw in Matthew 23:37: "How often I yearned to gather your children, as a mother bird gathers her young under her wings, but you refused me" (*New American Bible*).

Jesus criticizes the Jewish leaders but not because he is interested in human glory. The only glory worth seeking is that given by "the one who alone is God" (5:44). In the background of Jesus' defense we can hear the bitter polemic between John's community and "establishment" Judaism late in the first century. In this debate it is pointed out that the leaders have joyfully received the Baptist (5:35) and have even listened to false messiahs (those who come with their own authority, 5:43). Yet they refuse to love God and to offer to him that gift of self which alone wins his praise. They prefer self to God and thus are unwilling and unable to receive his Son. It is Moses himself, whom they pretend to follow, who will accuse them before God's throne (5:45–47).

REFLECTIONS. The relationship of the Son to the Father is one of the most difficult areas of doctrine. However, since this doctrine is both the basis of the Christian religion as well as the foundation of the spiritual life we are all called to live, it is crucial that we struggle to understand it. As we have seen, as late as the fourth century the Church was vigorously debating this question. The crux of the difficulty is this: the Scripture speaks of the equality (of nature) of the Father and Son, but it also speaks of a "subordination" of the Son to the Father. Arius gave these latter verses a false interpretation. In reaction against Arius later theologians have tended to neglect entirely the scriptural teaching on the Sonship of Jesus. Chapter five is a good example of the "problem" which Scripture poses. Study two verses:

Jesus answered them, "My Father is always working, and I too must work" (5:17).

So Jesus answered them, "I tell you the truth: the Son can do nothing on his own; he does only what he sees his Father doing" (5:19).

While the first verse affirms the equality of the Son with the Father, the second teaches the "subordination" of the Son to the Father. Both texts have their counterparts. In 10:30 Jesus will say that he and the Father are one. Yet 8:26 and 12:49 affirm that the Son does not speak on his own, and in many places Jesus insists that he does not come on his own but is sent by the Father. In 14:28 Jesus tells the disciples: "If you loved me, you would be glad that I am going to the Father; for he is greater than I."

Some theologians have been too quick to say that the subordination passages speak only of Jesus' humanity and not of his divine nature. The more ancient theology of the Church, however, understood that the "subordination" of the Son extends into the Trinitarian life itself. This enables us to remain in touch with the doctrine of the Church Fathers that the First Person of the Trinity (the Father) is the source of the Trinitarian life. This cannot be affirmed of the Second and Third Persons. They are the Word and the Spirit of the Father. As soon as you have said this, of course, you must affirm that the Father is not "more divine" than the Son or Spirit. Each shares totally and completely the divine nature. We are not doing a "favor" for God by ignoring part of what he has revealed about himself, even if that part (the "subordination" of the Son and Spirit) has in the past led to heresy (Arianism).

We are accustomed to thinking like this: the Father creates, the Son redeems and the Spirit sanctifies. This is easily remembered and is not too difficult to understand. Unfortunately, it is not faithful to what God has revealed about himself. It would be more faithful to understand the mystery in this way: the Father, Son and Spirit all create, all redeem and all sanctify. But each "works according to his Trinitarian role." Thus the Father creates only through the Son (as we saw in the prologue) and in the power of the Holy Spirit (see the role of the Spirit in Genesis 1).

The Father also redeems and sanctifies us, but always through his Son and in the power of his Spirit.

Human language is clumsy and very inadequate in expressing the mysteries of God and of his involvement in human history. Doctrinal formulas tell us more about what we cannot say than what we can say. However the Church's experience of Jesus, and through him of the Father and the Holy Spirit, impels her to proclaim her belief in the world. Likewise, the needs of devotion are served by a faithful expression of the truths of our salvation.

Thus, the answer to the question we have so often asked ourselves: What is truly different, unique about the Christian faith? The answer is: the experience of empowerment by the Spirit, the experience of sonship with Christ, the experience of standing in the intimate presence of the Father—this is the mystery and grandeur of the Christian life.

STUDY GROUP QUESTIONS

1. Verse 14 indicates a possible connection between the sick man and his sins. In your own experience do you find any connections between sin and sickness?

2. Read the passage on observing the Sabbath in Jeremiah 17:19–27. How might a contemporary family or community keep holy the Lord's day?

3. Jesus has come to raise us to life. In what ways does the "world" around us tempt us to remain lifeless?

4. How does each of the four witnesses (5:31–40) continue to testify to Jesus today? What other witnesses (people, events, places) have been important in your life?

5. St. Jerome said that ignorance of Scripture is ignorance of Christ. Share with your group one way in which Scripture has enriched your appreciation and love for Christ.

6. In what ways have you personally experienced the blessings of the end-time which are made present through faith in Jesus Christ?

Chapter Six

THE FOURTH AND FIFTH SIGNS

OVERVIEW. Although the setting for the events recorded in chapter five was Jerusalem during autumn, the events of chapter six are located in Galilee during the spring. This has led some scholars to argue that chapter six should be placed before chapter five in order to give a more suitable geography and chronology. Our commentary will follow the usual order, presuming that the author and editors of the Fourth Gospel were more concerned with the message of Jesus than with geographical accuracy.

The central event of this chapter is the fourth sign, the multiplication of bread. This is the one miracle that is clearly found in all four accounts of the Gospel of Jesus Christ. The way John arranges his material raises the question of the relationship of John with the Synoptic writers, particularly with Mark. A close examination of all four accounts of the Gospel will show that Mark and Matthew contain narrations of two multiplications, while Luke and John only narrate one multiplication of loaves. Furthermore, John's account strongly resembles Mark's account of the first multiplication (Mark 6:30–52). Thus, the question is raised, Did John have access to Mark's account of the Gospel, or were John and Mark using material from similar but independent traditions?

Our commentary will take the position that John did not rely on Mark. While there are many parallels and matching details in the accounts of Mark and John, this may best be explained by pointing out that the traditions behind each narration are reporting the same original event.

READ 6:1–21

COMMENTARY. The opening verses sketch the setting. Jesus is in Galilee. Having seen the healing miracles performed by Jesus, a large crowd follows him. The mention of Passover (6:4) indicates that John also uses this event to develop his theme of Jesus' replacing of the Jewish feasts. The transformation of the water to wine, another sign with eucharistic overtones, also took place before the Passover (2:13). Again, the Last Supper will take place just before the third Passover. As John systematically replaces the central Jewish rituals and feasts, remember that there is a double purpose in what he does. While there is a polemical element present (John debates with Jewish leaders), there is also the element of compassion. Many of those Jewish believers who followed Jesus are now excommunicated from the synagogue and cut off from their families (see Matthew 10:34–39). They are without the comfort and the joy of celebrating the great holy days. In order to confirm these believers in their commitment to Jesus and to comfort them in their loss, John will stress two points. First, in the replacement theme John shows them that what they celebrated in the great holy days they will find again, transformed in Jesus. Secondly, John will emphasize the close and loving ties that Jesus commands his followers to have with each other (the new commandment of 13:34, 15:23, 17).

Verse six is placed in parentheses, for it appears that it was not part of the original Gospel. The writer apparently wants to avoid any impression that Jesus asked the question out of ignorance. Hence the reference to Jesus' motivation: he asked in order to test Philip.

If one compares Mark 6:37–44 with John 6:7–13, one will notice that the eucharistic overtones are far more pronounced in John's account. Although the English words "gave thanks to God" are found in both accounts, the Greek words are different. John uses *eucharistēsas* in 6:11, the Greek word from which our word "eucharist" (thanksgiving) is derived. Although Mark recounts that the disciples distributed the bread to the large crowd (Mark 6:41), John records that Jesus himself distributed the bread to the people (6:11). While Mark writes that the disciples took the initiative in gathering the left-over food (Mark 6:42), John points out that Jesus commanded them to gather the left-over pieces (6:12). Finally, John's use of the Greek word for "pieces" is the same word the early Church used for the eucharistic particles.

Mark and John supply information that can deepen our understanding of the events surrounding the miracle of the multiplication of bread and fishes. Mark tells us that after the miracle Jesus "made" (i.e., forced) "his disciples to get into the boat and go ahead of him . . ." (Mark 6:45). John seems to supply the reason for this action of Jesus: the crowd, misinterpreting the sign, was on the verge of violence (6:14). There are implications of rebellion against Rome in the statement that the crowd was "about to come and seize him in order to make him king by force" (6:15). The crowd's statement, "Surely this is the Prophet who was to come into the world" (6:14), indicates that the people had interpreted Jesus' miracle in a political way.

The reaction of the people is not surprising. The element of liberation had always been associated with the celebration of Passover, since the first Passover took place in the context of winning freedom from the oppression of the Pharaoh. God had given the Hebrew people their prophetic leader, Moses. God had led them out of their bondage in Egypt. On their journey to the Promised Land God fed them with manna. We will see that when Jesus enters Jerusalem for the final Passover of his life (12:12–19), the people again misunderstand his action as a political move. Having ordered his disciples to leave by boat, Jesus slips away into the hills (6:15).

Later that night the disciples see Jesus walking on the water. This is the fifth sign recorded by John. In comparing Mark with John, we see that John's statement about the identity of Jesus is the central point. John wants to emphasize that Jesus is divine. He omits mentioning the struggle of the boat's crew, the time of night, and the ghostly appearance of Jesus. The incident is stripped down to its essentials: Jesus, walking on the waves, comforts the terrified disciples with the divine claim: "It is I!" (6:20).

Mark emphasizes the power of Jesus in stilling the storm and the incomprehension of the disciples (Mark 6:51–52). In John's account the boat arrives at its destination immediately after Jesus speaks the divine name (6:21). Note the connections between the accounts of Jesus walking on the water and the divine identity recorded in the Hebrew Scriptures.

JOHN 6:19–21	MARK 6:49–52	EXODUS 3:14
The disciples had rowed about three or four miles when they saw Jesus walking on the water, coming near the boat and they were terrified.	But they saw him walking on the water. "It's a ghost!" they thought, and screamed. They were all terrified when they saw him.	God said, "I am who I am. You must tell them: 'The one who is called I AM has sent me to you.'"
		ISAIAH 41:9–10
"Don't be afraid," Jesus told them, "it is I!"	Jesus spoke to them at once. "Courage," he said. "It is I. Don't be afraid!"	". . . I called you from its farthest corners and said to you, 'You are my servant.' I did not

Then they willingly took him into the boat, and immediately the boat reached land at the place they were heading for.

Then he got into the boat with them and the wind died down. The disciples were completely amazed, because they had not understood the real meaning of the feeding of the five thousand. . . .

reject you, but chose you. Do not be afraid—I am with you! I am your God—let nothing terrify you. . . ."

JESUS TEACHES ABOUT THE BREAD OF LIFE

OVERVIEW. Of the four evangelists, John has the most highly developed sacramental theology. We have seen how John wove baptismal and eucharistic themes into the Cana story and into the dialogues of Jesus with Nicodemus and the Samaritan woman. John will continue this technique in chapter six.

Because Jesus is the source of truth and life, Jesus' self-revelation occupies the center of the stage. This is important to see, for it will help us to understand the basic meaning of the words of Jesus as John reports them. While we are accustomed to read this chapter as if it were one long discourse on the sacrament of the Eucharist, there are two distinct sections. In the first section, verses 26 through 51a, the references which Jesus makes to himself as the "bread from heaven" basically pertain to the bread of his teaching. Jesus asserts that his message brings eternal life. In referring to both his message and his person, Jesus uses many themes from the Bible's Wisdom literature. In verses 6:51b–58, the words of Jesus specifically refer to the sacrament of the Eucharist. (There are three sentences in verse 51. The first two sentences are designated 51a. The third sentence is designated 51b. This division is important because it indicates where the first section of Jesus' discourse ended and the second section, pertaining to the Eucharist, began.) Thus, in this chapter "the bread from heaven" symbolizes two basic themes: Jesus' teaching and the sacrament of the Eucharist. But there is no decisive separation between word and sacrament; eucharistic themes are subtly woven into the fabric of the entire chapter. John wants the reader to see the relationship of the words and actions of Jesus to the liturgical practice of the community of late first-century believers. The community's sacramental activity is the continuation of Jesus' revelatory teaching and saving deeds.

READ 6:22–59

COMMENTARY. An examination of the movement reported in John 6:22–26 provides some difficulties in piecing together all the elements of this account, for example, the number of boats needed to transport 5,000 people in so short a time. John may be telescoping more than one incident. At any rate, it is the day after the miracle. The crowd has seen the disciples leave without Jesus (6:22). Apparently Jesus slipped away undetected, due to the confusion of the attempt to make him king, or under the cover of darkness. Then another group of people from Tiberias joins those who had spent the night in the place where the 5,000 had eaten (6:23). Both groups of people head for Capernaum where they find Jesus (6:25).

The setting for the dialogue between Jesus and the people is probably "the synagogue in Capernaum" (6:59). Although the exchange between the people and Jesus begins with the crowd's puzzlement regarding Jesus' presence in Capernaum, it immediately moves into a straight-forward rabbinic discussion (6:26–34). Then, after Jesus has given the people the bread of his teaching (6:35–40), their response turns into discontented grumbling (6:41–42).

In verse 26 Jesus goes straight to the point. They have sought him out merely because of the wonderful miracle which Jesus had worked on the day before; they have failed to understand that his miracles are signs that point beyond themselves to a deeper meaning. Jesus had told the Samaritan woman that the person who drank ordinary water would be thirsty again (4:13). He tells the crowd that ordinary food is perishable (6:27). Jesus promised the woman that the water he would give would satisfy her thirst forever (4:14). Jesus tells the crowd that the food (teaching) which the Son of Man will give them shall endure forever (6:27).

In hiking after Jesus and in rowing across Lake Galilee, the people have worked hard. It seems that Jesus is telling them to work at understanding his message rather than spending so much energy trying to obtain more bread from him (6:27). It is his message that is really important for it leads to eternal life. Jesus' teaching has this quality because the Father has sent him:

> *"I am telling you the truth: whoever hears my words and believes*
> *in him who sent me has eternal life"* (5:24).

The Father's testimony given on behalf of the Son was the subject of 5:19–47.

When the people ask Jesus what can they do to fulfill God's will, they have moved beyond a mere literal understanding of bread, but they still do not grasp Jesus' meaning. Since Jesus has told them to work for food that does not spoil, they misunderstand. They think that Jesus is telling them to do a particular work (action) that will enable them to obtain from God a miraculous food that does not spoil (6:28). (There was a popular expectation that when the messianic age arrived, God would give his people a new manna from heaven.)

In verse 29 Jesus tells them that there is a work they can do that will bring them "the food that lasts for eternal life" (6:27); that work is to believe in him. According to John's perspective, faith and works are not two separate realities; believing is a "work," an action, something a person does. Believing or having faith in Jesus is the work God wants of his people. At the same time, however, faith is also the gift of God: "No one can come to me unless the Father who sent me draws him to me" (6:44). In verse 30 the dialogue takes a more argumentative turn. Earlier the Jewish authorities had demanded a sign from Jesus (2:18). Now the people demand a miracle as the condition for their belief, i.e., their acceptance of his teaching (6:30). By asking for another manna miracle (6:31), the crowd is saying something like this: "We will believe you on the condition that you give us a demonstration of your power. Conform to our messianic expectations that in the new age God will give us bread in abundance." They want to put their faith in the signs Jesus can do rather than in Jesus and the message he comes to give.

This exchange probably took place in a synagogue. The discussion that follows between Jesus and the people follows the pattern of rabbinical interpretation of Scripture. In 6:31 the people cite Exodus 16:4, referring to the manna God gave in the desert (Exodus 16:4–36). Jesus then offers his own interpretation of the passage. "I am telling you the truth" (6:32) is the formula Jesus often uses to make an important point. Jesus then declares that the manna which came through the mediation of Moses was only a symbol of the real bread that God would give in the future: "What Moses gave you (the manna) was not the bread from heaven (the real revelation, the true teaching that Jesus has come to give). Jesus then strengthens his interpretation of the manna as a symbol of the real bread of his teaching by asserting that "it is my Father who gives you the real bread from heaven" (6:32). By asserting that his Father (God) is the one who gives the real bread, Jesus introduces another passage from the Hebrew Scriptures. This passage also relates Moses and the theme of the bread:

> *"Remember how the Lord your God led you. . . . He made you go hungry, and then he gave you manna to eat. . . . He did this to teach you that man must not depend on bread alone to sustain him, but on everything that the Lord says"* (Deuteronomy 8:2–3).

By referring to this biblical passage, Jesus points out that Moses himself had subordinated the manna miracle to the reality that was far more important: the words spoken by God. According to John, Jesus himself is the Word of God. Thus, the teaching of Jesus is not only about God but also from God. Therefore, the teaching of Jesus is the "real bread" given by God (6:33). The emphasis on giving in verse 33 illuminates another passage in which the Father gives the gift of his Son and the Son gives the gift of eternal life:

"For God loved the *world* so much that he *gave* his only Son, so that everyone who believes in him may not die but have eternal *life*" (3:16).

"For the bread that God *gives* is he who comes down from heaven and gives *life* to the *world*" (6:33).

Like the Samaritan woman, the crowd does not fully understand Jesus. She listened to Jesus as he offered her the "water" that would quench her thirst forever and then she asked for that water so that she would never have to come to the well again (4:14–15). The crowd asks for a continuous supply of the special bread from heaven: "Sir . . . give us this bread always" (6:34).

Jesus responds to their request on the level of his meaning: "I am the bread of life" (6:35). Although we have been accustomed to understand these verses as specific teaching about the sacrament of the Eucharist, verses 6:35–51a primarily refer to the message Jesus has come to reveal. While there are recognizable eucharistic overtones in these verses, it is the second section of the discourse (6:51b–58) that clearly refers to the sacrament of the Eucharist.

Isaiah recorded that God spoke of the significance of his word (Isaiah 55:10–11) shortly after he had extended his invitation to share in the messianic banquet and had promised a renewal of the Davidic covenant (Isaiah 55:1–3). Jesus applies these themes to himself. In Isaiah, God declared that his word will "do everything I send it to do" (Isaiah 55:11). Jesus, the Word of God, specifies what that mission is: to save all those given to him by the Father, to give eternal life to those who believe, and to raise these believers to life on the last day (6:39–40).

The people grumble. They do not agree with Jesus' teaching. In the context of a rabbinic discussion over the interpretation of Exodus 16:4–36, the crowd perceives that Jesus is probably claiming that he is the fulfillment of the text which states:

> *Then Yahweh said to Moses, "Now I will rain down bread for you from the heavens"* (Exodus 16:4, *Jerusalem Bible*).

As their ancestors complained in the desert (Exodus 16:2, 7–8), "the people started grumbling about him, because he said, 'I am the bread that came down from heaven' " (6:41).

In verse 45, Jesus seems to be freely citing the prophet Isaiah. Speaking to the inhabitants of a devastated Jerusalem, God declares, "I myself will teach your people and give them prosperity and peace" (Isaiah 54:13). Jesus interprets the passage in this way: those who learn from the teaching of God are those who come to Jesus (6:45). The theme from the prologue (1:18) is repeated in the assertion that the one sent from God is the only one who has "seen the Father" (6:46).

Verses 47–51a summarize Jesus' interpretation of the Exodus account of the manna and thereby bring to a close the debate introduced by the crowd in verse 31. The people had argued that Jesus should guarantee his message by performing a manna miracle like the one that happened under the leadership of Moses. Jesus has argued that a mere repetition of the manna miracle has no value in itself. The real significance of the manna is that it was a sign of the real life-giving bread God would give in the future. In verse 49 Jesus refers to the fact that ends the debate: the people who ate the manna are dead! That bread only had the ability to nourish physical life for a short time; it was not the bread of eternal life. Jesus and his teaching are "the bread that came down from heaven" (6:50). Wisdom, the personification of God's will, had called out, "Who is ignorant? . . . Come and eat my bread . . . Leave your folly and you will live . . ." (Proverbs 9:4–6, *Jerusalem Bible*). Jesus declares that whoever eats the bread he gives "will not die" (6:50). Three times during the course of his teaching Jesus has proclaimed that on the last day he would raise to life those who believed, those whom his Father had given to him (6:39, 40, 44). His teaching is indeed the true life-giving manna, the real bread from heaven.

Verses 51b through 58 are related to the sacrament of the Eucharist in a most explicit way. There were eucharistic overtones in the teaching of Jesus in verses 35–51a, but in these seven-and-a-half verses we find explicit references to eating *and* drinking, an apt description of the eucharistic liturgy. For the first time we find Jesus using the word "flesh" to describe the bread that he *will give* "so that the world may live" (6:51b).

Note that Jesus offers his teaching to the synagogue audience in the present tense: "I am the bread of life. He who comes to me will never be hungry" (6:35). But the bread of his flesh Jesus will give in the future (6:51b). Jesus is portrayed as looking ahead to the Last Supper, death and resurrection. Thus, the Word made flesh promises that he will give his own flesh in two basic ways: he will give himself up as a sacrifice on the cross; he will give himself in the eucharistic bread.

The response of the audience is significant. When Jesus interpreted the Exodus passage in a way that proposed his teaching as the real bread from heaven, the crowd grumbled (6:41). Now, as Jesus speaks of giving his flesh in the eucharistic bread, an "angry argument" begins (6:52). It is possible that these eight verses reflect one of the bitter conflicts between the synagogue and John's community. Let us examine the solemn answer that Jesus gives to those violently arguing, "How can this man give us his flesh to eat?" (6:52). Jesus asserts that eating his flesh and drinking his blood is the condition for possessing eternal life. Notice the similarity between the teaching Jesus gave to Nicodemus:

"I am telling you the truth: no one can enter the Kingdom of God unless he is born of water and the Spirit" (3:5).	"I am telling you the truth: if you do not eat the flesh of the Son of Man and drink his blood, you will not have life within yourselves" (6:53).

The deeper level of meaning in both assertions of Jesus has sacramental references, the one to Baptism, the other to the Eucharist. Since the Spirit had not yet been given, the references to Baptism could not have been understood by Nicodemus. But the reader of the Gospel did understand. Since Jesus had not yet given himself at the Last Supper and upon the cross, the Jewish audience in the synagogue could not have understood the eucharistic theology contained in verses 51b–58. Thus, the point at issue here is not whether Jesus did or did not speak these exact words in a synagogue in Capernaum sometime before his death. The point at issue is the nature of the eucharistic liturgy as it was understood by John's community late in the first century. Verses 51b–58 may have been included in the context of the synagogue debate in order to confirm Christian believers in their faith that the risen Jesus was totally present in the eucharistic bread and wine they ate and drank. It is likely that the Jewish community was highly critical of the community's eucharistic ritual. We can imagine members of the synagogue challenging the Christians with the question, "How can the crucified Jesus give you his flesh to eat?"

In the Hebrew Scriptures, the Jewish community could certainly find sufficient grounds for attacking the liturgical practice of the Christians. It was the Semitic understanding that the life of a creature was contained in the blood. For that reason, the Mosaic Law expressly forbade the eating of any meat with blood still in it. The Law stated:

> *If any Israelite or any foreigner living in the community eats meat with blood still in it, the Lord will turn against him and no longer consider him one of his people. The life of every living thing is in the blood* . . . (Leviticus 17:10–11).

But the Johannine understanding of the Eucharist is far deeper than what it appeared to be to outsiders. Flesh and blood were a Semitic way of speaking about the whole person. Eating Jesus' flesh and drinking his blood is a way of describing the intimate relationship of the believer with the risen Jesus. The sacrament (sign) of bread and wine contains the total reality of Jesus, risen and ascended to the Father, yet still present among his believing community.

The eucharistic liturgy is the Christian community's highest form of worship. Perhaps the eucharistic teaching of Jesus may be understood more deeply if it is related to his earlier discourse on true worship of the Father (4:21–24). Jesus had told the Samaritan woman that the day was coming when it would no longer be necessary to journey to sacred mountain or holy Temple. In this discourse Jesus declares,

> *"Whoever eats my flesh and drinks my blood lives in me, and I live in him"* (6:56).

Thus, not only would Christian believers be worshiping God "as he really is" (4:23, 24), i.e., as their Father, but the Christians would also be worshiping the Father in, with, and through the Son. (The words of the Concluding Acclamation in our present eucharistic ritual express the same thought. "Through him [Jesus], with him, and in him, in the unity of the Holy Spirit, all glory and honor is yours, almighty Father, for ever and ever. Amen.")

Returning to the book of Leviticus, note how the passage cited connects blood, sin, and sacrifice:

> *The life of every living thing is in the blood, and that is why the Lord has commanded that all blood be poured out on the altar to take away the people's sins. Blood, which is life, takes away sins. That is why the Lord has told the people of Israel that neither they nor any foreigner living among them shall eat any meat with blood still in it* (Leviticus 17:11–12).

The Baptist pointed out Jesus as the "Lamb of God who takes away the sin of the world" (1:29). Those who look upon the crucified Son of Man in faith will have eternal life (3:14–15). Eating the bread of the Eucharist and drinking the eucharistic wine, the sacramantal flesh and blood of Jesus, enables the believer to live "because of" him (6:57). "Blood, which is life, takes away sins" (Leviticus 17:11). The Jews may have criticized, perhaps even ridiculed the Christians for their liturgical ritual: "How can this man give us his flesh to eat?" (6:52). But the Christians understood another level of meaning in the teaching of Leviticus. The blood of Jesus is the sacrifice that takes away the condition of sin that had held humankind in bondage. The words of Paul well express the joy of those who celebrate the eucharistic liturgy:

> . . . *every time you eat this bread and drink from this cup you proclaim the Lord's death until he comes* (1 Corinthians 11:26).

Verse 58 links Jesus' teaching on the meaning of the Eucharist with his teaching on the significance of his message. In both the believer receives the "bread that came down from heaven" (6:58). Jesus promises that whoever "eats this bread will live forever" (6:58). From the earliest times the Eucharist has been called "the pledge of eternal life."

The words that Jesus taught "in the synagogue in Capernaum" (6:59) are celebrated in the eucharistic liturgy now, every day, in homes, churches and chapels, and everywhere on the face of the earth. The promise Jesus made, to give his flesh for the life of the world (6:51b), has come to pass.

THE WORDS OF ETERNAL LIFE
READ 6:60–71

COMMENTARY. In an earlier form of the Gospel, verses 60–71 probably followed the first part of the bread of life discourse (6:35–51a). Thus, the teaching that is "too hard" (6:60) refers back to the concluding words of Jesus, "I am the living bread that came down from heaven" (6:51a). Upon hearing their grumbling, Jesus challenges them: if you cannot accept the fact that I have come down from heaven, then what will be your response when I ascend back to heaven? (6:61–62). This return to heaven will happen with his being lifted up on the cross.

The teaching which the audience considers "too hard" is the message of Jesus. The people state that "this teaching" (6:60) is difficult to accept. They object: "Who can *listen* to it?" (6:60). Jesus replies that "The *words* I have spoken to you bring God's life-giving Spirit" (6:63). The mention of the life-giving Spirit refers us back to the teaching Jesus gave Nicodemus (3:6–8).

Verses 64 and 65 re-assert the teaching that no one can believe in Jesus unless God takes the initiative (6:44). The reference to the fact that many of Jesus' followers would no longer "go with him" (6:66) indicates that up until this point many had followed Jesus because of the signs he performed. By his teaching in the synagogue, Jesus has asked for a deeper commitment. He refused to give another sign. He demands a commitment to both his revealing message and his person. But the faith of these followers was incomplete and they did not want to invest themselves any further. Without the external support of miracles, their enthusiasm for Jesus dissolves. When faced with the decision (crisis) to move from mere faith in signs to real commitment to Jesus, they "turned back and would not go with him any more" (6:66).

When Jesus turns to the twelve disciples (symbolic of the twelve patriarchs of the New Israel), Peter responds: "You have the words that give eternal life" (6:68). Although many have been unable or unwilling to accept the teaching of Jesus, Peter recognizes that Jesus' doctrine leads to eternal life. (These same words of Peter are also appropriate for the readers of the Fourth Gospel.) Note that verses 68 and 69 represent the Johannine version of Peter's profession of faith at Caesarea Philippi (see Matthew 16:16–19). It is likely that the words of Peter, "Now we believe and know you . . . come from God" (6:69), convey the idea that Peter and the disciples (Judas excepted, as we see in 6:70–71) have moved from faith in signs to faith in Jesus. The title "the Holy One," is Peter's acceptance of Jesus as the Messiah, the anointed envoy of God. The parallel in Matthew's account reads: "You are the Messiah, the Son of the living God" (Matthew 16:16).

REFLECTION. It is possible to interpret 6:60–69 in another way than that described above. Verses 51b–58 may have been inserted to instruct other communities of Christian believers who did not accept the Johannine theology of the Eucharist. Thus verses 60 and 66 indicate that many followers of Jesus have rejected the hard saying regarding the Eucharist, "Whoever eats my flesh and drinks my blood has eternal life . . ." (6:54).

In addition to his own community, there are several other groups which John addresses in his account of the Gospel. We have seen his message for the disciples of the Baptist. Throughout the Gospel John is engaged in a polemical battle with Judaism. In chapters nine and twelve we will find John's harsh words directed toward the secret Christians, those who believe in Christ but who will not profess their faith publicly lest they be excommunicated from the synagogue (see 12:42–43). It is very possible that in 6:60–69 John may be taking issue with other early Christian communities, perhaps Jewish Christians who have publicly broken with the synagogue. These believers are not willing to go as far in belief as John has gone, either in his Christology of the divine, pre-existent Word, or in his assertion that the sacramental bread and wine consumed during the eucharistic liturgy are the flesh and blood of the risen Jesus. Perhaps these other Christians looked upon the ritual only as a memorial of the Last Supper or a meal of fellowship.

The presence of the various "audiences" in the Fourth Gospel, gives us a glimpse of the fascinating history of the early Church and its growth. It is possible that John's community was not in the mainstream of early Christian thought and practice. We catch glimpses of this situation in the Johannine letters, particularly in the third epistle where the Johannine writer complains that another Christian community refuses to accept missionaries from John's Church (3 John 9–11). It is possible that John's community was small and that other early Christian communities regarded it as "far-out," as a radical group, even as "troublemakers." We can imagine the secret Christians (still in the synagogue) asking, "Why can't they leave well enough alone? Why do they have to assert that God is no longer worshiped in Jerusalem?" (see 4:21). We can imagine others complaining, "Why does that community have to insist on the eternal pre-existence of Jesus as Word? It makes us look as if we followers of Jesus were worshiping two Gods!" We can imagine the consternation of still others, lamenting over the Johannine sacramental theology, "Why do they have to insist that the Eucharist is not only a meal of fellowship but also the way in which Jesus comes to each of us? Their talk of eating and drinking his body and blood gives the pagans the impression we're cannibals and gives the Jews the impression we're violating the Mosaic Law!"

STUDY GROUP QUESTIONS

1. In what ways is the eucharistic liturgy (Mass) similar to the multiplication of the loaves?

2. There are two basic sections of Jesus' teaching on the bread of life (6:35–51a and 6:51b–58). How does Jesus relate the manna given in the desert with his own teaching (6:35–51a)? How are the words of Jesus related to the eucharistic liturgy celebrated by John's community (6:51b–58)?

3. In what ways does chapter 6 help you to appreciate the Eucharist which we celebrate in our parish communities each Sunday?

4. It's been said that the most difficult feature of believing is the "incredible" goodness of the Good News. What do you find "hard" (6:60) in the teaching of chapter six? Does the difficulty lie in the ability of Jesus to give himself to us? Or is the difficulty found in accepting as true the extent of Jesus' love for you, a love that is so total that he wants to be united with you in the intimate union of your living in him and his living in you?

5. Jesus asks the twelve disciples, "And you—would you also like to leave?" Peter responds, "Lord, to whom would we go?" (6:67–68). Why were Jesus' disciples leaving him? What do we face in our own time that tempts us to leave Jesus and go somewhere else?

6. Jesus refused to give another sign because he wanted people to entrust themselves to him and his message rather than believe in proportion to the greatness of the sign (miracle) given. In what ways are we tempted to put more trust in externals instead of putting our faith in Jesus and his teaching?

Chapter Seven

JESUS AT THE FEAST OF TABERNACLES

OVERVIEW. In Chapters seven and eight the fourth evangelist continues to describe Jesus as the one who replaces the great Jewish feasts. Jesus goes up to Jerusalem for the feast of Tabernacles or Shelters. Some notes about this very popular Jewish feast will clarify the text.

Tabernacles was a week long celebration held in the fall, at the conclusion of the harvest. As time passed, the original harvest feast was "spiritualized"; that is, it was celebrated in memory of one of the great events in Israel's history. Tabernacles came to commemorate the period of Israel's desert wandering. Thus the pilgrims in Jerusalem lived in small shelters made of branches, to remind themselves of their earlier nomadic existence.

Two particulars of the feast are important in interpreting the words of Jesus in this and the following chapter. During the feast there were daily prayers for winter rains. Each day the worshipers processed to the Fountain of Gihon to draw out a pitcher of water. This was later poured over the altar as a supplication for rain and fruitful harvests. Secondly, the part of the Temple called the Court of the Women was brilliantly illumined by candles throughout the feast.

In these chapters Jesus is presented as Life (life-giving rain) and

Light (the illumined Temple). The dialogues are built around the Jewish objection to these claims. The reader might note the two "stages" which John uses to heighten the dramatic effect of his account. In the foreground Jesus is teaching and debating with the crowds of pilgrims. In the background the Jewish leaders are plotting his death.

READ 7:1–52

COMMENTARY. John notes that the Jerusalem "authorities were wanting to kill him" (7:1). From the first verse of this section the shadow of the cross stands clearly in the background. Galilean pilgrims were making preparations to set off for Jerusalem, and Jesus' relatives urge him to go. Their thinking demonstrates the natural or earthly mind which has great difficulty understanding the ways of God. Their suggestion in verses 3 and 4 may be related to the departure of many of the disciples in 6:66. Perhaps if Jesus does some spectacular miracles in Jerusalem, they reason, he can regain his lost popularity. The author notes that even Jesus' relatives did not believe (7:5), another fact which supports his insistence that the miracles/signs, by themselves, do not lead to faith.

Jesus' response concerns the "right time," another way of speaking about his hour. He does not act because of external forces (their persuasion or the opportunities to regain disciples) but because of the Father's will (at the right time). Characteristically, John portrays the relatives as missing Jesus' meaning. They understand Jesus' words in 7:8 on the earthly level. However, John intends a deeper level. Jesus is really speaking about his going to the Father, which can only take place at the hour of his death and glorification. That time has not yet come.

Jesus' departure marks his farewell to Galilee. The rest of his ministry will take place in Judea. He goes up to Jerusalem "secretly" (7:10). Again the evangelist may intend a twofold meaning. Jesus goes up alone, that is, separate from the pilgrim caravans. He also appears suddenly at the Temple (7:14), recalling the words of the prophet Malachi regarding the Day of the Lord:

> *The Lord Almighty answers, "I will send my messenger to*
> *prepare the way for me. Then the Lord you are looking for will*
> *suddenly come to his Temple. The messenger you long to see will*
> *come and proclaim my covenant"* (Malachi 3:1).

John notes that the crowds are divided (7:12). Such a reaction is typical in the Fourth Gospel. When the Light shines, people find themselves either in light or in darkness. There is no middle ground.

In 7:14–52 the evangelist seems to have gathered together attacks on Jesus and his replies, conflicts which probably took place at different times. Let us examine each of them individually.

(1) Surprised by his powerful teaching, the authorities question his credentials. It was common knowledge that Jesus had not attended a rabbinical "school." Nor did he cite the recognized masters. (A related text, Mark 1:22, notes that "the people who heard him were amazed at the way he taught, for he wasn't like the teachers of the Law; instead, he taught with authority.")

Jesus responds that he has studied with the very best Master, God himself! Despite the fact that he doesn't quote the great rabbis, he is not merely teaching his own opinions. The person who has surrendered his life to God's will can easily distinguish whether a teacher comes from God or gives his own opinions. The response in 7:17 is closely related to the teaching of 5:38–44. There Jesus teaches that the deafness of the authorities to the witnesses results from their lack of love for God and their desire for human glory. Both passages describe the basic disposition of heart necessary to receive Jesus: humility, obedience and love.

Jesus himself is a model for the disciple. His only desire is that the Father be glorified; thus the truth shines forth from him without any distortion (7:18). In verse 19 we catch an indication of the struggle between the Johannine community and the synagogue. The key word is the "you" in that verse: "Moses gave you the Law, didn't he?" Remember that in Matthew's account

Jesus sees himself in continuity with the Law. He has come not to repudiate it but to bring it to fulfillment (see especially Matthew 5:17–20). In John's account we recognize a clear distinction between Jesus and the Law. The prologue sets the tone in affirming: "God gave the Law through Moses, but grace and truth came through Jesus Christ" (1:17). In 7:19 Jesus does not say that Moses gave *us* the Law but that he gave *you* the Law. The shift in perspective between Matthew and John provides us with a clue to the situation of their audiences. Matthew's community was experiencing disunity with the synagogue, perhaps even some persecution. By the time John writes the situation seems to have become much worse. We catch glimpses of open hostility between the church and the synagogue. We will see in chapter nine that Jewish Christians are being excommunicated from the synagogue. In all probability, then, John portrays the conflict between Jesus and the Jewish leaders as more bitter than it really was, because of the escalated "warfare" between synagogue and Church late in the first century.

(2) In 7:21–24 we return to the argument over the Sabbath healing in 5:1–18. Jesus offers a different defense of that healing. The Mosaic Law commanded that a male infant be circumcised on the eighth day after birth (see Leviticus 12:3). The rabbis taught that this must take place even if the eighth day were a Sabbath. Jesus appeals to the Jewish leaders to judge his healing according to the spirit of the Law. If a circumcision can be performed on the Sabbath, cannot a sick person be healed on the Sabbath? After all, God gave the Law not to prevent salvation and wholeness, but to promote them. Similar defenses of Jesus' Sabbath activities can be found in Mark 2:23–28 and 3:1–6. But the Jewish authorities consistently judged Jesus' actions in a legalistic way instead of according to the purpose for which Moses gave the Law.

(3) There were several traditions about the Messiah in popular Jewish belief. According to one tradition, the Messiah would remain hidden until his dramatic manifestation before the people. In 7:25–31 we hear the crowd arguing about Jesus. Jesus must be ruled out as the Hidden Messiah, for it was well known that he came from Nazareth. Again we note the irony of John's account.

The crowds are thinking on an earthly level; they judge only by appearances. But Jesus is from above. His origin from the Father is, in fact, hidden from the crowd. Because he is sent by the Father, his destiny cannot be controlled by the Jewish leaders. They cannot arrest him before the hour (7:30).

(4) Another example of Johannine irony is evident in verses 32–36. As guards arrive to arrest him, Jesus speaks of the "little while longer" during which he will continue his ministry. This "little while" will be explained to the disciples during the Last Supper (16:16–22). Jesus then speaks of his return to the Father, but the authorities understand his words only on the earthly level. They sneer that perhaps he could get a better hearing among the Greek Gentiles. The irony is that they prophecy the direction which God's plan will actually take. By the time John writes, the Church has become predominantly Gentile. The haunting words of Proverbs 1:28–29 are being fulfilled in these verses:

> *Then you will call for wisdom, but I will not answer. You may look for me everywhere, but you will not find me. You have never had any use for knowledge and have always refused to obey the Lord.*

(5) In verses 37–39 we reach the climactic point of the chapter. Jesus chooses the most solemn moment of the week-long feast to make his most solemn and important statement. In the context of the procession and prayer for rain, he proclaims that he himself is the source of living water. Already we have seen Jesus' claim to be the giver of the water that leads to eternal life (4:14). In interpreting that passage we said the water probably referred both to Jesus' teaching (revelation) and to the Holy Spirit. It is possible that the streams of living water in 7:38 also refer to Jesus' teaching, since there are strong overtones of the Wisdom literature throughout this chapter. However, the dominant meaning of the water here is that it refers to the Holy Spirit. "Jesus said this about the Spirit, which those who believed in him were going to receive" (7:39).

The evangelist completes his account of Jesus' proclamation on the last day of the feast with the remark that Jesus' gift of the

Spirit was not yet available to believers, since Jesus had not yet been glorified (7:39). Even though Jesus has been pointed out as the one who will baptize with the Holy Spirit (1:34) and even though Jesus has been given the fullness of the Spirit by the Father (3:34), he will not become co-source of the Spirit with the Father until he has returned to the Father's side.

(6) Jesus' claim creates a division in the crowd (7:40–44). Some think that he must be the prophet which Moses promised. (See Deuteronomy 18:15; we have seen this opinion already in 6:14.) Others believe him to be the Messiah. Verses 41 and 42 are linked with 7:27, a verse referring to the tradition of the Hidden Messiah. Here we meet another of the messianic traditions, that of the Davidic Messiah. This tradition is more familiar to us from our Advent-Christmas readings. In our study of Matthew 2:5–6 we saw that he quoted the prophecy of Micah 5:2, according to which Bethlehem would be the birthplace of the Messiah. John is portraying here another example of the misunderstanding of the crowds. They think they know Jesus' birthplace; in reality, they do not know him at all.

(7) In the last section of this chapter John continues the backstage maneuvering which began in 7:32. The guards return without bringing Jesus as their prisoner. His teaching was too persuasive, too powerful (7:46). The authorities respond in disgust. The followers of Jesus, they argue, do not include those who know the Law but only the ignorant peasants, who are careless of the many demands which the Law imposes. The reference to God's curse in 7:49 probably has in mind the teaching of Moses in Deuteronomy 27:26: "God's curse on anyone who does not obey all of God's laws and teachings."

John concludes the chapter with another bit of irony. The leaders had boasted to the guards that none of *their* number had fallen under Jesus' spell (7:48). At just that moment Nicodemus speaks up in Jesus' defense. John's readers know what the Jewish leaders do not: that Nicodemus is a secret disciple of Jesus. Thus we see that Jesus' teaching did affect many people: members of the festival crowd, some of the Temple guards, even one among the leaders of Israel. However, in light of 12:37–42 we know that most of those who heard Jesus speak did not become believers.

REFLECTIONS. The traditional interpretations of 7:37–39 fall into two fairly clear groups: the Eastern Fathers held that the believer is the source of living waters, while the Western Fathers interpreted the verse in such a way that Jesus is the source. If we look closely, we can discover that theological differences provide the origin for these differing interpretations.

The Eastern Fathers nourished a more dynamic understanding of the Trinity. They maintained an orthodox sense of the "subordination" of the Son and Spirit to the Father. Their version of the "Gloria Patris" offers us a good example of their understanding. They prayed: "Glory be to the Father, through the Son, and in the power of the Holy Spirit." They taught that the Holy Spirit was a gift of the Father through the Son.

The Latin Fathers possessed a more static understanding of the Trinity. Emphasis was placed more on the co-equality of each Person than on the dynamic interrelationships of the Persons with one another. Thus they prayed the "Gloria Patris" in the form more familiar to us: ". . . to the Father, *and* to the Son, *and.* . . ." In their minds the Spirit could be seen as a gift of the Father or as a gift of the Son. After some centuries of debate the Latin hierarchy changed the traditional version of the Nicene Creed. In speaking of the Holy Spirit it now reads: "who proceeds from the Father *and* the Son," instead of "from the Father through the Son."

Admittedly there is not an enormous difference between the two understandings, and both are orthodox. It enables us to appreciate, however, why the Eastern Fathers would shy away from an interpretation in which the streams of water (symbolic of the Spirit) flowed from the heart of Jesus (7:38). They did not wish to understand Jesus as a giver of the Spirit in isolation from the Father. When we come to the Last Supper discourse we will see that the fourth evangelist provides support for both the Eastern and the Western theologies.

STUDY GROUP QUESTIONS

1. The Jewish Feast of Tabernacles (or Shelters) sets the context for the words of Jesus in chapters 7 and 8. In which church

feast do you experience the Word of the Lord spoken most powerfully?

2. Jesus only acted at the "right time" (7:6). Share from your own experience an instance in which you knew that it was God's time to act.

3. In the Fourth Gospel Jesus is consistently presented as one who creates division in the crowd. Some feel that this is a mark of a good leader. How do you view Jesus' leadership in this chapter? How does his style of leadership relate to that of any church leaders you may know?

4. Jesus speaks of the Holy Spirit as a stream of life-giving water (7:38). What image(s) would best describe the Holy Spirit for you?

Chapter Eight

THE WOMAN CAUGHT IN ADULTERY

OVERVIEW. You will notice that the text is enclosed in brackets. This indicates that it was not an original part of this Gospel. It is not found at all in the best manuscripts. Those which contain it do not agree; some place it after 7:36, others here (probably to illustrate 8:15), others at the end of the Gospel; still other manuscripts include it as part of Luke's Gospel. However, it was accepted as part of the Fourth Gospel by St. Jerome in his *Vulgate,* and from that time it has been considered a part of the canon of Scripture and thus as inspired by God.

In style this passage resembles the writing of Luke more than that of John. It is highly vivid and dramatic, and gives us a beautiful insight into the character of Jesus. Perhaps it is his quick and uncomplicated forgiveness of the woman which delayed the entrance of this narrative into the canon of Scripture. During the first centuries of the Church, penitential discipline was harsh and rigorous. It required many months, even years, of penance before a sinner could be received back into the community. Thus many doubted this story was a genuine part of the traditional teaching about Jesus.

READ 8:1–11

COMMENTARY. The picture of Jesus spending his evenings on the Mount of Olives and his days teaching in the Temple corresponds to Mark's portrayal of the last days of Jesus' ministry (see Mark 11). By bringing the woman to Jesus, the scribes and Pharisees are clearly attempting to trap him. Leviticus 20:10 demands the death penalty for adultery. However, the Romans would not allow their Jewish province the right of capital punishment. Thus Jesus must choose between counseling disobedience to Roman law and encouraging indifference to Mosaic Law (8:4–6).

This situation resembles the dilemma about paying taxes (Matthew 22:15–22 and parallels). As in that situation, Jesus refuses to choose either alternative. Instead, he invites any sinless leader to begin the stoning (8:7). Many attempts have been made over the centuries to explain Jesus' writing. According to the most popular but unlikely explanation, he wrote down the sins of the accusers. Others think that he wrote down his decision or that he simply traced figures in the earth to indicate disgust or disinterest.

The leaders are portrayed as zealous for the letter of the Law, but uninterested in its purpose. They lack the integrity to face Jesus' challenge and slip away, one by one. Augustine poetically describes the conclusion: *"Relicti sunt duo: misera et misericordia."* Jesus is not satisfied with a refusal to condemn the woman; he also encourages her repentance and conversion. In doing so he balances justice and mercy.

CONCLUDING DISCOURSES AT TABERNACLES

OVERVIEW. The location of the account of the adulteress in Chapter eight interrupted the sequence of Jesus' discourses at the festival of Tabernacles. As he did in chapter seven, the evangelist presents us with dialogue which probably took place on a number of various occasions. There are several "stopping points" within the chapter (e.g., verses 20 and 30), indicating that the evangelist may have woven together several short discourses. Many of the themes which we have already studied are continued in this section: witness, judgment, opposition of the leaders, polarization of the crowds. We hear a strong resonance of 1:11: "He came to his own country, but his own people did not receive him."

READ 8:12–59

COMMENTARY. Jesus begins the discourse with a proclamation which would have had profound meaning during the Feast of Tabernacles. On the evenings of the festival, giant candles illuminated the Temple area, and Jewish tradition held that there was not a house in Jerusalem which was not made brighter by these festal lights. As he had proclaimed himself the true water of life during the rain ceremonial, now Jesus announces that he is the true light. In the commentary on 1:5 we saw the importance of light as a sign of messianic times. We might add here a text from Zechariah: "When that time comes, there will no longer be cold or frost, nor any darkness. There will always be daylight, even at nighttime" (14:6–7).

The great lights of Tabernacles reminded the Jews that the light of their lives was the divine presence among them, particularly his presence in and through the Torah. Jesus proclaims that now his teaching (his revelation of God) is the light of life. The one who follows Jesus' teaching does not walk in darkness (that is, does not lack guidance on the journey).

As they did in 5:31, the Jewish leaders reject Jesus' claim because it is self-testimony. Jesus' response (8:14–18) might be paraphrased in these words: "You are correct that an individual's unsupported word is not admissible in a law court. My own word, however, is valid, because I know my origin and destiny. You judge only what appears on the surface, without knowing who I really am. In addition, you judge in a condemning way. I do not judge in order to condemn. Yet those who reject my light will by that very act be judged. And that judgment will be valid, because it is the Father's judgment also."

We have already seen that Jesus speaks of judgment in two ways, both of which appear in this passage. Jesus does not judge in the sense of condemning people (8:15; 3:17; 12:47). However, as the light of the world, Jesus' presence and teaching demand a response of acceptance. By rejecting the light a person automatically judges him/herself (8:16; 5:10–30; 9:39; 12:48). This judgment has eternal consequences.

Verses 21–30 may originally have been a separate dialogue between Jesus and the leaders of Israel. We hear a tone of urgency in these words. Jesus again tells them that he will soon return to the Father. Unless they seize the opportunity to welcome the light, they will lose the gift of eternal life. It is interesting that "sins" is singular in the Greek. For the Johannine school there is only one sin: the refusal to believe in Jesus (which is at the same time the refusal of life).

As they had in 7:35–36, the leaders misunderstood Jesus' meaning. In their ignorance, however, they touch on a profound truth (8:22). Jesus' death will not be suicide, but it will involve a laying down of his life for others. Verses 23 and 24 explain the urgency of the choice which confronts not only the Jewish leaders but ultimately every person. Only the One whose origin is "from above" has the power to free people from sin, from the life-unto-death. The path to eternal life is found only in believing that Jesus bears the divine name, I Am Who I Am.

It will be helpful to study several passages from the Jewish

Scriptures in order to understand the significance of 8:24, 28 and 58. When God appeared to Moses in the burning bush and sent him to rescue the Hebrews, Moses asked in whose name he was to go.

> God said, "I am who I am. You must tell them: 'The one who is called I Am has sent me to you' " (Exodus 3:14).

For ancient peoples, knowledge of a name gave power over the thing named. Thus to know the name of one's god was to insure that one's prayers would be heard. Although scholars cannot be certain, it seems that God's answer is a refusal to give his name to Moses: "I Am Who I Am." The true God cannot be manipulated, even by prayer. In time the Hebrew for I-Am-Who-I-Am was shortened and put into the third person, He-is; thus it became the name by which the Hebrews knew God—Yahweh. (The *Good News Bible* always translates Yahweh as Lord. The *Jerusalem Bible* retains the Hebrew word itself.)

The name Yahweh never implied a supreme being who was far removed from the trials of his people. For the Israelites the name Yahweh was always closely connected with the mighty acts of deliverance by which he had saved them. In another word of God to Moses we hear this:

> "Say, this, then to the sons of Israel, 'I am Yahweh. I will free you of the burdens which the Egyptians lay on you. I will release you from slavery to them, and with my arm outstretched and my strokes of power I will deliver you. I will adopt you as my own people, and I will be your God. Then you shall know that it is I, Yahweh your God, who have freed you from the Egyptians' burdens' " (Exodus 6:6–7, *Jerusalem Bible*).

For this reason some scholars think that the Hebrew of Exodus 3:14 should be translated I-Am-He-Who-Causes-To-Be, or as I-Will-Be-For-You-Who-I-Will-Be.

Chapters 40–55 of Isaiah are filled with a sense that Yahweh alone is God and that there is no other. In the Greek version of the Hebrew Scriptures (the Septuagint), several of these passages are translated using the phrase *egō eimi* "I Am," as if it were a divine title. We meet this same Greek phrase in verses 24, 28 and 58 of this chapter. Clearly, Jesus is claiming for himself the title which belongs to Yahweh. The implications are not lost on his Jewish audience. They first question him further (8:25), and in the end they attempt to stone him for blasphemy (8:59; see Leviticus 24:16).

Jesus has been trying to tell them who he is (8:25), but they are unable to hear. So Jesus looks ahead to the Passion for the second time:

> *"When you lift up the Son of Man you will know that 'I Am
> Who I Am' "* (8:28).

In Mark Jesus looks ahead to his death three times (Mark 8:31, 9:31, and 10:33). The parallel in the Fourth Gospel can be found in the three-fold prophecy of the lifting up of the Son of Man (3:14, 8:28 and 12:32). This "lifting up" includes both the lifting of Jesus onto the cross and the return of the Son to the bosom of the Father. In this glorification Jesus will be recognized as the One who rightly shares the divine name. His death, as the ultimate sign of his obedience, will prove that Jesus' entire life has been one of obedience to the Father. He has not acted on his own (8:28) but always in concert with the Father. Thus he has never really been separated from the Father (8:16 and 29). John concludes this section with the comment that many of Jesus' hearers believed in him. It will be important to remember this, since the final section of the discourse will portray a deep and bitter separation between Jesus and some of the Jews.

The final section of this chapter (8:31–59) introduces Jesus' radical questioning of whether the Jews are true descendants of Abraham or even authentic children of God. The dialogue develops through the typical Johannine method of using the objections of Jesus' opponents to introduce a clarification. There are indications that John articulates these themes in such a way as to appeal to Jews who believed in Jesus but were hesitant to abandon their Jewish heritage. By the time John wrote, it was no longer possible to believe in Jesus and remain within the synagogue.

The dialogue begins with the theme of freedom. The path to freedom is discovered only by the person who abides in the teaching of Jesus. The words "obey my teaching" literally mean "abide in my word." To abide in the word means much more than to hear it or even to memorize it. It means to take it into oneself until it becomes a part of one's very flesh and blood, until it becomes the motivating force of every word and action. Only this person—by definition a disciple—knows the truth about human life, knows the ultimate faithfulness of the Father. It is this inner knowledge of the heart which makes the disciple free.

The Jewish nation was frequently enslaved during its long history. Yet Jewish believers took pride in being children of Abraham, the friend of God (see Isaiah 42:8). They alone among the nations of the world possessed the Law, the key to the mind of God. Thus they respond indignantly to Jesus' words about freedom: "We have never been anybody's slaves" (8:33). The Christian Scriptures never question that the Jews were a specially chosen people. It seems, however, that Jewish awareness of their privileged status had degenerated into a presumption of guaranteed divine providence. Matthew 3:7–10 presents John the Baptist's reaction to this type of thinking. Jesus' critique (8:34–41) is similar but even stronger. Only Jesus can set people free from real slavery, that is, slavery to sin.

Another way of expressing freedom is through the concept of

being "at home" in the Father's house. Such a gift can only come from the true Son of the Father. If the Son invites you to be at home, "then you will be really free" (8:36). Jesus admits that the Jews are physical descendants of Abraham. Yet their actions demonstrate that they are still slaves to sin (8:37). In verse 38 Jesus begins a radical indictment of his audience.They think they are descendants of Abraham and children of God; in fact, as their actions prove, they are children of the Devil.

The "works" of Abraham in 8:39 may be a reference to Genesis 18:1–8, in which Abraham welcomed the three visitors, and in so doing welcomed God himself. Jesus comes as God's messenger, but the Jews do not welcome him (one of Abraham's works); instead they are trying to kill him (one of the Devil's works). For the first time in the Fourth Gospel the Devil emerges as the real adversary of Jesus. It will become clear in the hour of the Passion that Jesus' struggle is not with the Jews but with Satan. In seeking Jesus' death the Jews are doing Satan's work. In 8:44 the Devil is characterized as a murderer and the father of lies. This links us again with Genesis, chapters 3 and 4. There we read of the original sin, which results from the lie of the snake (Genesis 3:4), and of the expression of the sin in the murder of Abel (Genesis 4:8).

To this radical accusation the Jews respond that Jesus is a Samaritan and has a demon (8:48), which probably means that he traffics in magic or evil spells and that he is insane. Jesus denies these attacks in the confidence that the Father will vindicate him (8:49–50). He then reaffirms that the only path to life lies in obedience to his teaching (8:51). The Devil has unleashed into the world the poison of murder and lies. The word of Jesus is the only antidote.

John concludes the discourse with a masterful comparison of Jesus and Abraham. Already Jesus has claimed to be greater than Jacob (4:12–13) and Moses (5:46). Now Jesus' audience senses in his words a claim to surpass even Abraham. Note the irony of their question: "Who do you think you are?" (8:53). Jesus' response is by now familiar to us. He is not seeking personal glory. If his audience knew the Father, they would recognize Jesus' true status (8:54–55).

The comparison with Abraham is full of biblical memories.

Abraham rejoiced in God's promise, that in him all nations would be blessed (Genesis 12:1–3). He "saw" the time of Jesus' coming in the birth of Isaac. Both he and Sarah were too old to have children, yet God announces that he will give them a child. Abraham laughed at the impossibility of the idea (Genesis 17:17), but his laughter was always interpreted by the rabbis as a laugh of joy. We see a similar understanding at work in Hebrews 11:13: "It was in faith that all these persons died. They did not receive the things God had promised, but from a long way off they saw them and welcomed them. . . ."

In this way Jesus affirms that he himself is the fulfillment of the entire history of Israel. Again his Jewish listeners understand his words only on a human level. How can he, obviously yet a young man, have seen Abraham? Again Jesus claims for himself the divine name, "I AM." The phrase "before Abraham was born" reminds us of the opening verses of the prologue (1:1,3) as well as of the second verse of Psalm 90:

> *Before you created the hills*
> *or brought the world into being,*
> *you were eternally God,*
> *and will be God forever.*

Jesus' words in 8:58 were clearly heard by his listeners as a claim to divinity. Accordingly they search the still unfinished Temple for stones with which to put him to death. The evangelist indicates to his readers that chapters 7 and 8 constitute a unit. At the beginning of the Feast of Tabernacles Jesus secretly came up to Jerusalem (7:10). Now, in hiding, he leaves the Temple (8:59). During the feast he has proclaimed himself the source of living water, the light of the world, and I Am Who I Am.

REFLECTION. The Fourth Gospel is very harsh in its attitude toward the Jews of Jesus' day. Looking back, we are astonished at their seeming hard-headedness, at their failure to perceive what is so clear to us. As we read John's Gospel we need to keep reminding ourselves that he writes from the perspective of the 90's. Jesus' claims were astonishing, and Jewish religious consciousness was unable to fit them into its traditional understanding of what God had revealed about himself. We are outraged that they would pick up stones against Jesus. Yet the Law demanded that God's honor be protected against blasphemy.

Jesus did express disappointment in the reaction of his people. He did condemn, at least in some of the Jewish leaders, a blindness and a hardness of heart. These traditions, however, come to us through the crucible of the struggle of the early communities of Christians to remain within Judaism. Properly understood, the Gospels do not authorize us to judge Judaism harshly, either in its first century form or as it exists today. One of the tragic ironies of history is that the followers of the One who alone is full of loving-kindness and faithfulness have not yet ceased to persecute God's chosen people.

STUDY GROUP QUESTIONS

1. How can the saying of Jesus in 8:7 be applied to parish life? To family life? How could Jesus say, "I do not condemn you" (8:11)?

2. What might it mean to "walk in darkness" (8:12)?

3. In 8:15 Jesus says, "I pass judgment on no one." However, 5:22, 27 and 30 speak of Jesus' judgment. How can these seemingly contradictory passages be reconciled?

4. Jesus uses of himself the title, "I Am Who I Am." What titles of Jesus (e.g., Lord, Savior, Master, Prince of Peace, Son of the Father) are most important for you?

5. What meaning does Jesus' saying, "the truth will set you free" (8:32), have for your daily living?

6. As the "father of all lies" (8:44), the Devil tries to lead God's people astray. In what ways does the enemy lie to us today?

Chapter Nine

JESUS HEALS A MAN BLIND FROM BIRTH

OVERVIEW. Usually a miracle story centers attention on Jesus. In the cure of the man born blind, it is not Jesus but the former blind man who is the center of attention. This ninth Chapter is an outstanding example of the way the early Christian communities dynamically handed on the traditions of the sayings and deeds of Jesus, adapting those traditions to their own situations. Matthew, Mark and Luke record several incidents in which Jesus gives sight to the blind. However, we cannot tell which of the Synoptic healings John is narrating. John's account of Jesus' cure of the man born blind takes a different approach than the Synoptic writers.

Although the Pharisees are portrayed in a negative manner, justice demands that we keep in mind that they were dedicated and conscientious people. The very least we could say for the Pharisees is that they were more the victims of circumstances than evil-intentioned villains. When the Jewish-Roman war of 66–73 A.D. destroyed the Temple and wiped out the Sadducees, the Pharisees were the only ones who could provide religious leadership for the Jewish people. They did so by providing the stability of learning and authority. Fidelity to God was measured by means of the strict observance of the Law of Moses. Since fidelity to the person and teachings of Jesus was the heart of the

Christian disciple's faith, there was no way that the Law could occupy the central position. Thus the Christian Jews became a threat to the whole process by which Judaism was struggling to re-define her identity in terms of the faithful observance of the Mosaic Law. Recognizing this threat, the Pharisees seem to have made a decision to force the Jewish Christians out of the synagogue. This chapter recounts Jesus' cure of a blind man in terms of the meaning of that cure for a persecuted community of Christians living in the 90's.

READ 9:1–41

COMMENTARY. The chapter may be divided into seven scenes. In the first scene, Jesus and his disciples see a blind beggar. Perhaps referring to Exodus 20:5, "I bring punishment on those who hate me and on their descendants down to the third and fourth generation," the disciples ask Jesus if the man's blindness was caused by himself or his parents. Jesus does not accept the simple either/or explanation of the blind man's suffering. It is not necessarily sin that caused the man's blindness. The author of Job had concluded that there is no rational formula that can explain the relationship between the justice of God and the suffering of the innocent (see Job 42:1–6). Jesus points out that there can be other purposes in human suffering: "He is blind so that God's power might be seen at work in him" (9:3).

The assertion of Jesus, "I am the light for the world" (9:5), is soon to be demonstrated in action. Jesus kneads spittle and clay, rubs the man's unseeing eyes, and sends him to wash his face in the Pool of Siloam. And "the man . . . came back seeing" (9:7).

The blind man has become a symbolic expression of Jesus' mission. The Word was sent by the Father to be "the real light—the light that comes into the world and shines on all mankind" (1:9). As the Father sent Jesus, so Jesus sent the blind man to wash in the pool named "Sent" (9:7). The man born blind bears forever the effects of God's power at work in Jesus.

As is so characteristic of John's writing, sacramental themes are woven into the account of the words and actions of Jesus. Just as the washing of his face with water brings sight to the blind man,

so the water of baptism brings enlightening faith to those becoming the disciples of Jesus. The Greek word which is translated "rubbed" in verses 6 and 11 also means "anointed." The ritual anointing of the person being baptized has been an action of the baptismal ritual since the earliest days of the Church. Even more significant is the fact that John specifies that the name of the pool means "Sent." Thus the pool itself is a symbol of Jesus, the one sent by the Father. The blind man's washing of his face (his face expressing his identity) in the pool named "Sent" expresses that he has been baptized in Jesus. When he returns "seeing," he has a new identity.

The second scene involves the now-sighted man born blind and his neighbors. Being able to see has so changed the man's appearance that his neighbors are not sure he is the same person "who used to sit and beg" (9:8). (The baptismal theme in the background reminds us that he does have a new identity; he has been born of water and the Spirit, 3:3–8.) When the former blind man identifies himself, "I am the man," the first interrogation begins: "How is it that you can now see?" All the man knows about Jesus is his name and the instructions he gave (9:11).

When the man's neighbors take him to the Pharisees, the third scene begins. But the Pharisees are not interested in the miraculous restoration of sight to the man blind from birth. They single out two violations of the Sabbath Law. Kneading was a work forbidden on the Sabbath. In mixing the mud to put on the blind man's eyes, Jesus broke the Sabbath Law. Furthermore, some Pharisees held that if a person's life was not at stake, then it was unlawful to cure that person on a Sabbath. With these two counts against Jesus, some Pharisees declare that he "cannot be from God" (9:16). Other Pharisees are less quick to pass a judgment and a deadlock results. (Note how prominent in this chapter is the familiar Johannine theme of the divison which Jesus creates among people.) To resolve the controversy, the Jewish leaders call the man back for further interrogation: ". . . well, what do you say about him?" (9:17).

Until this precise moment, the blind man had not taken a position with regard to Jesus. Now, surrounded by hostile authorities, some of whom have already decided that Jesus is not from God, the cured man takes a stand: "He is a prophet" (9:17). In spite of the intimidating circumstances, the man bears witness to Jesus. Recall that Nicodemus had stated, "No one could perform the miracles you are doing unless God were with him" (3:2). To acknowledge Jesus as a prophet is to assert that Jesus is "from God."

With the man's confession of Jesus, the division among the Pharisees ceases. The whole interrogation takes a strange turn as the Pharisees become unwilling to believe that the man had been born blind in the first place (9:18). Looking for evidence that the man never was blind, they call the man's parents for questioning.

The fourth scene involves the blind man's parents. Trying to disprove the blind man's claim, his parents are called to the witness stand. Their behavior is significant from the point of view of the events taking place in the 80's and 90's. Note they will admit only that the man is their son. They deny all knowledge of both the healing itself and the person who did the healing. Extremely anxious to avoid further questioning, they ask to be excused by pointing out that their son is capable of telling them what they want to know (9:20).

John explains the anxiety of the blind man's parents:

His parents said this because they were afraid of the Jewish
authorities, who had already agreed that anyone who said he

*believed that Jesus was the Messiah would be expelled from the
synagogue (9:22).*

It is likely that verse 22 refers to a decision made by the Rabbinic Academy at Jamnia about the year 85. Established shortly
before the Jewish-Roman war, this academy played an increas-
ingly significant role in the preservation of Judaism in the chaotic
years following the destruction of the Temple. John's reference to
the agreement to expel from the synagogue those who professed
that Jesus was the Messiah is probably related to the decision
made by the rabbis at Jamnia. The Pharisees of Jamnia were
struggling to preserve Judaism from dissolution by emphasizing
the Mosaic Law and the authority of those who interpreted the
Law. Since the Christian Jews did not fit into the pattern being
established, the Jewish leaders sought a way to force the issue.
The means chosen were the introduction of a new form of the ancient synagogue prayer known as the Eighteen Benedictions.

The twelfth benediction asked God to do away with the Naza-
renes and the Minim (the Christians and the heretics). With the
introduction of the revised form of the Eighteen Benedictions, the
die was cast. For most Christian-Jews it meant a bitter choice between Jesus or Judaism, between faith in Christ the Messiah or
fidelity to Yahweh according to ancient feasts, rituals and the
Sabbath. These difficult years witnessed the birth pangs of the
Christian religion. Many Christian Jews left family and friends as
well as the synagogue (see Matthew 10:26–39). A few Christian
Jews remained, praying the Eighteen Benedictions when they had
to, concealing their faith in Jesus as best they could. The author
of the Fourth Gospel strongly disapproves of those who are secret
Christians. This is evident in his words (particularly 12:42) and in
the way the former blind man destroys the argument of the
Pharisees in verses 24–34.

In the fifth scene the man born blind is interrogated for the
third time (once by his neighbors and twice by the Pharisees).
Not able to deny that the man was born blind and that he had
been healed, the Pharisees try to coerce the man to bear witness
against Jesus. They put him under oath to tell the truth. Before

he can speak, however, the Pharisees state their own judgment: "We know that this man who cured you is a sinner" (9:24).

Here the Pharisees judge by human standards. (Those who break the Law are sinners. Jesus is therefore a sinner.) Refusing to agree with their judgment, the healed man relies on his experience (9:25). When his interrogators continue to press him, he becomes the one who interrogates them. With biting irony, the man asks them if their great interest in what Jesus did is the result of their desire to become his disciples (9:27).

The injection of discipleship into the argument further reveals the late first century tension between Church and Synagogue. The Pharisees insult the man. They remind him of his ignorance by stating that they are the learned disciples of Moses, whereas he is the disciple of "that fellow" (9:28). To demonstrate the insignificance of such discipleship, the Pharisees point out that they "do not even know where he comes from!" (9:29).

Instead of intimidating the man born blind, the designation of being "that fellow's disciple" has the opposite effect. The unlearned beggar unleashes an eloquent counterattack that leaves the position of the Pharisees in shambles. Testifying from his own experience, he destroys their case against Jesus. First, he refutes their judgment that Jesus is a sinner: "You do not know where he comes from, but he cured me of my blindness! We know that God does not listen to sinners; he does listen to people who . . . do what he wants them to do" (9:31). Secondly, he refutes their conclusion that Jesus is not from God: "Since the beginning of the world nobody has ever heard of anyone giving sight to a blind person. Unless this man came from God, he would not be able to do a thing" (9:32–33).

The Pharisees have lost the argument. All they can do is take refuge in the shopworn theological opinion (refuted by the author of Job) that misfortune is the direct result of sin (9:34). Unable to tolerate the blind man's profession of Jesus and the consequent challenge to their authority, the Pharisees eject the former blind man from the synagogue (9:34).

It is obvious that the blind man is a hero for the Johannine community. He also symbolizes the kind of witness a disciple of

Jesus is called to give. Such a disciple is ready to suffer insult, persecution, even excommunication for the sake of Jesus. Noting the baptismal themes woven into the narrative, we see that the man born blind symbolizes what happens when a person is given a new identity by being anointed and bathed in the water that is Jesus (9:6–7). This episode also demonstrates what happens when a person is given the understanding of "heavenly things" as the result of being born of water and the Spirit (see 3:3–12).

In the sixth scene of the Johannine dramatization, the blind man is about to be questioned for the fourth time. Jesus himself will ask the question, in order to reveal himself more fully to the man who has been given the gift of sight. Then Jesus asks, "Do you believe in the Son of Man?" (9:35). The readiness of the man to believe in the Son of Man (9:36) is most significant. The title, "Son of Man," is integrally related with the greatest sign of all, the crucifixion and glorification of Jesus. In all the three prophecies of the Passion and glorification (see 3:1; 8:28; and 12:34–35) this title is used. When the "hour" of "the Son of Man" does come, the full identity of Jesus will be revealed. His loving obedience to the will of his Father (12:27) as well as his love for his disciples and for the world will be manifested on the cross (see 3:16; 13:1). Thus to believe in Jesus as "the Son of Man" is to accept Jesus as the one who has been sent by the Father to save the world. With this background on the significance of the title, "the Son of Man," we can clearly recognize the climax of the entire episode:

> *"Tell me who he is, sir, so that I can believe in him."*
> *Jesus said to him, "You have already seen him,*
> *and he is the one who is talking with you now."*
> *"I believe, Lord!"* (9:36–38).

The man born blind has reached the end of his journey to faith in Jesus.

In the beginning the man knew only the name of the one who cured him of his blindness (9:11). Afterward he acknowledged that Jesus was a prophet (9:17). Now he recognizes Jesus as Son of Man, and as Lord (9:35, 38). The wording of his profession of faith, "I believe, Lord," is probably a first century baptismal profession. It is very close to the teaching of Paul:

> *I want you to know that . . . no one can confess, "Jesus is Lord,"*
> *unless he is guided by the Holy Spirit* (1 Corinthians 12:3).

The seventh scene serves as an epilogue. As Jesus states the paradox that he has come so that the blind should see and that those who see should become blind, some Pharisees take offense (9:40). On the one hand, as Light of the World, Jesus has given sight to the man blind from birth. On the other hand, Jesus brings judgment against those who refuse to see. The concluding verse brings us back to the beginning of this narrative. There Jesus had asserted that the man's physical blindness was not caused by sin (9:2–3). Here Jesus teaches that sin does cause spiritual blindness (9:41).

REFLECTION. Some kind words for the Pharisees are appropriate. These men, usually rabbis, were part of a movement that developed during the century prior to the birth of Jesus. They were devout laymen who studied the Hebrew Scriptures in order to find ways of applying the will of God to every aspect of daily living. There were several schools of opinion among the Pharisees. During the time of Jesus the school of Shammai (favoring a strict interpretation of the Law) and the school of Hillel (favoring a more flexible interpretation of the Law) were the most influential.

We do the fourth evangelist no disservice if we try to view the hostility between Church and Synagogue from a broader perspective. The Pharisees did make a momentous contribution to the survival of Judaism in the time following the destruction of the Temple. With nineteen centuries of hindsight, one can see that it was the delicate attention to the smallest detail of God's Torah that enabled Judaism to endure as a cohesive community of believers. Zealous fidelity to God's Law as interpreted by the rabbis held Judaism together in spite of centuries of continuous persecution.

If John were to address us today, he might well describe the perdurance of Judaism as a sign that God has always been with his first Chosen People. John might also take a less critical view of the Pharisees' insistence on the thorough observance of the Sabbath Law, even in their discussion of the lawfulness of Jesus' work of kneading clay to put on the blind man's eyes. Perhaps if John had been aware of how twentieth-century Christians observe their Sunday Sabbath, he might even have pointed out that Christians have something to learn from the Pharisees about the one day of the week which believers are called to dedicate to God.

STUDY GROUP QUESTIONS

1. In what ways does John's account of the healing of the man born blind bring out the significance of baptism?

2. What does the fear of the blind man's parents tell us about the historical situation of the Johannine community living in the 90's (9:18–23)?

3. What aspects of our own time and locale might correspond to the pressures being exerted upon the Johannine community in the 90's? In what ways are we tempted to compromise our faith in Jesus?

4. In our own day, which persons or groups might correspond to the blind man whose plight is blamed on his sin or his parents' sin (9:1–2)?

5. In our city or town or place of employment, what could we do that would correspond to the witness of the blind man to Jesus (9:24–34)?

6. The situation that produced the hostility between the Christian community and the Synagogue lasted only for a limited span of time. State what you think is the better course of action: (1) Since that situation no longer exists, simply gloss over the hostile

attitude that once existed; (2) acknowledge that such bitter hostility did exist, but then point out the causes, and work toward a better Jewish-Christian relationship in our own day. If #2 is preferred, what practical approaches might be taken by a parish community?

Chapter Ten

JESUS AS THE GATE
OF THE SHEEPFOLD AND GOOD SHEPHERD

OVERVIEW. In this chapter John continues to enrich his Christology, giving us the images of Jesus as the gate which gives access to the Father (10:7–10) and as the true shepherd of Israel (10:11–18). John also continues the polemic against the Pharisees. Leaders of the synagogue, the Pharisees are linked with the uncaring religious and political leaders of Israel's past (symbolized by the hired man, the thieves and the robbers).

From a chronological perspective, the chapter clearly contains two parts. The material in 10:1–21 looks back to the events associated with the Jewish Feast of Tabernacles, celebrated in the fall. The material in the second part (10:22–41) has a winter setting. It is Hanukkah, the Feast of the Dedication of the Temple.

READ 10:1–21

COMMENTARY. The first six verses presuppose a familiarity with shepherding customs in first century Israel. Shepherds, for the purpose of protecting many flocks at once, built large, stone-walled corrals. Thus, during the night many shepherds could keep their individual flocks safe from thieves and beasts of prey with a minimum of effort. The gatekeeper served as a sentry. When morning came, the various shepherds would return, identify themselves to the gatekeeper and go into the sheepfold. Once inside, the shepherd would call his sheep with a particular chant or whistle; some shepherds would call each sheep individually by some pet name. Recognizing their pastor's voice, the sheep that belonged to a particular shepherd's flock would follow him out of the fold and be led to the place where they would pasture. It is this typical scene that Jesus describes in verses 1–5.

However, the scene is so familiar to Jesus' audience that they do not understand his point (10:6). It would be as if one of our own contemporaries told us this story: "A man parked his car in a downtown garage. When morning came, he presented the parking ticket to the attendant, paid the fee and drove his car away." The mere telling of the incident has little significance. Further explanation would be needed so that the audience could understand.

Although verse 6 refers to Jesus' example as a "parable," verses 1 through 5 could be described more accurately as an allegory, i.e., a story in which each key image and action has a symbolic meaning. As Jesus explained the meaning of his story about the sheep, the gatekeeper, and the shepherd, the audience could see the references to the prophetic words of Ezekiel. Addressing Ezekiel, God declared:

> *". . . denounce the rulers of Israel. Prophecy . . . to them: You are doomed, you shepherds of Israel! You take care of yourselves, but never tend the sheep. . . . I will take my sheep away from you and never again let you be their shepherds. . . . I, the Sovereign Lord, tell you that I myself will look for my sheep and take care of them in the same way as a shepherd takes care of his sheep that are scattered and are brought together again. I will bring them back from all the places where they were scattered on that dark, disastrous day . . . I will lead them back to the mountains and streams of Israel and will feed them in pleasant pastures. . . . I myself will be the shepherd of my sheep, and I will find them a place to rest. I, the Sovereign Lord, have spoken"* (Ezekiel 34:2–15).

These prophetic words had been addressed to the Jewish exiles in Babylon (587–539 B.C.). The message was one of consolation and explanation. The exiles were suffering because Israel's corrupt leadership had led the people astray (see Ezekiel 33:25–29). The consequent failure to observe the Covenant brought upon all the "dark, disastrous day" (Ezekiel 34:12), the destruction of Jerusalem and the deportation of the survivors in 587 B.C.

By the time of Jesus, the prophetic words of Ezekiel not only referred to the corrupt shepherds who led Israel just before the invasion of the Babylonians but also to the self-serving Jewish leaders during the time of the Maccabees. At that time corrupt Jewish leaders, such as Simon, and the high priests Jason and Menelaus (see 2 Maccabees 4:1–29), paved the way that led to the desecration of the Temple:

> *It was then that there emerged from Israel a set of renegades who led many people astray. "Come," they said, "let us reach an understanding with the pagans surrounding us. . . ." This proposal proved acceptable, and a number of the people eagerly approached the king, who authorized them to practice the pagan observances. So they . . . disguised their circumcision, and abandoned the holy covenant . . .* (1 Maccabees 1:11–16, *Jerusalem Bible*).

Jesus, however, refers to the words of Ezekiel as an indictment of the religious leadership of his own day. At best such leadership is symbolized by the hired men (10:12–13); at worst, the leaders are referred to as thieves and robbers (10:8, 10). Since Jesus is the only gate, any other person seeking access to the sheepfold must climb the fence. By this stealthy act, such persons acknowledge their evil intention. Their interest in the sheep is only self-interest. As thieves and robbers they come to steal and destroy (10:8, 10). In contrast to their destructive purposes, Jesus comes to give "life—life in all its fullness" (10:10). In Jesus' declaration that he gives life in all its fullness, several themes converge. Jesus is the gift of the Father that brings eternal life to the world (3:16); Jesus is the giver of the life-giving water (4:14; 7:38); Jesus is the bread of life (6:35ff).

Against this background we see the bold Johannine view of Jesus. He is the one true leader; there is no other. As John has asserted again and again, Jesus is the one way into the full presence of God. Without Jesus, there is no complete access to God. The sheep in the corral can only get to the pasture lands by going through the gate:

"Whoever comes in by me will be saved; he will come in and go out and find pasture" (10:9).

Verse 11 introduces the second theme, that of Jesus as the good shepherd. Instead of the gate through which both sheep and shepherd must pass, Jesus now describes the shepherd who brings his flock into and out of the corral. The phrase "good shepherd" can also be translated as "noble shepherd" or "model shepherd." The "model shepherd" possesses two essential qualities. First, he is willing to die for the sheep (10:11). In comparison with Jesus, who suffers death for the sake of those he comes to lead and save, other leaders (the Pharisees) are but hired men (10:11–13). Secondly, the good shepherd knows his sheep and his sheep know him just as "the Father knows me and I know the Father" (10:14–15). Four times in these two verses Jesus uses the verb to know. The relationship spoken of by Jesus is one of mutual experience and commitment. To know in the biblical sense, means to live in intimate communion with the other. Jesus is willing to die for his disciples because he knows and loves each one personally. The model for his relationship with the disciples is this perfect intimacy with the Father.

As he so often does in the Fourth Gospel, Jesus claims equality

with Yahweh in these verses. In Psalm 23, notice how each of the aspects of Yahweh's role as shepherd now belongs to Jesus:

> *"The Lord is my shepherd; I have everything I need. . . . He*
> *gives me new strength. He guides me in the right paths. . . . Even*
> *if I go through the deepest darkness, I will not be afraid, Lord, for*
> *you are with me. . . . You prepare a banquet for me . . . and fill*
> *my cup to the brim. I know that your goodness and love will be*
> *with me all my life . . .* (Psalm 23:1–6).

Verse 16 has been interpreted in different ways down through the centuries. In our own time we are accustomed to read these words of Jesus in the context of the ecumenical movement. Christian Churches are striving to discern ways in which our faith in Jesus unites us more closely with one another. However, in the context of the Fourth Gospel, the reference of Jesus to those "other sheep" seems to refer to the Gentiles. The Gentiles belong to Jesus because, as the one through whom all creation came to be (1:3), the whole world is his. John's community already includes a large portion of Gentiles. But the remaining Gentiles are not yet part of the one flock (that is, the Church) because they have not yet heard his message and believed. Someday, however, the Gentiles "will listen to my voice, and they will become one flock with one shepherd" (10:16).

There is a second interpretation of this passage that merits attention. Perhaps the fourth evangelist presents the risen Jesus addressing other Christian communities. While these Christians have already accepted Jesus as the Messiah, as "the Holy One who has come from God" (6:69), they have not yet perceived Jesus as the eternal Word of God. Thus these non-Johannine communities are already the sheep of Jesus, but they are not yet "in this sheep pen," i.e., they do not yet believe with the depth of faith of the Johannine community. Thus, there is "one shepherd," Jesus, but there is not yet "one flock," that is, a union of all believers in the common belief that Jesus is the divine Word of God. The use of the future tense, "they *will listen* to my voice, and they *will become* one flock," is perhaps indicative of John's hope that one day all Christians will be united in the same deep faith in Jesus.

In verses 17 and 18 Jesus asserts that his death is a voluntary one. This fact is crucial, for it is the foundation of the Johannine view of Jesus as the revelation of God's love. The giving of Jesus, whether in the Incarnation or upon the cross, is solely the gift of God's own initiative. As the Fourth Gospel will emphasize again and again, no created thing brings Jesus to the cross. Neither Judas, nor the soldiers, nor the Jewish authorities, nor the power of Rome, nor the evil "ruler of this world" has any real role in bringing about the death of Jesus. They may play an instrumental role in the death of Jesus on the cross; but it is Jesus who accomplishes that which both he and his Father will to happen. This is John's inspired understanding of the death of Jesus. Not only is the Father glorified in the revelation of his love for the world, but the Son is also glorified. Because Jesus died voluntarily, all people will know that he gave up his life out of love for us, the shepherd for his flock.

The people are divided in their response to Jesus (10:19). Those who disagree with him suggest that he is "crazy" (insanity and demonic possession were usually identified). Others, referring to the healing of the man born blind, side with Jesus (10:21).

JESUS AND THE FATHER ARE ONE

OVERVIEW. The Feast of Dedication is the background for the second section of chapter ten. Jesus will speak of the sheep his Father has given to him. In speaking of the mutual love that he and his Father have for these sheep, Jesus implies that he shares in the reality of God. Recognizing the implications of Jesus' teaching, the Jews, striving to be faithful to the Mosaic Law, attempt to stone him for blasphemy. Thus, the final verses of this chapter (10:31–42) look ahead to the trial and death of Jesus. It is likely that in an earlier edition of the Fourth Gospel the account of Jesus' public ministry was concluded here. Jesus' ministry thus ends where it began—in the very place where John the Baptist first gave witness to Jesus (10:41–42).

READ 10:22–42

COMMENTARY. The last indication of the chronology of Jesus' deeds and preaching had been the reference to the eighth day of the Feast of Tabernacles (7:37). Now it is December. Jesus and the people are celebrating the re-dedication of the Temple, also known as Hanukkah or "the Feast of Lights."

Since the Maccabees had won both religious and political liberation for Israel, the question addressed to Jesus has both religious and political overtones:

"Tell us the plain truth: Are you the Messiah?" (10:24).

The question is a significant one. Not only does it provide Jesus with the opportunity to review his previous claims, but it also links the teaching Jesus is about to give with his future trial and condemnation: "he ought to die because he claimed to be the Son of God" (19:7).

Jesus reminds his audience that he is God's envoy; the signs he has done are not his own but his Father's (10:25). Verses 26 to 30 develop the third metaphor of Jesus' parable (10:1–5), that of the sheep. His sheep hear his voice; they follow him; they receive eternal life; they cannot be snatched away (10:27–28). Jesus concludes his discourse by asserting that both he and his Father are united in their mutual care for the sheep: "The Father and I are one" (10:30).

As John has indicated earlier (5:17–18; 8:58–59), the crowd is quick to perceive the implications of Jesus' words (10:31). As they prepare to stone him for claiming to share in the power of God, Jesus defends himself by challenging them to specify which of his good works merits his being put to death (10:32). The people respond that the issue is not his works, but his blasphemy: "You are only a man, but you are trying to make yourself God!" (10:33).

Jesus responds (10:34) to this accusation by citing Psalm 82, a psalm which records God's reproach of the dishonest judges of Israel:

> God . . . gives his decision. . . .
> "You are completely corrupt. . . .
> 'You are gods,' I said; 'all of
> you are sons of the Most High'
> But you will die like men . . ." (Psalm 82:5–7).

God himself refers to the judges as "gods" because they were appointed to give decisions in his name. God calls them his "sons" because their authority was from him, a fact which placed them in a special relationship with him. Having cited the Psalm, Jesus states that they can no more accuse him of blasphemy than they can change the Scripture (10:35). Neither can they accuse him of blasphemy for having said, "I am the Son of God" (10:36).

Subtle but strong assertions undergird Jesus' statements. If the corrupt judges could be called "gods" because their judgments expressed the words of God, then how much more Jesus can be called God, for he is the eternal Word of God. If the dishonest judges could be referred to as the "sons of the Most High" because the authority of their office placed them in a special relationship with God, then how much more the Father's only Son deserves to be called "the Son of God!"

As the Word of God, Jesus is the Father's envoy "sent . . . into the world" (10:36). Jesus claims that God approves the works he does. Israel has had her share of false shepherds and corrupt judges. Now the roles of shepherding and judging converge in Jesus. He is the model shepherd and the true judge. The same themes of shepherding and judging converge in Ezekiel's prophecy of a messianic king from David's line:

> "... I will rescue my sheep and not let them be mistreated
> anymore. I will judge each of my sheep and separate the good
> from the bad. I will give them a king like my servant David to
> be their one shepherd, and he will take care of them" (Ezekiel
> 34:22–23).

Finally, Jesus boldly challenges his audience to recognize that "the Father is in me and that I am in the Father" (10:38). As the crowd tries to seize Jesus again, he slips away, seeking the safety of the territory beyond the Jordan (10:39–40).

If there was an earlier and shorter edition of the Fourth Gospel that existed before the complete account we now have, the bold theological challenge of Jesus is a fitting conclusion to Jesus' public teaching:

> *". . . you should at least believe in my deeds, in order that you may know* once and for all *that the Father is in me and that I am in the Father"* (10:38).

For the moment Jesus has escaped the hostile Jewish leaders. In a few months the third Passover of Jesus' public ministry will arrive. Then Jesus will again travel to Jerusalem. Once there he will suffer the cross and be exalted in glory. Verses 40 to 42 would thus conclude the first section of the Fourth Gospel, the Book of Signs. The reference to the Baptist and the place where he once baptized (10:40) recalls the witness he bore to Jesus during the opening days of Jesus' public ministry (1:19–51). The welcome extended to Jesus by those living outside the boundaries of Judea (10:41–42) echoes the poignant words of the Prologue:

> *He came into his own country, but his own people did not receive him. Some, however, did receive him and believed in him . . .* (1:11–12).

REFLECTION. You might have heard the saying, "Grace builds on nature." The saying basically means that God relates to us as we are, as human beings. Since Jesus declared, "I have come in order that you might have life—life in all its fullness" (10:10), a brief exploration of the relationship between "life in all its fullness" and the human emotion of happiness is appropriate matter for meditation.

Throughout our lives we seek to be happy. We experience happiness now and then, here and there, in bits and pieces. But we yearn for permanent happiness.

But in human life the experience of happiness is never complete. The achievement of a long-sought goal, the victory of the athlete, the union of two persons in love and marriage, the birth of a son or daughter—all these are the occasions of intense happiness. Yet in each instance the happy person soon discovers that there is more to life than what has already been experienced.

Different people seek happiness in different ways—in security, in contentment, in abundance of material goods, or even in ecstasy. But contentment and security are at the mercy of changing circumstances. Abundance does not bring lasting happiness. Ecstasy is not the normal way of human living; it cannot be sustained. Still others seek happiness in escape from constant change and demands of human living. Yet how can happiness exist as a lack of activity, a lack of personal commitment, a lack of life? Whenever authentic happiness is experienced, we find that it is related to knowing, striving, and loving commitment.

The author of the Fourth Gospel might encourage us to relate happiness to Jesus' promise of life in all its fullness. Complete happiness is not available on this earth. One could respond to this fact by looking to the future. One might say something like this: "Perfect happiness will come in heaven. I'll make the best of life in this 'vale of tears,' and look forward to life after death." Saint Augustine beautifully sums up this view in his prayer, "You have made us for yourself, O Lord, and our hearts are restless until they rest in thee."

The fourth evangelist offers us another perspective. Jesus offers life to the full now, during our life on earth. Authentic happiness comes from our union with Jesus. In knowing him, in loving him, in offering our lives to him in service of others—this is where happiness is found. Heaven will continue in greater intensity what has begun here on earth.

If this is true, then our daily lives are often poorly directed. We seek lasting happiness where it cannot be found. John would encourage us to relate our daily life to the person and values of Jesus. No matter what challenges and difficulties face us on a given day, if we live those moments in union with Jesus, we are in touch with lasting life, with eternal life. It is true that the emotion of happiness cannot accompany every moment of our day. However, our longing for happiness can enkindle in us a greater desire for union with Jesus (and through him with the Father and the Holy Spirit). As we grow in union with the Lord Jesus we discover more and more clearly that he is the source of life-giving water; that he is the bread which gives life; that he, alone, is the light which illumines our journey to the Father.

STUDY GROUP QUESTIONS

1. How do you experience Jesus as the good shepherd? Which verse of Psalm 23 best describes your experience?

2. Share with each other the way these three verses relate the themes of the Father's love for us, the Son's love for us, and John's understanding of the cross:

> *For God loved the world so much that he gave his only Son, so that everyone who believes in him may not die but have eternal life* (3:16).

> *The bread that I will give him is my flesh, which I give so that the world may live* (6:51b).

> *No one takes my life away from me. I give it up of my own free will* (10:18).

3. Relate the statement of Jesus, "What my Father has given to me is greater than everything, and no one can snatch them away from the Father's care" (10:29), to the possibility that we might use our freedom to turn away from the Father and from Jesus.

4. In light of the last Reflection, how would you describe "life in all its fullness" (10:10)?

Chapter Eleven

JESUS, THE RESURRECTION AND THE LIFE

OVERVIEW. If 10:40–42 concluded the Book of Signs at one time, chapters 11 and 12 must be considered a very happy addition. These pages contain a powerful summary of the themes of the first ten chapters. The largest part of Chapter Eleven is devoted to the account of the death and raising of Lazarus. This is Jesus' seventh and final sign, a sign that points clearly to the power of Jesus to grant eternal life. Throughout the passage we hear echoes of Jesus' words in 5:25–29:

> *"I am telling you the truth: the time is coming—the time has already come—when the dead will hear the voice of the Son of God, and those who hear it will come to life. . . . Do not be surprised at this: the time is coming when all the dead will hear his voice and come out of their graves. . . ."*

Eternal life is not withheld until the end-time. For those who believe in Jesus it is available now; and the same power which grants eternal life assures the believer of resurrection from the dead on the last day.

John's catechetical genius is evident in this passage. He has taken the tradition of the raising of Lazarus of Bethany and created a highly dramatic "proof" of Jesus' claim to continue the Father's work of giving life. He gives us a wealth of detail and moves the account forward through lively dialogues between Jesus and Martha and Mary and the disciples. Instead of presenting the narrative and following it with a discourse (his usual approach), John here blends narrative and discourse into a unity.

READ 11.1–44

COMMENTARY. Bethany was close to Jerusalem. Mark 11:11 and 14:3 mention that Jesus stayed in Bethany when he visited Jerusalem. Luke 10:38–42 remembers a meal that Jesus shared with Martha and Mary. Verse 2 expects the readers to be familiar with the tradition of Jesus' preburial anointing, which the evangelist will record in chapter 12. The message which the sisters send is very similar to the "request" of the mother of Jesus in 2:3:

Jesus' mother said to him, "They are out of wine" (2:3).	The sisters sent Jesus a message: "Lord, your dear friend is sick" (11:3).

Note that in both accounts the "request" is met with what seems like a rejection at first hearing, and in both Jesus goes beyond the expectations of his mother/friends to work a sign which manifests his glory. Without question the evangelist wants to link in our minds the first and last signs.

Jesus' statement in 11:4 provides the theological basis for interpreting this final sign. Though Lazarus will die from the illness, physical death will not have the final word. The word of Jesus (11:43) is more powerful than death. It is possible that the author intends death to have a double meaning: physical death and the spiritual death which is the heritage of those who are not enlivened by the Son of God.

Certainly the glorification of the Father and the Son (11:4) has a twofold meaning. On one level, the raising of Lazarus glorifies God by manifesting his power (see 9:3) and by demonstrating that Jesus shares in this awesome power of giving life, thus winning him the praise of all who see or hear of it. On a deeper level, the raising of Lazarus provokes the hostility of the Jewish authorities and leads to Jesus' death. It is Jesus' death in the Fourth Gospel which truly glorifies him and his Father.

John wants his readers to understand that Jesus' failure to hurry to Bethany is not due to indifference. Thus he pointedly reminds us of Jesus' love for Lazarus and his sisters (11:5). Throughout the passage we are impressed with the emphasis on Jesus' love for his friends from Bethany. The evangelist has arranged his narrative so that when Jesus decides to return to Judea (and thus to his death), he himself takes the initiative (as opposed to responding to the sisters' request).

Verses 7–16 seem complicated, because John has combined two themes: the danger of a return to Judea (11:7–10 and 16) and Jesus' desire to go to the aid of Lazarus (11:11–15). The readers should connect verses 8–10 with 9:2–5. In both places we hear the urgency in Jesus' voice. The time for acting grows short; the night draws near. During the time of darkness, the power of the Prince of this world will be allowed to work its will upon the Son of Man. The same urgency accompanies the choice of the prospective disciple: the opportunity to accept Jesus as the light of life will not be present forever. The person who rejects the light can only stumble through the darkness. Jesus' words are reminiscent of the word of warning spoken so many centuries earlier by the prophet Jeremiah:

> *People of Israel, the Lord has spoken!*
> *Be humble and listen to him.*
> *Honor the Lord, your God,*
> *before he brings darkness,*
> *and you stumble on the mountains;*
> *before he turns into deep darkness*
> *the light you hoped for* (Jeremiah 13:15–16).

Jesus returns to Judea because he is obedient to the mission which the Father sent him to accomplish. Every choice of his life is made in light of the hour which approaches.

On another level of meaning, Jesus returns to Judea because of his love for Lazarus. The word "friend" in verse 11 is better translated "beloved." The same word is used in the conclusion of the Third Epistle of John:

> *Peace be with you. The beloved here send you their greetings; greet the beloved there, each by name* (3 John 15, *New American Bible*).

Within the Johannine churches "the beloved" may have been a common title for fellow Christians. It may be, then, that the fourth evangelist intends that we understand Lazarus not only as an historical person whom Jesus loved but also as a symbol of every believer. Thus, as Jesus loved Lazarus, so he loves each of his followers. During the Last Supper Jesus will make it clear that his disciples are his friends.

As usual the disciples misunderstand Jesus' meaning (11:11–15). This provides the evangelist with the opportunity to clarify further the importance of this event. As at Cana, Jesus' sign will not only glorify him but will also lead the disciples to "believe" in him. (Compare 2:11 with 11:15.) Jesus is not speaking about an initial or immature faith as he did at Cana. Through the sign of the raising of Lazarus, the disciples will come to a greater maturity of faith; they will learn that Jesus' authority extends even beyond the boundaries of the grave.

In the Fourth Gospel, Thomas the Twin appears only in situations involving Jesus' death and resurrection. The author may intend that Thomas' words in verse 16 express the path every disciple is called to follow. Paul records a similar teaching in Galatians: "I have been put to death with Christ on his cross, so that it is no longer I who live, but it is Christ who lives in me" (2:19–20). The words of Thomas may also express the attitude each disciple is called to develop. Again the words of Paul complement Thomas' commitment to Jesus: "The attitude you should have is the one that Jesus had. . . . He was humble and walked the path of obedience all the way to death—his death on the cross" (Philippians 2:5–8).

Verses 17–27 introduce Jesus' arrival in Bethany and his dialogue with Martha. The four days mentioned in 11:17 would be important to those familiar with rabbinic theology. According to the rabbis, the soul of a dead person remained near the body for three days. After that it departed for the nether world. Thus there is no question that Lazarus is truly dead. In Palestine the deceased were buried on the day of death. Grieving followed the burial, for at least a week, possibly for as long as a month. The grieving was accompanied by wailing and loud expressions of sorrow.

On Jesus' arrival Martha hurries out to meet him. John's portrait of the sisters matches that of Luke 10:38–42. While Martha acts as "hostess," Mary sits (thus the Greek text) at home (11:20). When she does come to meet the Master, however, she falls at his feet (11:32). Martha's faith is deep. Her profession, however, should be interpreted in light of 11:39. She believes that Jesus could have healed her brother, but her statement in verse 22 is not an expectation of the raising of Lazarus. Jesus' action will burst the boundaries of her faith. We must admit, though, that she does expect something, for she recognizes Jesus' closeness to the Father. Perhaps we should compare her confidence with that of Mary at Cana (2:5).

Jesus promises the resurrection of Lazarus, but Martha understands his words as a conventional truth with which friends comforted mourners. Belief in a resurrection on the last day did not emerge until two hundred years before Christ, but by his time it was widely accepted by the average person. Martha's misunderstanding provides Jesus with the opportunity to clarify his meaning.

Jesus' proclamation and Martha's response (11:25–27) are among the most beloved verses in the Scriptures. They should be read in light of the teaching in 5:24–29 and 6:40, 54. The verb "die" is used in two senses. Perhaps a diagram will help:

11:25–26

"I am the resurrection"	"Whoever believes in me will live (will be raised to eternal life) even though he dies (physical death)."
"I am the life"	"Whoever lives (present physical life) and believes in me will never die (spiritual death)."

As we have seen frequently in the Fourth Gospel, the realities of the end-time are already present for those who believe in Jesus. The believer does not have to wait until the last day for the gift of life that conquers death. That gift is given now (11:25). Such life is eternal life; its recipient will never die spiritually (11:26). Martha responds not so much to Jesus' doctrinal statements as to his person. She affirms her belief in him through three titles which were introduced to the readers of the Fourth Gospel in the first chapter. Messiah, Son of God and He-who-is-to-come. The final sign will impart an even deeper meaning to these traditional Jewish expectations.

The account of Mary's meeting with Jesus may have been added in a later stage of the Gospel's history, for it repeats his meeting with Martha. The Greek verb used in 11:28 ("is here") is related to the word *parousia.* This became the word by which the early church referred to the coming again of the Lord on the last day. John may intend that Martha's words symbolize the summons that comes to every Christian at death ("the Teacher is here . . . and is asking for you") and that Mary's response ("she got up and hurried out to meet him") prefigures the response of every faithful believer. Lazarus, although already four days in the tomb, will hear the Teacher's voice and will hasten to respond (11:43–44). He is the first to experience that the last day has already arrived for those who believe in Jesus.

Jesus' response to Mary in 11:33 has been the subject of many interpretations. Translated literally, the Greek reads: "he groaned in spirit and troubled himself." The verb "groaned" carries a connotation of anger. It is used several times in the Synoptic Gospels in the context of the healing of the sick. Jesus is not angry at the sick person but at the power of evil which is manifest in the sickness. This seems to offer the best model for the interpretation of Jesus' groan in 11:33. He groans in anger because of his confrontation with the ultimate effect of evil, death.

The second verb, "troubled himself," is used of Jesus in 13:21 (at the prospect of Judas' betrayal) and of the disciples in 14:1, 27 (they are told not to be troubled at the prospect of Jesus' departure from the world). Face to face with the kingdom of Satan, manifested in the death of Lazarus, Jesus looks forward to his

Passion and is filled with deep emotion. (See the Gethsemane accounts in Mark 14:33 and Hebrews 5:7.)

The brief wording of verse 35 carries profound meaning. (See the Reflection section.) Even the visitors from Jerusalem notice the depth of Jesus' love for Lazarus. Since Jesus knows that he will raise Lazarus, he weeps not out of sorrow at Lazarus' death but out of sorrow for those who will remain in death because of their lack of faith. Luke 19:41 remembers that Jesus also wept over the failure of Jerusalem to respond to him.

In verse 37 the evangelist deliberately connects the raising of Lazarus with the healing of the man born blind. Jesus is both light and life for those who believe in him. Jesus approaches the tomb and orders the stone taken away. Martha is horrified, evidence that her faith is still too narrow. Is she here a symbol of all of us in those moments when our faith is weak and we place limits on the power of God? Jesus reminds Martha that only the believer can see God's glory (11:40; note that once again the evangelist emphasizes the themes of faith and glory).

Jesus' prayer in 11:41–42 makes evident the continuing relationship of the Father and the one whom he has sent. There is a remarkable parallel with the prayer of Elijah, offered many centuries earlier in a similar moment of confrontation with evil:

> *At the hour of the afternoon sacrifice the prophet Elijah approached the altar and prayed, "O Lord, the God of Abraham, Isaac, and Jacob, prove now that you are the God of Israel and that I am your servant and have done all this at your command. Answer me, Lord, answer me, so that this people will know that you, the Lord, are God and that you are bringing them back to yourself."*

> *The Lord sent fire down, and it burned up the sacrifice, the wood, and the stones, scorched the earth and dried up the water in the trench. When the people saw this, they threw themselves on the ground and exclaimed, "The Lord is God; the Lord alone is God!"* (1 Kings 18:36–39).

Jesus does not "need" to ask the Father as Elijah does; he prays in order that those around him will recognize that he acts not on his own but always in union with the Father. The prayer makes it clear that the miracle is the work of both Father and Son. Jesus does only what the Father does and acts with his authority. Jesus does not seek human praise and honor for himself; his sole desire is to lead Israel to know the Father. God sent down physical fire in response to the prayer of Elijah; now he sends down the fire of life upon the grave of Lazarus in response to the prayer of his Son.

With characteristic brevity the evangelist records the great act of power. The miraculous in itself is not important but only the reality to which it points. The verb used for Jesus' loud call (11:43) will be used in chapters 18 and 19 for the shouts of the crowd, as they seek Jesus' death. Jesus' shout brings forth life, while the shout of the crowd leads to death.

As Lazarus emerges, the words of 5:28–29 find their first fulfillment: "Do not be surprised at this; the time is coming when all the dead will hear his voice and come out of their graves...." The gift of physical life is the sign of Jesus' ability to grant eternal life in the present moment and to raise the dead on the final day. The completion of Jesus' life-giving work is shared with Lazarus' family and friends. "Untie him," Jesus told them, "and let him go" (11:44). The Christian community's role of unbinding and letting go those whom Jesus has brought to life is essential. Without it, people continue to walk around in shrouds.

REFLECTION. Most of us have been affected by the heresy of Deism, which first emerged in the sixteenth century. Deism taught that God set the world in motion and then stepped back to watch as a detached observer. When we are faced with trials and sufferings, it is tempting to take a deist position. God doesn't care about what is happening to us, we think. Perhaps we become angry, because it seems that God doesn't lift a finger to rescue us.

One response to suffering is to accept Deism as the truth, as the way things are. Another response is to accept as true what God has revealed about himself in his beloved Son. John 11:35 is the shortest verse in the Bible. "Jesus wept." But what a wealth of meaning it contains! The Lazarus account demonstrates with every verse the tremendous love of God for us. He does not love us in the abstract, but as individual persons. He weeps for our unredeemed condition, for the effects of sin upon our lives.

Greek theology speculated that God could not change, could not feel pain, could not be moved to tears. Jesus, weeping at the tomb of Lazarus, reveals that God is not at all like that. If God is not moved to joy at our response of love, if he is not moved to tears by our refusal to obey and love him, then what can it mean to affirm that he loves us?

Some have responded that only the humanity of Jesus loves with emotion, that his divinity is untouched by the "guts" of human life. Unfortunately this approach has infected much of our theology and spiritual writing. However, Jesus Christ reveals what God is like precisely as a human being. The Fathers of the Church loved to talk about the "juxtaposition of opposites" in Christ. We affirm human things about the divine nature (God wept at the tomb of Lazarus), and we can affirm divine things about the human nature (the man, Jesus of Nazareth, raised Lazarus from the dead).

What should create our "image of God" is not what we think God should be like but what God has revealed about himself in the ministry, death and glorification of Jesus Christ. The next time we are tempted to feel discouraged because of God's "remoteness" from our plight might be the best time to meditate on John 11:35.

THE RESULT OF THE GREAT SIGN

OVERVIEW. According to the Synoptic tradition, the cleansing of the Temple was the action which united the opposition of the Jewish leaders against Jesus. Mark 11:18 notes: "The chief priests and the teachers of the Law heard of this, so they began looking for some way to kill Jesus. They were afraid of him, because the whole crowd was amazed at his teaching."

As we have seen, John places the cleansing at the beginning of the ministry. It is the raising of Lazarus, in the Fourth Gospel, which galvanizes the leaders into action. Jesus' gift of life results in his own death. At first glance the reader might be puzzled at the prominence given to the raising of Lazarus, since the Synoptic Gospels do not record this event. The answer lies in understanding this as yet another example of the catechetical genius of the fourth evangelist. He chooses one sign out of the many which Jesus worked, and dramatizes it as the exact moment at which the Jewish leaders made their fateful decision.

To our modern historical minds, this may seem like a distortion of the facts. We need to remember two things: first, that "history" in our contemporary sense is a very modern idea. Ancient people were far more concerned with the meaning of events than with the "bare facts." Secondly, none of the evangelists attempts to write a "biography" of Jesus. They are very selective in what events they record, and even these are recorded in order to convey the deeper meaning (the theology) which the evangelist perceives in these events. While Matthew, Mark and Luke understood that the Temple cleansing (together with Jesus' teaching) motivated the leaders to decide to kill him, John perceives that it was the raising of Lazarus which precipitated the momentous decision.

READ 11:45–57

COMMENTARY. As usual, John notes that Jesus' action creates diverse reactions in the crowd. Many of the onlookers begin to believe (11:45). This indicates another parallel with the account of Elijah's prayer. When the skeptical Israelites saw the fire from heaven, "they threw themselves on the ground and exclaimed, "The Lord is God; the Lord alone is God!" (1 Kings 18:39). John does not share with us the psychological reaction of the crowd in Bethany. There must have been a profound sense of awe, even of terror. It does not surprise us that many began to believe that Jesus was indeed sent from God.

What may surprise us is the reaction of the priests and Pharisees. We need to remember that the relationship of Palestine with Rome was a fragile one. The Jewish people were allowed to practice their religion freely, as long as this did not disrupt political stability. Palestine in the time of Jesus had witnessed a series of revolutionary Jewish groups, each hoping to foment a revolution and overthrow Roman rule. The Sanhedrin feared that Jesus could become such a revolutionary leader (11:47–48). Again we note the irony in John's account: the early Church believed that it was precisely because of Jesus' death that the Romans destroyed the Temple and laid waste to Jerusalem in 70 (Matthew 24:1–2, 15–25).

The key to this section lies in the prophecy of Caiaphas. Jewish tradition accepted the possibility that a person could prophesy without being conscious of it. In addition, the Torah spoke of the special ability of the high priest to determine God's will (Exodus 28:30). Thus the early Church carefully preserved in memory the words of Caiaphas. On one level his statement had a pragmatic meaning: it was easier to dispose of one revolutionary than to chance the wrath of Rome. On a deeper level, as John notes (11:51), Caiaphas foretold the salvific nature of Jesus' death on behalf of Israel.

In 10:16 we read of Jesus' desire to reach out to those who were not part of the Jewish fold. Now John teaches that Jesus' redemptive death would embrace all people, Jew and Gentile alike. The phrase translated as "scattered people of God" literally reads "children of God." This reminds us of the theology of the prologue. People receive "the right to become God's children" (1:12) through their faith in the Word. John reminds us that if people can be united by humanitarian ideals, how much more profundly they can be united by the lifting up on the cross of the Son of Man (12:32).

Verses 55–57 provide a transition into chapter 12. This Passover is the third of Jesus' public life. It will witness the final confrontation of Jesus with the powers of darkness. Jews who lived in close contact with Gentiles could easily lose their ritual purity. For example, contact with a grave defiled the believer and necessitated seven days of purification. As Jesus waits with his disciples in Ephraim, pilgrims begin to gather in Jerusalem for the rites of purification (11:55). They remark to each other about the danger to Jesus if he should come to the feast. He would come, not out of foolhardiness but out of obedience to the Father's plan. The hour was near.

STUDY GROUP QUESTIONS

1. Lazarus' illness "happened in order to bring glory to God" (11:4). Discuss experiences in your life in which you believe an objectively evil event (sickness, accident, sin) resulted in God's glory. Discuss situations in your life in which Jesus seemed to wait "two more days" (11:6) before hearing your cry for help.

2. Share with the group one concrete effect for you of Jesus' teaching, "I am the resurrection and the life" (11:25).

3. "Jesus wept" (11:35) contains a wealth of meaning. Express some of the implications this statement has for you.

4. Share with one another how verses 11:39–40 might express the limitations of our own faith. How would you go about moving beyond the boundaries of Martha's faith?

5. Lazarus seems to symbolize every Christian. In what ways can we carry out Jesus' command to unbind other members of our community?

6. Verse 11:50 can be called "the Caiaphas principle": the individual who threatens the status quo ought to be sacrificed for the sake of the majority's desire to have things remain the same. Does this principle operate in our society? In what ways? Can we do anything positive to protect those whose rights are subjugated for the sake of the status quo?

Chapter Twelve

THE ANOINTING AT BETHANY

OVERVIEW. With Chapter Twelve John concludes the Book of Signs. The two narratives (the anointing and the triumphal entry into Jerusalem) and the discourse all focus on the meaning of his death. Lazarus has a prominent place in the account of the anointing; he, too, is a victim of the plot of the leaders against Jesus. As the decision of the Sanhedrin expresses the refusal to believe, Mary's action symbolizes the response of loving faith.

READ 12:1–11

COMMENTARY. It is the final week of Jesus' life, and he returns to Bethany. By adding the phrase "the home of Lazarus, the man he had raised from death" (12:1), John underlines the connection between the raising of Lazarus and the anointing. As the raising of Lazarus "causes" Jesus' death (11:45–53), so the anointing anticipates his burial. The expense of the perfume emphasizes the extent of Mary's love and gratitude.

The Synoptic tradition records two anointings. That recounted in Mark (with Matthew a close parallel) resembles the passage in John 12. Luke 7:36–38 records an anointing of Jesus' feet (after a washing by tears and drying by hair) by a sinful woman. It seems clear that the oral tradition which the fourth evangelist has received has confused some details from the separate events. This explains the very unusual anointing of Jesus' feet instead of his head, and Mary's immodest behavior of loosening her hair, not to mention the senseless act of wiping off the expensive ointment. The author must have recognized the inconsistencies, but he has allowed them to stand because they serve his theological purpose.

Together with Mark, the fourth evangelist interprets the Bethany anointing as a preparation for Jesus' burial. Mary does not plan it this way; her intention is simply to perform an act of love for the Master. Jesus, however, realizes the closeness of his death and defends her action as an unrealized preparation of his body for burial (12:7). The text of verse 7 has provided many difficulties for commentators. An alternative translation (which may not be the original wording but probably catches the meaning more accurately) is provided by the *Jerusalem Bible:* "So Jesus said, 'Leave her alone; she had to keep this scent for the day of my burial.' " She did not sell it and give alms to the poor, Jesus says, because she was to use it in a prophetic preparation for his burial. Thus the significance of the anointing of Jesus' feet: you anoint the head of a living person but you would anoint the feet of a corpse.

The disciples' grumbling in Mark's account has become Judas' protest in the Fourth Gospel. Both Matthew and John portray Judas in a poorer light than Mark. The tradition may have darkened his name as the memory of his betrayal was handed on. As we have seen, Jesus defends Mary's action. The opportunity to aid the poor is never absent, but the chance to prepare Jesus for burial would not come again (12:8). Jesus' teaching here is in close harmony with rabbinic theology. The rabbis distinguished two kinds of good works: works of mercy (such as burying the dead) and works of justice (such as aiding the poor). They taught that works of mercy were more perfect. Some Christians have tried to use Jesus' saying as an excuse to avoid the works of justice. Jesus' words are very similar to the teaching of Deuteronomy 15:11, and we should interpret them in that light:

> *Of course there will never cease to be poor in the land; I command you therefore: Always be open-handed with your*

brother, and with anyone in your country who is in need and
poor (Jerusalem Bible).

JESUS' TRIUMPHAL ENTRY INTO JERUSALEM

OVERVIEW. This event of Jesus' life is familiar to us from the Synoptic Gospels. (See the parallels in Matthew 21:1–11; Mark 11:1–11 and Luke 19:28–40.) Our tendency is to assume that all the accounts are saying the same thing. As we are learning, however, the evangelists often approach the same event from different theological or pastoral perspectives. We will study John's account of the triumphal entry in light of the accounts of the Synoptic evangelists.

As you read the text, note the ways in which John differs from his predecessors: (1) the initiative for a triumphal procession begins with the crowds rather than with the body of disciples. John specifically tells us that the enthusiasm of the crowd was stirred by the raising of Lazarus. (2) The order of events is changed: Jesus finds the donkey after the crowd's acclamation. In the Synoptic tradition Jesus requests the animal and mounts it. Only then do the disciples begin to acclaim him. (3) The crowd holds branches of palm trees. (Luke does not mention any branches, while Matthew and Mark simply mention branches.) All of these changes will affect our interpretation.

READ 12:12–19

COMMENTARY. During the time that Jesus spent in Ephraim (11:54) word reached Jerusalem about the raising of Lazarus. As a result a large crowd goes out to meet Jesus as he approaches the Holy City for the Passover festival. Taking in hand palm branches, they greet him in the words of Psalm 118:25–26. The palms probably symbolize the nationalistic feelings of the populace. Examine the texts of First Maccabees 13:51 and Second Maccabees 10:7 to see how palm branches were closely associated with Jewish victories over political and religious enemies. Note also that John adds the phrase "God bless the King of Israel," which is not part of Psalm 118. In this way John indicates that the crowd is welcoming Jesus as a political figure, as one who could be another Judas Maccabeus in liberating his people from foreign domination. Once before the crowd misunderstood one of Jesus' signs (the multiplication of the loaves) and wanted to make him king (6:14–15). Now they have misunderstood the sign of the raising of Lazarus, and come out from Jerusalem to greet their political liberator.

Only then does Jesus seek out the donkey. He fulfills the prophecy of Zechariah, part of which John cites (very freely) in 12:15. A study of the full passage will help us see the meaning of Jesus' action.

> *Rejoice, rejoice, people of Zion!*
>> *Shout for joy, you people of Jerusalem!*
>> *Look, your king is coming to you!*
> *He comes triumphant and victorious,*
>> *but humble and riding on a donkey—*
>> *on a colt, the foal of a donkey.*
> *The Lord says,*
> *"I will remove the war chariots from Israel*
>> *and take the horses from Jerusalem;*
>> *the bows used in battle will be destroyed.*
> *Your king will make peace among the nations;*
>> *he will rule from sea to sea,*
>> *from the Euphrates River to the ends of the earth"*
> (Zechariah 9:9–10).

By his prophetic action Jesus both accepts the crowd's acclamation (he is a king) and rejects it (he is not a political figure; his kingship is not of this world). Jesus enters Jerusalem as a king of peace, a source of salvation. The Jews seek their nationalistic interests, but Jesus will accomplish his work for all peoples. (Look back to 11:52 and forward to 12:32.)

John notes that the disciples did not understand what was happening any more than the crowd (12:16). They also seem to have originally expected Jesus to be a political figure. Even after the resurrection they can ask him: "Lord, will you at this time give the kingdom back to Israel?" (Acts 1:6) Only after Jesus' glorification (which includes the sending forth of the Spirit of Truth) did they understand that Jesus' kingship was universal and was to be accomplished only through his death and resurrection. In using the phrase "they remembered" (12:16), the evangelist wants to remind us of another misunderstood event, Jesus' prophecy that he would rebuild the temple in three days (2:19–22). That prophecy, as well as the triumphal entry, could be put into perspective only in light of Jesus' exaltation through death.

In verse 17 we have yet another mention of Lazarus. The author may be emphasizing that Jesus conquers death (the raising of Lazarus) only by dying himself. Great crowds had gone out to Bethany (12:9) and great crowds now meet Jesus on the outskirts of Jerusalem. The Pharisees are frustrated and provide us with another ironic statement: "Look, the whole world is following him!" (12:19). Here John is again affirming the universal nature of Jesus' kingship and is preparing us for a pivotal turning point in the ministry: the arrival of the Gentiles to see Jesus (12:20).

SOME GREEKS SEEK JESUS
READ 12:20–36

COMMENTARY. Immediately following the lament of the anguished Pharisees, "Look, the whole world is following him!" (12:20), some Gentiles asked to see Jesus. The Gentiles symbolize the universality of Jesus' mission. He has been sent not only for the Jews, but for all people. When the Greeks arrive to see Jesus (John often uses "see" for "believe"), he recognizes that the hour of his passion and glorification is at hand. This "hour" is the moment in which Jesus will accomplish both the salvation of the world and the glorification of the Son of Man. The glory of Jesus is not a selfish grasping for human honor. The hour of glorification involves great renunciation. For this reason Jesus interprets his hour by means of a parable about a grain of wheat.

The point of the parable is this: either the grain "remains" nothing but itself or it bears fruit. The planting of the seed is the condition for the future harvest. In the context of the arrival of the searching Gentiles, the production of "many grains" (12:24) probably refers to the universal application of Jesus' redeeming death and resurrection.

Restating the parable of the grain of wheat in plain language (12:25), Jesus applies the parable's meaning to those who would be his disciples. "Loving" and "hating" one's life is a Semitic expression that indicates one's priorities. We have already seen the implications of the statement, ". . . people love the darkness rather than the light" (see 3:18–20). To prefer one's own self to all else is a form of self-idolatry. Such preference is a choice to remain only a single grain; it is the refusal to become any more than what one already is by human birth. Since "What is born of the flesh is flesh" (3:6, *Jerusalem Bible*), those who prefer self to all else will perish in death's destroying power.

But, on the other hand, "Whatever is born of the Spirit is spirit" (3:6, *Jerusalem Bible*). The baptismal theme, being born of the Spirit, matches perfectly with the discipleship theme expressed in Jesus' teaching about "hating one's life in this world" (12:25–26). If "loving" one's life is the refusal to become more than one already is by human birth, then hating one's life expresses a willingness to change by accepting "birth from above" (3:3, 5). Being willing to change, that is, being willing to die to self-centeredness, is the pre-condition for rising to new life. In this way, one keeps his or her life "for life eternal" (12:25).

Verse 26 further develops the meaning of discipleship. Notice the similarities in both Mark and John regarding Jesus' teaching about those who follow him:

"If anyone wants to come with me . . . he must forget himself, carry his cross, and follow me" (Mark 8:34).	"Whoever wants to serve me must follow me, so that my servant will be with me where I am" (John 12:26).

Verses 27 and 28 contain John's version of the prayer of Jesus in the Garden of Gethsemane. Jesus' prayer is placed before, not after, the Last Supper. Taking Mark's account as representative of the Synoptic tradition, note the similarities and differences between the Synoptic and the Johannine accounts:

"Father," he prayed, "my Father! All things are possible for you. Take this cup of suffering away from me. Yet not what I want, but what you want" (Mark 14:36).

"Now my heart is troubled—and what shall I say? Shall I say, 'Father, do not let this hour come upon me'? But that is why I came—so that I might go through this hour of suffering. Father, bring glory to your name!" (John 12:27–28).

Jesus can foresee what is coming. He is a hunted man; his enemies are many. If he continues to proclaim his message, those in power will kill him. In Mark, Jesus refers to the suffering he faces. In John, Jesus states that his "heart is troubled." The humanity of Jesus is seen in both accounts. However, the Synoptic tradition records the fear and dread of Jesus, while the Johannine tradition emphasizes his single-mindedness. In Mark Jesus requested that the Father take away the cup of suffering. John writes that although he was tempted to ask the Father to do so, Jesus did not ask it.

It is John's understanding of the cross that best explains the differences between the Johannine and Synoptic accounts of Jesus' prayer. The cross expresses the mission of Jesus. The cross is, above all, the revealing moment, because it brings about the glorification of both the Father and the Son. Jesus has come to glorify the Father, i.e., to reveal, to manifest the Father to the world. On the cross Jesus reveals the Father's great love for humankind: "God loved the world so much that he *gave* his only Son, so that everyone who believes in him may . . . have eternal life" (3:16). The Father has given his Son in a two-fold sense: in the Incarnation and upon the cross. Thus, the cross is the climax of Jesus' mission. He has been sent "into the world to be . . . its savior" (3:17). Jesus, therefore, refuses to ask his Father to spare him from his hour of imminent suffering. Were he to do so, he would be weakening his total commitment to doing the will of his Father (see 4:34).

Furthermore, the cross is the moment of Jesus' own glorification. He will be revealed as the good shepherd who comes to give his life for his sheep (10:11). The cross is the means by which Jesus manifests his own great love for his disciples and for the world. Just as there are no external pressures or forces that will bring Jesus reluctantly to the cross, so also there is no inner hesitation on the part of Jesus in accepting his hour. Jesus expresses his internal attitude in his prayer: "Father, bring glory to your name!" (12:28).

Just as Jesus finished his prayer of praise, the crowd hears thunder (an ancient symbol for the speech of God). In accordance with the Johannine perspective, the Father answers Jesus by testifying to the signs that Jesus has given ("I have brought glory to it") and by affirming Jesus as he faces the ultimate glorification of the cross and resurrection ("I will do so again"). But the crowd, lacking deep faith in Jesus, cannot comprehend the Father's affirmation of his Son's mission. Even though the voice of the Father was meant for them (12:30), some merely heard thunder, while others had only a vague idea of the thunder's significance ("An angel spoke to him!").

In verses 31 to 33 Jesus anticipates his Passion for the third time. John stresses the cosmic dimensions of Jesus' being lifted up on the cross. First, the world finds itself facing judgment; secondly, the Prince of this world (Satan) is about to be overthrown; thirdly, everyone will be drawn to Jesus (12:31–32).

The Greeks have said, "We want to see Jesus" (12:21). They will see him on the cross. Everyone looking at the crucified Jesus will have eternal life (see 3:14–15). John has reflected for many years on the beautiful words of Jesus in verse 32. From the vantage point of his mature insight, John offers us a powerful image for our meditation. Jesus has foretold the kind of death he would suffer. When Jesus is physically lifted up on the cross, his very posture will express the deepest meaning of his crucifixion: with outstretched arms Jesus will draw all people to himself.

The crowd objects. They expect that the Messiah "will live forever" (12:34). It is likely that they are referring to Scripture passages that speak of the descendant of David who will be Israel's everlasting king. For example:

*A child is born to us!. . . And he will be our ruler. . . . He will
rule as King David's successor . . . from now until the end of time*
(Isaiah 9:6–7).

The crowd then challenges Jesus, "How . . . can you say that
the Son of Man must be lifted up? Who is this Son of Man?"
(12:34). Although Jesus did not specifically refer to himself by the
title, "Son of Man," in referring to his death (12:32), John asso-
ciates this title with each of the three prophecies of the death of
Jesus (3:13; 8:28; 12:32). In the first century the Jewish people understood the title in two different ways. On the one hand, "Son
of Man," simply meant a human being, that is, someone born of
human parents. Thus, God addresses Ezekiel as "Son of Man," or,
as the Good News Bible translates it, as "Mortal man" (Ezekiel
2:2; 3:1). On the other hand, the title can also refer to the mysterious figure of heavenly origin depicted in Daniel. This person-
age receives a universal authority from God:

> *As the visions during the night continued, I saw one like a son of
> man coming, on the clouds of heaven; when he reached the Ancient
> One and was presented before him, he received dominion, glory and
> kingship; nations and peoples of every language serve him. His
> dominion is an everlasting dominion that shall not be taken away,
> his kingship shall not be destroyed* (Daniel 7:13–14, *New
> American Bible*).

Thus, in the second way of understanding, the title has messianic features. The crowd may have used the title to question Jesus about his messianic claims.

Note the answer Jesus gives to the crowd's questions about the
Son of Man. Jesus refers to himself as "the light" who will be
present only a little longer (12:35). Here we find an allusion to the
cure of the man born blind. Recall that in the beginning of chapter nine Jesus declared that he was the light of the world (9:5).
The climax of that whole incident of the cure of the man born

blind was the man's acknowledgement of Jesus as "the Son of Man":

> *"I believe, Lord!" the man said, and knelt down before Jesus*
> (9:38).

For Christians the title, "Son of Man," had a new meaning. It also signified that Jesus was divine.

The crowd had asked, "Who is this Son of Man?" Jesus has indirectly answered them. The Son of Man is the eternal Word, "the source of life" that "brought light to mankind" (1:4). The Son of Man is the one who enables all people to become "the people of the light" (12:35). Recall that Jesus began speaking of his death when he had heard that some Greeks had come to "see" him (12:21). Isaiah's description of God's servant is most appropriate:

> *The Lord said to me, "I have a greater task for you, my servant.*
> *Not only will you restore to greatness the people of Israel who have*
> *survived, but I wll also make you a light to the nations—so that*
> *all the world may be saved"* (Isaiah 49:6).

REFLECTION. Catholics have been accustomed to interpret verses 25–26 solely in terms of the calling to the priesthood or to the life of the religious brother or religious sister. But the fact is that all baptized Christians are called to live out this teaching of Jesus. The willingness to "hate" (love self less than . . .) one's life characterizes the daily life of every Christian, in whatever state of life he or she finds himself or herself. As the teaching of the Second Vatican Council expressed it, the call to holiness is universal. It is addressed to every one of us:

> *It is therefore quite clear that all Christians in any state or walk*
> *of life are called to the fullness of Christian life and to the*
> *perfection of love. . . . The faithful should use the strength dealt out*
> *to them by Christ's gift, so that, following in his footsteps and*
> *conformed to his image . . . they may wholeheartedly devote*

themselves to the glory of God and to the service of their neighbor
(*The Dogmatic Constitution on the Church* no. 40).

REFLECTION. For the second time in the Fourth Gospel we encounter the adversary of Jesus. In 8:44 he was described as the
Devil, a murderer and the father of lies; in 12:31 he is called the
ruler of this world. John has taught us that the Father made all
things through his Word (1:3) and that he has given to Jesus all
authority for giving life and judging (5:19–30). How, then, can
John say that anyone other than Jesus is the ruler of this world?
In answering this question we will come to an understanding of
John's view of the relationship between sin and salvation, Satan
and Jesus.

It is at the moment of the primal sin that the world begins to
have another ruler than the Word. Adam and Eve (whose names
mean "Man" and "Mother of Life") refuse God's will, and in so
doing they bring upon themselves all the consequences of their
sin: separation from God, pain, and death (Genesis 3:16–19). Keep
in mind that in its early tradition Israel did not identify the serpent of Genesis 3 with Satan. In fact, Satan does not appear on
the pages of Scripture until the book of Job is written, about 450
B.C. Even here, Satan is not portrayed as opposed to God; he is
that servant of God whose function is to "test" the faithfulness
of human beings and then report back to God (Job 1:6–8).

The identification of Satan with the serpent of Genesis first occurs in the book of Wisdom, written about 150 years before the
birth of Jesus. There we read that "it was the devil's envy that
brought death into the world" (Wisdom 2:24, *Jerusalem Bible*). Jesus
described Satan as a murderer "from the very beginning" (8:44).
Satan is indeed the primal murderer since, according to Wisdom,
it was at his instigation that death had come to the human family.
Furthermore, the designation of Satan as "a liar and the father of
lies" (8:44) alludes to the serpent's lie. Eat the fruit God has forbidden, the serpent said, and "You will not die" (Genesis 3:4).

Now, however, the hour of Jesus has arrived. Now he will receive great glory (12:23). Now he will cast out the ruler of this
world (12:31). By becoming the grain of wheat that dies, by being

lifted up on the cross, Jesus regains what rightfully belongs to him: "authority, honor, and royal power, so that the people of all nations, races, and languages would serve him" (Daniel 7:14). It is a dominion of love and justice, not a domination of strife and sin. As Satan's hateful envy and the disobedience of Adam and Eve have brought death to the world, so Jesus' loving obedience brings life to those who believe.

Yet, while we live in a redeemed world, we continue to be born with free will. Each of us, in God's mysterious providence, has the capacity either to utter the defiant cry, "I will not serve," or to make our own the words of Mary: "I am the Lord's servant," said Mary; "may it happen to me as you have said" (Luke 1:38).

THE MYSTERY OF BELIEF AND UNBELIEF, SUMMARY (READ 12:37–50)

COMMENTARY. Jesus has gone into hiding (12:37). When the people see him again he will be a prisoner. Verses 37–43 bring to a conclusion the section of the Gospel known as the Book of Signs. (12:44–50 has been added by the final editor as an appendix.) There is sadness in this summary of Jesus' public ministry. In spite of all Jesus did, "they did not believe in him" (12:37). The author of the Fourth Gospel, like the other members of the early Church, was all but scandalized by the fact that the majority of Jesus' own people did not accept him. The followers of Jesus searched the Scriptures for an explanation. They found it in Isaiah's account of his calling to be the Lord's prophet. About seven centuries before the birth of Jesus, Isaiah had written:

> In the year that King Uzziah died, I saw the Lord. . . . I said, "There is no hope for me! I am doomed because every word is sinful". . . . Then one of the creatures . . . touched my lips with the burning coal, and said, ". . . your sins are forgiven." Then I heard the Lord say, "Whom shall I send? Who will be our messenger?" I answered, "I will go! Send me!" So he told me to go out and give the people this message: "No matter how much you listen you will not understand". . . . Then he said to me, "Make the minds of these people dull, their ears deaf, and their

eyes blind, so that they cannot hear or understand. If they did,
they might turn to me and be healed" (Isaiah 6:1–10).

The logic of this passage seems strange to those of us unfamiliar with the Semitic way of thinking. Jewish theology often displays great leaps in logic, going from present fact to ultimate cause, i.e., God. The gist of Isaiah's account is this: since God foresaw the people's future rejection, then God must have willed it to happen.

John uses the citation of Isaiah as an epilogue for Jesus' public ministry. What were the original circumstances in which Isaiah wrote did not matter. John simply declared, "Isaiah said this because he saw Jesus' glory and spoke about him" (12:41). With some variations, all four accounts of the Gospel refer to the same passage of Isaiah as the explanation for the non-acceptance of Jesus by the majority of Jewish people (see Mark 4:11–12; Matthew 13:13–15; Luke 8:8–9).

In those sad years in which the communities of Church and Synagogue wrestled with each other for the one identity of being God's true people, there seemed to be no other resolution to the conflict. Each side declared that it was the faithful community; each community called the other faithless. These poignant verses at the ending of the Book of Signs reflect that conflict.

Turning from his explanation of why large numbers of the Jewish people did not accept Jesus, John now directs his attention toward another group, those who believe in Jesus but who nevertheless remain members of the synagogue (12:42–43). John is highly critical of these Jewish authorities, because they will not openly profess their faith in Jesus. Like the parents of the man born blind (see 9:22), these Jewish-Christian believers remain silent lest they "be expelled from the synagogue" (12:42). John has very hard words for these secret Christians. He accuses them of loving, that is, preferring human approval rather than the "approval of God" (12:42). "Approval" has a meaning similar to "honor" or "glory." Whereas the man born blind glorified God by professing Jesus in spite of the opposition of the Pharisees, the secret Christians are described as refusing to honor/glorify God because they feared the Pharisees.

The last seven verses (12:44–50) constitute a summation of the key themes of the Fourth Gospel: Jesus is the envoy sent by the Father; the choice before all of us is judgment or eternal life; to believe in Jesus is to accept him as the light of the world. Jesus asserts that his words are the words "the Father has told me to say" (12:50). In sum, Jesus is the Word of God. He has come to reveal his Father to the world.

REFLECTION. Verses 42 and 43 give us a glimpse of how difficult the last decades of the first century were for both the Jews loyal to the synagogue and the Jewish followers of Jesus. In a Judaism stripped of the Temple, observance of the Mosaic Law had become the deciding factor between belonging to the Jewish community and excommunication from that community.

On the other hand, the public profession of Jesus as Messiah and Lord has become the touchstone for being a true disciple according to John and his community of believers (see 9:38, 20:28, 20:31). From John's point of view, the Pharisees, the authorized teachers of the Law, deserved much blame (see 9:22, 12:42). And yet, in God's mysterious providence, and in that late first-century crucible of suffering and decision, Christianity became a religion with its own unique identity.

Looking back, we can perceive that there was a great deal of turmoil of one kind or other in the early Church. John has hard words for secret Christians (12:43). The disciples of Jesus argued among themselves (Mark 10:41–45). Paul publicly opposed Peter (Galatians 2:11). Jewish-Christians from Jerusalem clashed with the Christian believers in Antioch (Acts 15:1–15).

Thus, the events of the first century tell us much about what we can expect in the twentieth. In the wake of the changes brought about in the Catholic Church by the Second Vatican Council, many of us found ourselves longing for the "peaceful" period before Pope John XXIII and the Council. In the light of our Church history we see that the Church has always been undergoing some development, often with accompanying controversy. For example, in the decades immediately after the death of Jesus, some Jewish Christians insisted that the Gentile converts keep the Mosaic Law, even to the extent of being circumcised before they could enter the Christian community. These believers wanted, as far as possible, to keep things the way they had been. We can imagine that these believers argued against allowing Gentiles into the Church, because they would jeopardize the Jewish character of the community. Moderates argued for adapting to the new circumstances: God had done something totally new in Jesus. These Christian Jews did not want the Mosaic Law to be a barrier preventing the Gentiles from embracing Jesus in faith.

The early Church made the decision for greater openness even though all the consequences were not foreseen. In the long run the Jewish Christians who opposed the development were correct in their logic but not in their theology. What they feared and what the moderates did not foresee happened: the Church became predominately Gentile. God does not think human thoughts. Originating in Judaism, the Church went out to embrace the Gentile world. In the ultimate analysis, God accomplishes his purposes.

A generation ago, Pope John XXIII called for an ecumenical council. Some Cardinals preferred the way things were. They argued that such a council would bring dark days upon the Catholic Church. We can imagine the enormity of the decision that Pope John faced. With courage and with trust in the Spirit of truth, John went ahead with plans to hold a council for the purpose of up-dating the Church.

Thus, the pattern discerned in the early days of the Church has continued through our history. There have always been divergent points of view within the community of believers. In the wake of the developments that have taken place in the Church since the beginning of the Second Vatican Council, faith and courage are again needed as we seek to discern and do the will of God. As believers, we face a two-fold task: to contemplate in faith what God has brought about in his mysterious providence and to grapple with the resulting new challenges we all face. While we have no divine blueprint telling us how to solve these challenges, we do have a description of the manner in which are to seek solutions. In chapter 14 we will hear John's insistence on the single commandment which Jesus left to his disciples: that they love one another.

STUDY GROUP QUESTIONS

1. Jesus seems callous to the plight of the poor when he says, "You will always have poor people with you" (12:8). Read Deuteronomy 15:7–11. In light of this text, what are the full implications of Jesus' statement in 12:7–8?

2. The same people who on the occasion of Jesus' entry acclaim him (12:13) will call for his crucifixion just a few days later (19:15). How do we often behave in exactly the same way?

3. Share with your group the way in which you understand and apply to your life the teaching of Jesus in 12:24–26.

4. Discuss why John's "theology of the cross" is central for the understanding of the Fourth Gospel (see 12:27–28, 31–33).

5. John's harsh words for the secret Christians (12:42–43) reflect some of the tensions that existed in the early Church. What are some of the tensions we experience in the Church of our day? Share with each other how you might ease existing tensions in parish and diocese.

Chapter Thirteen

JESUS WASHES HIS DISCIPLES' FEET

OVERVIEW. Chapter Thirteen marks a turning point in the Fourth Gospel. Jesus no longer teaches large groups of people. Having concluded his public ministry, he now reveals his deepest thoughts to his friends. In word and action (the footwashing) Jesus shares his most intimate teaching and his humble love. John intends that his readers give their intense attention to what Jesus shares with his disciples during these last hours before his death. The setting is charged with deep intimacy and great affection.

As we reflect on the example and teaching Jesus gives during the Last Supper, we could ask ourselves what we might say on a similar occasion. What would we want to share with spouse, children, family or friends on the evening of a dangerous journey or even in the face of death? In asking ourselves how we would want our loved ones to remember us on such an occasion, we will penetrate more deeply the solemnity of the revelation Jesus gives his disciples during the final hours before his Passion and death. We will also more clearly perceive how painful the betrayal of Judas was to Jesus.

As you read the story of the Last Supper you will see that John does not give an account of Jesus' institution of the sacrament of the Eucharist. Yet John is describing the same meal as the Synoptic writers, for we see the same details in all four Gospel accounts: the Passover features, the prediction of Judas' betrayal, and the prophecy regarding Peter's denials. John has already developed his eucharistic theology in chapter six. There John linked together the sign of the multiplication of the bread, the teaching of Jesus about his life-giving message, and the sacrament of the Eucharist, the pledge of eternal life.

READ 13:1–20

COMMENTARY. On this night and the following day Jesus will reveal to his disciples the full extent of his love for each of them. The first verse solemnly asserts that Jesus "loved them to the very end," that is, he loved them to the fullest extent possible: the gift of his life for them. While the entire Fourth Gospel is an account of the immeasurable love of the Father and the Son, the depth of this love is most clearly expressed during the Last Supper. A comparison between the Johannine account and the early preaching of Peter shows how much more profound is John's interpretation of the crucifixion of Jesus:

In accordance with his own plan God had already decided that Jesus would be handed over to you; and you killed him by letting sinful men crucify him. But God raised him from death . . . (Acts 1:23–24).	It was now the day before the Passover Festival. Jesus knew that the hour had come for him to leave this world and go to the Father. He had always loved those in the world who were his own, and he loved them to the very end (13:1).

In John, it is not a question of Jesus' being killed or murdered. Jesus dies voluntarily. Jesus goes to his death knowing that his hour has come, knowing that he was returning to his Father, and lovingly offering his life for his disciples. The love with which Jesus lays down his life is the key to the meaning of the symbolic washing of the disciples' feet.

The second verse sets the stage for the action that follows. The meal has begun. The final clash between light and darkness, between Jesus and the ruler of this world is imminent. On one side Judas, at the instigation of Satan, plans to betray Jesus. On the other side, Jesus, in complete communion with his Father, prepares his disciples. Jesus wants them to understand that his death is both the glorification of his Father and the manifestation of his love for his friends.

Although the passage dealing with the footwashing is generally understood as an example of humility, the action narrated by John symbolizes much more. While some commentators point to the baptismal themes that are woven into the action of Jesus' washing his disciples' feet, the most basic meaning of the footwashing pertains to the cross, the ultimate sign of Jesus' love. This is clear when we note the relation between verses 3 and 4:

> *Jesus knew that . . . he had come from God and was going to God.*
> So he rose *from the table* . . . (13:3–4).

Girding himself with a towel, Jesus then "began to wash the disciples' feet" (13:5). Because the footwashing follows immediately after the assertion that Jesus knew he was about to return to his Father, verses 3, 4 and 5 are integrally linked together. Thus, the footwashing serves two purposes. It is primarily related to the death of Jesus (13:3–11) and, after this, the footwashing is intended to serve as an example of how the disciples should humbly serve one another (13:12–20). Let us examine the first and most basic meaning of this sign, namely, the cross as the ultimate symbol of Jesus' love.

In first-century Israel the washing of feet was either a lowly task done by a slave or it was an act of tender affection performed by one's spouse or children. When Jesus rose from the table to wash his disciples' feet, he brought together these two aspects of humble service and tender love. Thus the action of washing his disciples' feet was an anticipation of what he would do on the cross. There the crucified Jesus would manifest the total extent of his love ("he loved them to the very end"—13:1). Upon the cross Jesus would serve the world by casting down Satan (12:31) and by drawing all people into his saving embrace ("I will draw everyone to me"—12:32).

The profound meaning of this symbolic action is brought out in the exchange between Jesus and Peter. Peter asks, "Are you going to wash my feet, Lord?" Jesus answers, "You do not understand now what I am doing, but you will understand later" (13:7). The answer Jesus gives links the footwashing with earlier symbolic actions such as the cleansing of the Temple (2:18–22) and the triumphant entry into Jerusalem (12:12–16). The disciples will understand the meaning of these three actions only in the light of Jesus' death and resurrection. What Jesus knows, Peter will only realize later on: that his submission to Jesus' washing of his feet is the symbolic acceptance of Jesus' death as an act of love for him and for every disciple. As John had indicated earlier, to accept the death of Jesus, i.e., to look upon the crucified Jesus with the eyes of faith, is to be saved:

> *As Moses lifted up the bronze snake on a pole in the desert, in the same way the Son of Man must be lifted up, so that everyone who believes in him may have eternal life* (3:14–15).

It is because the footwashing is a symbol of his crucifixion that Jesus insists upon washing Peter's feet: "If I do not wash your feet," Jesus answered, "you will no longer be my disciple" (13:8). The words of Jesus can also be translated this way: "If I do not wash you," Jesus answered, "you will have no share in my heritage" (13:8, *New American Bible*). The "heritage" or "portion" of Jesus is eternal life. In effect Jesus is saying, "Peter, if you do not accept this gesture as a symbol of my death for you, then you cannot share in the effects of my saving death."

Missing the point, Peter declares that he'll take a bath if that's what Jesus wants (13:9). Anticipating the cleansing power of his

death on the cross, Jesus tells Peter that he is already clean (13:10). The one exception is Judas. Even though Jesus washed Judas' feet (Jesus died for him as well as the other disciples), Judas is not clean. Judas has already planned to betray Jesus (13:2).

We can also see a two-fold meaning in Judas' act of betraying Jesus. It literally means that Judas will "hand Jesus over" to his enemies. However, in the context of the dialogue between Jesus and Peter, Judas' betrayal also means that Judas is giving up everything related to Jesus; Judas is refusing to receive a portion or share in Jesus' heritage (see 13:8). For a few moments Peter outwardly refused to accept the symbolic cleansing Jesus offered, but Judas did the opposite. He visibly accepted the footwashing while inwardly rejecting the meaning of Jesus' loving gesture. Jesus, the good shepherd, offered to lay down his life for Judas, but Judas refused the gift.

Verse 12 begins to unfold the second meaning of the footwashing, i.e., an example of humble service. Jesus, the Lord and Teacher, gives his disciples an example of how they should humbly serve one another (13:13–15).

We can learn much about John's understanding of the Church from his usage of this saying of Jesus (13:16). John sees the Church as a community in which the disciples of Jesus imitate his example by serving one another. These verses also represent John's views on the manner in which the community's leaders should serve the members of their flock. The image of Jesus as the "good shepherd" brings together both meanings of the footwashing, that of humble service and that of dying for his disciples. Thus Jesus not only serves by guiding his sheep to their pasture, but he also lays down his life to protect them (see 10:11–16). In the entire Fourth Gospel there are only two instances in which Jesus pronounces that a person will be blessed or "happy" if he or she puts into practice a particular action. Here is the first instance: the disciple will be blessed in the action of humbly and lovingly caring for others (13:17). The second instance is located at the end of the Gospel when Jesus will declare that those who believe in him (even if they have not seen him during his earthly life) are also blessed (20:29). It is interesting to note how simply John states his understanding of the kind of behavior that characterizes those who belong to the community of the Church: humble service. Matthew develops the same theme in the discourse of Jesus on the use and abuse of authority (18:1–19:1).

Verse 18 returns to the betrayal theme. Jesus cites Psalm 41:9, "The man who shared my food, has turned against me." The psalm probably refers to David's trusted counselor, Ahithophel, who betrayed David by taking the side of Absalom in his rebellion against his father (see 2 Samuel 15:31; 16:23; 17:1–4). Afterward Ahithophel hanged himself (2 Samuel 17:23).

Verse 19 links the betrayal of Judas with the death and resurrection of Jesus. Faith in Jesus is the basic issue. Only after Jesus is crucified and risen will the disciples be able to believe:

When you lift up the Son of Man, you will know that "I Am Who I Am" (8:28).	I tell you this now before it happens, so that when it does happen, you will believe that "I Am Who I Am" (13:19).

REFLECTION. No matter what we do to make a living, whether we are students or business executives, whether we are salespersons or homemakers, whether we are artists or parents, we all have two things in common: we all have daily responsibilities, and we all encounter other persons during the course of the day. If we are disciples of Jesus, we have a third area in common: the opportunity to serve others in accordance with the loving and humble example of Jesus (13:15–16).

But to do this is not easy. Like all matters concerning Jesus, a choice must be made. To a great extent we are the ones who decide which perspective to take regarding daily responsibilities. We can view our daily tasks as part of "the rat race." This is a common option. Or we can choose to see with the eyes of faith: whatever we do on the job or in the home is an opportunity to serve others according to the example of Jesus. If we could begin to see each aspect of our daily living from the perspective of faith in Jesus, how fresh and full of meaning our daily lives would be! To strive seriously after and pray for this attitude is to experience what Jesus promised. "Now that you know this truth, how happy you will be if you put it into practice!" (13:17)

JESUS AND JUDAS
READ 13:21–30

COMMENTARY. Jesus, under great emotional distress, declares that one of his own disciples will betray him. The same word that described Jesus' feeling about the death of his friend, Lazarus (11:33) is used to describe the anguish Jesus now faces (13:21).

The disciples are taken by surprise to hear that one of their own number is a traitor. Peter asks "the one whom Jesus loved" (13:23) to find out who it is. This is the first reference in the Fourth Gospel to the disciple "whom Jesus loved." Although this beloved disciple is never identified by name, tradition reports that the beloved disciple is John, one of the twelve, the son of Zebedee, and the one whose authority stands behind the Fourth Gospel.

In response to this disciple's question, Jesus affirms that his betrayer is the one to whom he will offer a piece of bread. The action has a two-fold meaning. On one level, it indicates to the beloved disciple the one who plans to betray Jesus. On another level, the act of giving bread to another is a sign of affection and friendship. Thus, Jesus offers Judas a gesture of reconciliation. But Judas refuses to be reconciled:

As soon as Judas took the bread, Satan entered into him (13:27).

Having failed in this final effort to win Judas back, Jesus seems to give Judas permission to do what he has decided: "Hurry and do what you must!" Having sided with Satan, Judas goes into the night (13:30). Thus, Judas becomes a symbol of those who prefer the darkness to the light (see 3:18–20). Rejecting Jesus, the light of the world, Judas plunges into the night, which is now his native element.

INTRODUCTION TO THE LAST SUPPER DISCOURSE

OVERVIEW. These verses provide a bridge between the narrative of the Last Supper (13:1–30) and the Supper Discourse (14:1–17:26). Since verses 31–38 introduce so many of the themes which will be developed in later chapters, we may consider them to be the introduction to the discourse.

In handing on the memory of the Last Supper, the disciples were guided by their strong conviction that the words of Jesus at the Supper were intended not only for them. In a real way Jesus was speaking to all his disciples, those who were present on that night in Jerusalem and those not yet born. After the Resurrection, the first disciples proclaimed Jesus' Last Supper teaching with more mature faith and insight. They came to a full appreciation of Jesus' words at the Supper only after the Resurrection. This provides us with an excellent example of Jesus' promise that the Spirit of Truth would bring the disciples to a full understanding of what Jesus had taught.

Inspired by the Spirit, the fourth evangelist has given to the Church a channel through which Jesus speaks to every believer, regardless of how long after the Last Supper he or she lives. The Church has always regarded the Last Supper discourse with a special reverence and affection. Perhaps this is because we need to hear again and again its assurance that the Master has not left us orphans, that he continues to dwell within the community of believers and within the heart of each disciple. Perhaps more than any other portion of the Fourth Gospel the teachings of the Supper discourse need to be studied prayerfully.

READ 13:31–38

COMMENTARY. Judas leaves the Light of the world to plunge into darkness (13:30). In one sense the Passion has already begun, since Judas leaves to do the work of Satan. Thus the hour is now. "Now the Son of Man's glory is revealed" (13:31). The tragedy of Judas' betrayal leads to the glorification of Jesus.

The hour of Jesus' glory is envisioned by the fourth evangelist as a process. It began with the arrival of the Gentiles (12:20–23) and continues as Jesus gathers his disciples for the last time before his death (13:1). "Glory" means that God's presence becomes visible through an act of power. Jesus tells the disciples that this glorification will happen in two ways (yet they are two sides of the same coin). First, the Father's glory becomes manifest in the death/resurrection of his Son. Already the presence of the Father has become visible in the powerful works of Jesus' ministry. Jesus has always sought the Father's glory. Now his perfect obedience unto death brings the Father's glory to perfection. As the Son of Man is lifted up on the cross, the presence of the Father to his children and his love for them becomes manifest.

Secondly, God will reveal the glory of Jesus (13:32). The lifting up of Jesus involves not only his obedient suffering but also his victorious return to the Father's side. In this way the Father vindicates his Son's trust and manifests Jesus' life as truly that of the Son of God. The same glory is being revealed, whether the Father's glory in the Passion of the Son or Jesus' glory in his return to the Father.

Jesus' glorification will involve his departure from the disciples. With verse 33 he begins to prepare them for this. His tenderness is evident in the term "my children," which is used frequently in the First Epistle. Jesus had told those who refused to accept him that they could not follow him, because their lives were oriented toward eternal death (8:21). His separation from them will be final, but his separation from the disciples will be only for a time (13:36 and 14:3).

Jesus' departure will create a new relationship, not only between himself and his disciples but also among the disciples themselves. The new commandment is given to guide the new relationship of the disciples to one another. Since the Torah had mandated love for neighbor (Leviticus 19:18), how are we to understand the newness of Jesus' command? It is new because the Covenant from which it flows is new. Yahweh gave the original ten commandments to Israel as a way of living out the Covenant relationship which he had established with them at Sinai. Now, as Jesus prepares to inaugurate the New Covenant, he leaves with his faithful disciples a new commandment. As the New Covenant enables its participants to know and love God more fully, so it enables the disciples to love one another more fully. The words of Jesus, "As I have loved you," envision the completion of his Passion. Thus, disciples are to love "to the very end" (13:1). There is to be no limit to the love of the disciples for one another; they are to love to the end of their lives, to the end of their strength, with the generosity of Jesus' love for sinners. Jesus is not only the standard and measure of this love, he is its source. Only the person who is born from above, who possesses the Spirit of Jesus can love in this way.

The very newness of such love establishes the credentials of the disciple (13:35). The "world" will recognize the origin of this love, since it recognizes that it is incapable of loving in this way. Christian love will challenge the world to choose between darkness and light. One of the Fathers of the Church, Clement of Alexandria, spoke of this love as the face and image of Christ the Savior in us. Only this love can open the hearts of all people and draw them to the truth.

Jesus is the pioneer of salvation. He must tread the way to the Father alone. Yet "later" the disciples can follow him (13:36). The original disciples will follow in a literal manner, laying down their physical lives as Jesus did. Thus 13:36 is related to 21:19, which looks forward to Peter's martyrdom. Peter thinks he is ready now, and his bold statement contains yet another Johannine irony: "*I* am ready to die for *you!*" (13:17). Peter fails to understand his own weakness and also the difficulty of the task. Jesus' return to the Father is accomplished only through his struggle with the Prince of this world. Only after Jesus' victory, only after the pioneer of our salvation has marked out the path, can the disciples follow.

REFLECTION. In the Sinai Covenant Yahweh gave Israel ten commandments by which they could live out their union with him. In the Covenant of the Last Supper Jesus gives only one command. There is a startling implication. Love among the disciples is the *only* way of living out union with Jesus. Many of us have become experts in giving lip service to the new commandment and then living much as the "world" does. We commend ourselves if we can manage to be polite to other believers, if we can maintain a sort of camaraderie within the parish.

We would probably have to admit that there is little love-to-the-very-end going on in our parishes. It might be important for each one of us to ask himself/herself these questions: Do I have much appreciation for what the new commandment involves? Have I ever prayerfully asked what it means to love "as I have loved you"? Do I have any intention of living according to the new commandment of Jesus? What differences would occur in my family and in our parish life if we began to obey the new commandment?

Dietrich Bonhoeffer has spoken of "the cost of discipleship." We tend to ignore the new commandment because it is so hard, because it demands our total time and energy and being. For the most part we try to respond to Jesus' great love for us at the cheapest possible price. We try to "get by" with as little as possible. If we go to church, if we keep the ten commandments, if we say a few prayers, we tell ourselves, "that should do it."

It is true that the new commandment is difficult. But the power of God is in proportion to the cost. As Jesus' love is the new standard, so his ability to love is the new source of Christian life. Remember the dialogue of the disciples with Jesus in Mark 10:26–27:

> *At this the disciples were completely amazed and asked one another, "Who, then, can be saved?"*
>
> *Jesus looked straight at them and answered, "This is impossible for man but not for God; everything is possible for God."*

STUDY GROUP QUESTIONS

1. "Jesus performed this first miracle in Cana in Galilee; there he revealed his glory and his disciples believed in him" (2:11). Discuss how this statement is related to 13:1, 31–33.

2. In what situations are we like Peter, protesting that Jesus cannot wash our feet (13:6–8)?

3. As disciples, we are called to live out the teaching of Jesus in 13:13–17. In what ways can we practice this teaching in our family and parish communities?

4. How is Jesus' "new commandment" new? Share with each other the different ways this new commandment can be observed in home and parish.

5. In the departure discourse Jesus shares his most intimate teaching with his friends. What parting words would you want to leave with those you love?

6. In what situations are we like Peter, boasting of our fidelity to Jesus (13:37)? Are the results similar?

Chapter Fourteen

JESUS IS THE WAY TO THE FATHER

OVERVIEW. The major overview for the entire Supper Discourse was given in the last section of Chapter Thirteen. The verses from 13:31 to 14:31 probably constituted the entire discourse in the first "edition" of the Fourth Gospel. We have divided the section into three parts: 13:31–38 (introduction); 14:1–14 (Jesus as way to the Father); and 14:15–31 (the dwelling of the Spirit, Jesus and the Father within the believer).

In 14:1–14 John continues and develops the themes of the introduction, especially that of Jesus' departure. As we will see in 14:14–31, Jesus departs in order to fulfill the Father's plan of establishing a new form of presence (a permanent abiding) among his people.

READ 14:1–14

COMMENTARY. Jesus begins by reassuring his disciples. In the face of his departure they are not to be "worried and upset." Jesus' words would be better translated, "Do not let your hearts be troubled." We have seen the Greek word translated "troubled" in several passages. In 12:27 Jesus' heart was "troubled" as he anticipated the hour; in 13:21 he was "deeply troubled" because of Judas' betrayal. In each case Jesus is troubled as he anticipates the hour of his struggle with Satan. The disciples, however, are not to be troubled. Jesus' death is at the same time his victory over death; by his seeming "defeat" he conquers the Prince of this world. Thus the disciples are instructed to stand firm in God and in their Master (14:1b; remember that "belief" means being rooted in God's own faithfulness).

Jesus departs that he might return. He is the forerunner of salvation and he goes before the disciples to prepare a dwelling place; then he will return and bring them to be with him (14:2–3). These two verses provide us with another example of the multiple levels of meaning in the Fourth Gospel. Notice how the words of Jesus have a threefold meaning:

Rooms in the Father's house	Jesus' return to take the disciples
1) heaven	at the end of time
2) heaven	at the personal death of the disciple
3) spiritual union with the Father in Jesus	in the present experience of the disciple

Jesus has been speaking of his destination: the Father. In verses 4–7 he begins to speak about the way. He uses Thomas' lack of understanding as an opportunity for one of his most profound claims:

> *I am the way, the truth and the life; no one goes to the Father except by me* (14:6).

Jesus' own "way" is that of loving obedience to the Father, even to death on the cross. For the disciples, Jesus himself is the way. There is no union with the Father except through union with Jesus. The concept here is very similar to that of another of the great "I am" statements: "I am the gate. Whoever comes in by me will be saved. . . . I have come in order that you might have life—life in all its fullness" (10:9–10).

Jesus is the way because he is the truth. The believer can approach the Father through Jesus because Jesus reveals the Father.

The truth sets the believer free (8:32) because the truth is not a set of propositions or doctrines but is Jesus himself. Jesus is the way because he is the life. The whole purpose of our journey on the way is life with the Father, life eternal. Jesus is himself this life (11:25). To be with him is already to experience life with the Father, to see the Father (14:7).

Again, one of the disciples fails to understand. Philip probably thinks of a glorious manifestation of God such as that sought by Moses (Exodus 33:18–23). Jesus chides him gently: the disciples still have not understood. (It is probable that the confusion expressed by Philip continued into the evangelist's own day. Thus there are two audiences for whom this teaching of Jesus is intended. First, John directs these words of Jesus to the Johannine community; secondly, these words of Jesus are meant to help other Christian communities develop a deeper appreciation of Jesus as the one who shares in the divine nature of God.) Jesus' reply to Philip is one of the most memorable in the Scripture: "Whoever has seen me has seen the Father. . . . Do you not believe, Philip, that I am in the Father and the Father is in me?" (14:9–10).

Even in the Covenant with Israel, the messenger whom Yahweh sent carried his authority and in some way made him present. In Jesus, however, there is an absolute identity between his word and that of the Father, between his works and those which the Father performs (14:10bc). Jesus *is* the Word of the Father (1:14, 17). (We should also remember that in the Hebrew Scriptures God's Word possesses a dynamism of its own. For this reason, God's Word is understood as a deed or an action, as well as a verbal reality. Thus we can say that Jesus *is* God's Deed, his Work.) Because Jesus totally reveals the Father, the person who sees Jesus sees the Father also. (Remember that "seeing" here means more than physical sight; to "see" Jesus is to believe that his words and signs point to his unity with the Father; it is to accept him as the One sent by the Father to draw believers into union with himself.)

As Jesus does the works of the Father, so those who believe in Jesus will do these works also (14:12). Indeed, the believer will do even greater things, because Jesus is going to the Father. The idea of our doing "greater things" might puzzle us. Jesus has healed the crippled, given sight to the blind, raised up the dead and revealed the Father. How can believers do greater things than these? The key to understanding can be found in 5:20: "For the Father loves the Son and shows him all that he himself is doing. He will show him even greater things to do than this, and you will all be amazed." Until his return to the Father, Jesus' works are only signs of his power to give eternal life. The streams of life-giving water (the Spirit) cannot be poured out until Jesus is raised to glory (7:39). When he returns to the Father, Jesus will do greater works than he has done during the ministry. But he will accomplish these greater things *through those who believe,* through the preaching and sacraments of his Church.

REFLECTION. In 14:1 Jesus encourages his disciples (is it a command?) to avoid being troubled and anxious. Despite our Lord's teaching, how many of us are continually worried and upset over all kinds of things! Your study group might find it profitable to discuss this statement: the disciple of Jesus should be marked by a certain kind of freedom from tension and anxiety.

None of us will fully achieve this freedom in this life any more than we will fully accomplish the goal of laying down our lives for one another. It may be important, however, to perceive it as a goal, as a gift of our union with Jesus. Of course we are human beings with the full range of human emotions; we will experience sadness, the stress of some situations, the deep concern for our futures and the futures of those whom we love. However, the Christian is a person who is not dominated by his or her emotions. Can we not see that giving in to excessive anxiety contradicts our discipleship just as fully as giving in to anger or lust or jealousy?

Freedom from anxiety flows from belief in the victory of Jesus over every form of evil. The disciple sinks his/her roots deeply into the truth. The familiar analogy of the tree applies here. Since its roots penetrate the ground only a few inches, an immature tree can be blown over by a strong wind. The mature tree, however, sinks its roots deep into the soil. Strong winds may bend it a little but cannot really harm it. Faith in Jesus does not remove us from

the human condition. We will always experience trials and suffering. But as we mature in faith these difficulties affect our inner
peace less and less. We remain serene and confident, even in the
face of sickness and death, knowing that we participate in Jesus'
victory over evil.

THE ABIDING OF THE SPIRIT, JESUS AND THE FATHER

OVERVIEW. The final verses of 14:1–14 spoke of the post-as-
cension role of the disciples: continuing the ministry of Jesus. In
14:15–31 Jesus explains how the disciples will be equipped for
their task. As faith was emphasized in verses 1–14, love becomes
the focus of these verses.

This passage can be divided into two parts: verses 15–24 and
verses 25–31. The first part (14:15–24) contains a threefold pattern, each section of which is devoted to the abiding with the disciples of one of the divine Persons: the Spirit (15–17), the Son
(18–21) and the Father (23–24).

READ 14:15–31

COMMENTARY. In these verses John becomes almost tiresome
in his insistence that love and obedience must be joined together
in the life of the disciple. There may have been those in the Johannine community who were advocating love without fidelity
to the commandments, for the author of the First Letter reminds
his readers: "our love for God means that we obey his commands" (1 John 5:3). Commandments (plural, 14:15) would not
mean something different from the single commandment of love
given in 13:34. (See 15:10 and 12 for another example of the inter-
changeability of commandment and commandments.) Jesus
speaks here of the life-style which his command to love will introduce.

Loving Jesus and keeping his commandments prepares the disciples for a further gift. At Jesus' request the Father will give "another Helper" (14:16) to stay with the disciples. This is the first
of five passages within the Supper Discourse which refer to the

Holy Spirit. "Another" is the operative word. It indicates that the Spirit will continue the work of Jesus. The Greek word *paraklētos* ("Helper") literally means called-to-one's side. It is used of Jesus in 1 John 2:1: "But if anyone should sin, we have, in the presence of the Father, Jesus Christ, an *intercessor* who is just" *(New American Bible)*.

While Jesus is our Paraclete with the Father, the Holy Spirit becomes the Paraclete/Helper on earth. Until his death it was Jesus who revealed the truth to his disciples. After Jesus ascends to the Father, the Spirit "reveals the truth about God" (14:17a). Because the world is hostile to God, it blinds itself to the presence of the Helper; but the disciples recognize his presence because the Spirit dwells within them (14:bc). The evangelist uses here the same verb for the abiding presence of the Spirit as he has used for the indwelling of Jesus in the disciple. Note that the noun form of this verb is used in 14:23 to describe the Father's presence within the disciples.

In 14:18–21 Jesus speaks of his own presence with the disciples after his departure. At the death of a rabbi, his disciples were often said to be orphaned. But Jesus promises: "When I go, you will not be left all alone; I will come back to you" (14:18). Verses 19 and 20 seem to have a double fulfillment. Initially these promises are fulfilled in the Resurrection appearances of Jesus. The world no longer sees him, but the disciples both see him and draw life from his Risen Life. But after the ascension the promises cannot be fulfilled through a physical "seeing" of the Risen Lord. Then disciples will "see" the Lord through his indwelling presence.

Verse 21 re-emphasizes that the Christian life cannot be reduced to an experience of the presence of the divine Persons. Only obedience to Jesus' commandments prepares a person to receive the gifts which God desires to give. Judas' question (14:22) regards the end-time: How can Jesus' appearance in glory be missed by the world? Jesus responds that the blessings of the end-time are already anticipated for the believer. Jesus and the Father reveal themselves to the believer through an interior indwelling of which the world remains ignorant (14:23). The words translated "live with" in verse 23 could be literally translated "make a room." Thus the believer does not have to wait until personal death or the end-time for one of the "rooms in my Father's house" (14:2) which Jesus goes to prepare. That which will be the essence of heaven—dwelling in the presence of Jesus and the Father—is already possessed! For this reason the Little Flower could say that "all the way to heaven is heaven."

In verses 27–31 Jesus returns to the theme of his departure. Again he encourages the disciples not to give in to the temptation of becoming troubled or anxious or fearful. Fears and anxieties are the fruits of placing one's trust in the world and its values. Trust in Jesus produces another fruit: peace. We should not equate the peace of Jesus with an absence of worries or troubles. The peace (or in Hebrew "shalom") which Jesus envisions embraces the full harmony which comes from union with God. In the Hebrew Scriptures "shalom" expresses the gift of salvation. Our tendency is to think of salvation as if it were only a personal reality, a gift given by God to the individual soul. In Scripture, however, salvation is a communal gift, in which the individual members share. We might sum up this scriptural perspective in this way: because the gift of salvation/peace is given to us, it is given to me. Thus, God saves the Chosen People. (But an individual can choose to exclude himself/herself from this gift.) In a similar way "shalom" is primarily a gift for the community. It establishes a harmonious and loving relationship not only between Yahweh and his people but also among the holy people in their relationship to one another and to the world around them. Thus Israel looked forward to peace as a gift which the Messiah would bring when he came to dwell among the Chosen People. The connection of all these themes can be seen in the familiar verse from Isaiah:

> *How beautiful on the mountains,*
> *are the feet of one who brings good news,*
> *who heralds peace, brings happiness,*
> *proclaims salvation,*
> *and tells Zion,*
> *"Your God is king!"* (Isaiah 52:7, *Jerusalem Bible*).

Jesus can bestow the messianic gift of peace/salvation because now the hour has begun. Far from being discouraged in the face of Jesus' departure, the disciples should rejoice (14.28). Jesus cannot complete the work he has been sent to do until he returns to the Father. From the moment of his glorification the Son becomes the source of all the Father's gifts.

Jesus' return to the Father will complete his victory over the Prince of this world (14:30–31). Their struggle is really not an equal one, for Satan has no power over Jesus. However, Jesus loves the Father and so will be obedient to his plan, obedient even unto death. In this way even the world must recognize Jesus' loving faithfulness to the Father.

Verse 31, "Come, let us go from this place," is probably the ending of the Last Supper Discourse in the earlier edition of the Fourth Gospel. It seems that the final editor wanted to add material from the Johannine tradition (now contained in chapters 15–17) without making any changes, so he let the original conclusion remain as it was. This explains the fact that there are two conclusions to the discourse, 14:31 and 18:1.

REFLECTION. We are tempted sometimes to romanticize the days in which Our Lord walked the earth. We think: if only I had lived then! If only I had heard him teach and seen one of the miracles. How much more committed I would be, how fervent, how selfless!

In light of 14:15–21, we would have to say such thinking misses the point. If the original disciples *alone* could say, "He has dwelt with us!" then all believers since the ascension would be second-class Christians. If Jesus' return to be with the disciples applied only to the period between the Resurrection and the ascension, then we are truly unfortunate because we did not live in Palestine during the first third of the first century.

But the truth is this: we are not second-class Christians! We can claim, as truly as could the original disciples, that Jesus has returned to dwell with us. He has not left us orphans! And yet it is true that the presence of Jesus in his risen body lasted only a short time. How does he return to be present with us? The answer of the Fourth Gospel is this: through the gift of the other

Helper. Jesus dwells with his disciples through the power of the Holy Spirit. Just as Jesus brings us into the presence of the Father, so the Spirit draws us into union with Jesus.

As we will see, the Spirit does not innovate. He is not interested in his own glory. He wants only to lead people to Jesus. He does not teach a new doctrine but brings to remembrance what Jesus has taught. We might say that as Jesus is the way to the Father, so the Holy Spirit is the "way" to Jesus. Paul's teaching, in 1 Corinthians 12:3 says the same thing in different words. We will paraphrase it here: no one can say "Jesus is Lord" (recognize him as the Son of God and surrender one's life in obedient service) except in the power of the Holy Spirit (through the indwelling presence of the Paraclete).

STUDY GROUP QUESTIONS

1. Discuss the following statement: Freedom from being "worried and upset" (14:1) is a good sign that a person is a disciple of Jesus.

2. How is Jesus the way *for you;* the truth *for you;* the life *for you?*

3. For us disciples who do not see him in his earthly life, how can we understand Jesus' teaching that to see him is to see the Father (14:9)?

4. How are the "even greater things" (14:12) which Jesus promised happening in your parish? in your town or city?

5. In what ways has the Holy Spirit been "another Helper" (14:16) in your own life?

6. Describe an occasion in which the Holy Spirit taught you or helped you "remember" the teaching of Jesus (14:26).

7. In what ways is the peace of Jesus (14:27) different from the peace of the world?

Chapter Fifteen

THE VINE AND THE BRANCHES

OVERVIEW. In this beautiful passage Jesus speaks of his relationship to the disciples and of the common life which they share. The image of the vine and its branches carries many resonances from the prophetic books of the Jewish Scriptures. There Israel is pictured both as a vine (Ezekiel 15:1–6; 17:5–10; and 19:10–14) and as a vineyard (Isaiah 5:1–7 and 27:2–6). While Yahweh lavishes great care and tenderness on his vineyard/vine, the fruits are either bitter or non-existent. Israel, although chosen by God, does not fulfill its role as God's vine. Thus Jesus claims to be the real vine, the true vine. (This is a good example of the way in which the Fourth Gospel applies to Jesus the titles and images which belong to Israel.)

The image of vine and branches has as its primary meaning the intimate love and friendship of Jesus and his disciples. (Note how dominant in this passage are the words of union: remain united to me, love, friends, joy.) There is also a secondary meaning of these verses: the sacrament of the Eucharist. Thus the vine in John 15:1–17 symbolizes the eucharistic wine, source of life for the disciples. Note that during Mark's account of the Last Supper, Jesus speaks of the wine which has become his precious blood as "the fruit of the vine" (Mark 14:25).

READ 15:1–17

COMMENTARY. In the Overview section we saw something of the richness in the metaphor of the vine and branches. By proclaiming himself the real or the true vine, Jesus makes at least three claims: (1) that he fulfills in himself the role of divine Wisdom as the fruitful vine; (2) that he replaces Israel, the unfruitful vine; and (3) that he is the source of heavenly (from above) nourishment as opposed to earthly (from below). In addition, the image of the vine emphasizes the profound intimacy of Jesus and his disciples. The branches are an integral part of the vine. The same life which flows through the vine also enlivens the branches.

As the gardener, the Father both breaks off the unfruitful branches and prunes the fruitful ones. The following diagram will help explain the Father's action:

AGRICULTURAL TASK	TYPE OF BRANCH
1) In February or March the gardener breaks off the branches that cannot bear fruit.	The unfruitful branch refers to the disciple who has somehow lost the life which Jesus gives.
2) In August the gardener prunes the branches, so that all the nourishment of the vine will flow to the fruit-bearing branches.	The fruitful branch refers to the disciple who lives by the life of Jesus (obedience, love). To bear more fruit is to grow in union with Jesus and to spread this life to others.

The original disciples were pruned or made clean by the teaching of Jesus (15:3). This verse should be linked with the statement made by Jesus in 13:10. By washing his disciples' feet, he has made them clean. Both Jesus' word and his saving death remove from the disciples all obstacles to their full sharing in eternal life.

As part of the real vine, the life of the disciple is not static. Once enlivened, the disciple must choose (even daily) to be sustained by life from above. Thus Jesus teaches the disciples that they must *remain* in union with him. (Note that the phrases "remain united to" and "remain in" are used ten times in verses 4–

10.) Apart from Jesus no fruit can be produced (15:4–5; see the Reflection section for a development of these themes).

We have already commented on the "dualistic" viewpoint of the fourth evangelist. He sees things in sharp distinction, as either black or white. Thus, the alternative to remaining in Jesus and bearing fruit is to be broken off (15:2), thrown out and burned (15:6). There is no neutral ground. For the fourth evangelist, abiding in Jesus is so crucial, so central to the purpose of life that rejecting union with Jesus is the equivalent of choosing death.

The disciple must choose either life in Jesus or death apart from him. Verses 7–17 describe the blessings which accompany the choice to abide in the life of the vine. Note that the evangelist uses the same verb "remain" to describe both the disciple's abiding in Jesus and the presence of Jesus' words abiding in the disciple. This has profound implications. The words of Jesus are to make their home in the disciple. As the food we eat becomes a part of our very flesh and blood, so the words of Jesus should dwell in the disciple as a part of his/her very being. When this happens, the disciple's mind and will are in perfect communion with the Master's, and thus every request can be granted.

The Father's glory has been revealed both in the ministry of Jesus and in his death (12:28 and 13:31). In 15:8 it is the obedience and love of the disciples that glorify the Father. Note that here Jesus is speaking as if his death/resurrection has already been accomplished. Such fruitfulness brings joy to the Father's heart. It also provides the credentials of the disciples. Their fruitfulness is the evidence that they are truly the disciples of Jesus.

In 15:12–13 Jesus will again emphasize that the mutual love of the disciples must be patterned on his love for them, a love unto death. In 15:9 Jesus shares with them the mystery of this love: his love for them is the same love the Father has for him! By dwelling as branches in the vine the disciples are introduced not only to the powerful human love of Jesus. They also become participants in the mystery of the Trinitarian love. As the Father loves his beloved Son, so Jesus loves his disciples, and so the disciples love one another. No wonder the Fathers of the Church spoke of the Christian life as a process of "divinization"! No wonder the great saints of the Church spoke of the excitement of being disciples of Jesus. We become immersed in the dynamic movement of love in such a way that we ourselves become channels of divine love and life for one another.

Reason enough for rejoicing! The joy of the disciples flows from their union with Jesus (15:9–11). As Jesus leaves to the disciples the gift of his peace (14:27), so also he shares with them the heritage of his own joy (15:11). Jesus' joy springs from his loving obedience and union with the Father, and it leads him to lay down his life for those he loves (15:10–14). In the same way the joy of the disciples comes to its fulfillment only in love for one another (15:12). Again Jesus compares the love within the Christian community with his own self-gift. The love of the disciples is expressed in the laying down of their lives for one another (15:13).

Be careful not to misunderstand the "if" clauses in 15:10 and 14. These verses do not mean that dwelling with Jesus and being his friend depend on our obedience. We cannot earn these graces. Jesus' love-unto-death creates the community of his friends, that is, the community of all those (including ourselves) who dwell with him. The obedience of the disciples is simply the natural response to Jesus' initiative. (The Greek word which is translated as "friend" in verses 13–15 might be more accurately translated as "the beloved.")

A servant knows the general directions and plans of his master, but he does not know his master's personal thoughts and desires. Since Jesus loves his disciples, he does not relate to them in this impersonal way. On the contrary, he reveals to them the secrets of his heart. All of his "conversations" with the Father are shared with his disciples (15:15).

In first-century Palestine one who wished to become a disciple generally chose the rabbi with whom he would study. Such is not the case with the disciples of Jesus. He takes the initiative in choosing them as disciples and he appoints them to their ministry. In the Greek the words "give" (15:13) and "appointed" (15:16) are different forms of the same verb. This indicates that the disciples are sent out to continue Jesus' mission of laying down his life for the community. As seen in 14:13–14 and 15:7–8, whatever the disciple prayerfully requests from the Father is unfailingly given when those requests are primarily concerned about doing the greater works (14:12) and bearing lasting fruit (15:8 and 16).

REFLECTION. In reflecting on the Christian life we can easily envision a false distinction between being and doing. We often distort the meaning of discipleship by speaking of people who are Christians but who do not live out their faith, who do not obey the commandment of Jesus. When the Fourth Gospel speaks of bearing fruit in 15:2–5, we tend to think of bearing fruit in terms of doing good works (as if the doing could be separated from being in union with Christ, the true vine). But such a separation would not have occurred to the fourth evangelist. For him there was no middle ground between full Christian life (being a fruit-bearing part of the vine) and spiritual death (being a broken-off branch).

Our contemporary distinction between being a Christian (that is being in Christ, belonging to the vine) and bearing fruit (living in obedience and love) distorts the teaching of Jesus. It enables us to "water down" the quality of Christian life. It allows us to play the games in which we give "lip service" to Christ (Mass on Sunday, a contribution to the collection basket, perhaps service on a parish committee) while living very worldly, pagan lives.

If we hear what the Spirit speaks through John, then we realize that Christian living cannot be divided into being and doing. Relation, not separation, is the crux of Christian life. To bear fruit simply means to be part of the vine; to be part of the vine is to abide in Jesus; to abide in Jesus is to obey his word; and to obey his word is to lay down one's life in love for other disciples. Such is the grandeur—and the terrible responsibility—of the Christian life!

Perhaps the reason why we find it so hard to live this life is that we do not allow ourselves to be loved by Jesus. Verses 9–12 link both fidelity to his commands and love for the Christian

community with Jesus' love. Without the energizing and trans-
forming power of the love of Christ we are incapable of obedience and love.

The spiritual tradition of the Church has some valuable sug-
gestions about how to receive the love of Jesus. (1) Don't allow
your sinfulness to become a barrier to his love. We tend to give
up when we feel unlovable. Jesus loves the sinner more than ever!
Jesus' "thing," we might say, is to love us precisely at this time.
(2) It is important to spend some time each day at the Master's
feet. His love for us is always alive and present, but we need to
become more aware of it. We can be so busy raising children and
earning a living that we make ourselves, in effect, unavailable to
Jesus. In addition to our prayers of praise and petition, we should
spend some time each day simply being present to Jesus and
available to his love. In this way we will discover how to integrate our daily responsibilities (family and job) with an awareness of his abiding love.

THE WORLD'S OPPOSITION
TO JESUS AND HIS DISCIPLES

OVERVIEW. Jesus has come into the world as both its light and
the source of its life (see 1:3–5). But many choose to live as if they
were lords and masters unto themselves. They "love the darkness
rather than the light" (3:19). As the world has rejected the person
and message of Jesus, it will also reject his disciples.

Jesus has spoken of the deep and intimate relationship shared
between himself and his disciples (15:1–17). Now Jesus prepares
his friends for what they will face from those who stand in opposition to him (15:18–27). Keep in mind that the author of the
Fourth Gospel is not only recording the words of Jesus, he is also
applying those words to the situation of the community in the
last decade of the first century. The followers of Jesus have already experienced persecution in Rome while Nero was the Roman emperor. In the 90's Christians are being ejected from the
synagogue and are suffering a more widespread persecution set in
motion by the Emperor Domitian.

READ 15:18–27

COMMENTARY. The identity of Jesus and his disciples (symbolized by the unity of the vine and its branches) is the basis for the world's hostility toward the disciples. John is using "world" not in its positive sense (as the context of both human life and as the people God loves), but in its negative sense, as the sum total of sinful opposition toward God:

> *If you belonged to the world, then the world would love you as its own. But I chose you from this world, and you do not belong to it; that is why the world hates you* (15:19).

Jesus then reminds his disciples of what he said when he had finished washing their feet: "Remember what I told you: No slave is greater than his master" (15:20). These words, which appear in Matthew's account of Jesus' missionary discourse (see Matthew 10:24), are found in two different contexts in John's account of the Last Supper Discourse. In the first instance the Master asked his disciples to serve one another humbly as he had served them (13:16). In the second instance the Master prepares his disciples for the persecution they will receive because they follow him (15:20).

John's arrangement of the saying of Jesus, "No slave is greater than his master," and the missionary context given to this saying in Matthew (see Matthew 10:16–25) tell us something significant about the early Church's understanding of discipleship. Following Jesus was a public, not a private matter. For this reason John is severely critical of the secret Christians, those who believed in Jesus, "but because of the Pharisees they did not talk about it openly, so as not to be expelled from the synagogue" (12:42). John tells us that it is not enough merely to believe in Jesus. The disciple's faith has to manifest itself in the way the disciple lives.

The conditional sentences in verses 22 and 24 stress the gravity of the world's sin and the consequent vehemence of the world's hostility. According to John, the rejection of Jesus is sin in its most radical form. The Father's sending of the Son was the turning point in human history, for the Son came to reveal the Father. Thus, in hating the Son, the world also hates the Father (15:23). In verse 24 Jesus refers to those of his own people who have deliberately refused to accept the witness of the "deeds my Father gave me to do," the deeds that "speak on my behalf and show that the Father has sent me" (5:36).

While John's application of the words of Jesus may seem excessively harsh on those who did not believe in Jesus, we must bear in mind that John thinks in the most comprehensive terms. All is black or white, truth or falsehood, acceptance or rejection. In John's perception, there are only two modes of existence. Either we belong to Jesus or we belong to the realm dominated by Satan, the Prince of this world. Although this is actually an oversimplification of reality, it enables John to state quickly and clearly the ultimate value at stake: eternal life with God. That life is worth the risk of everything we hold dear, whether it be one's family, one's community, one's traditions, or even one's life itself.

In contrast to the world that judges Jesus falsely, that is, hates Jesus "for no reason at all" (15:25), the disciple will speak the truth about Jesus. It is the Spirit, the Helper, who comes from the

Father, that will enable the disciples to speak the truth about Jesus (15:26). Jesus, whom John the Baptist had singled out as "the one who baptizes with the Holy Spirit" (1:33), promises to send the Spirit to his disciples (15:26). These words are intended to encourage his disciples to face the suffering they will receive when others recognize that they belong to Jesus (15:21).

REFLECTION. Most of us, at one time or another, have expressed criticism of the institutional aspects of the Catholic Church. The usual form this criticism takes is the contrasting of the poverty of Jesus with expensive cathedrals, Vatican art treasures, lavish vestments, costly living quarters of those who have taken the vow of poverty, and the like. Those of us who were not involved in the decision to build a cathedral, etc., are rather free with such critical contrasting, for it makes us feel that we are the "real" Christians.

But the words of Jesus shatter such false confidence in our own individual life-styles. Instead of looking at external things, we must ask ourselves if the quality of our belonging to Jesus is of such caliber that the world knows who we are. We may have to admit that our discipleship is kept at such a low profile that few people, if any, recognize that we are his followers.

In 1974, the American Catholic Bishops gave us "A Review of the Principal Trends in the Life of the Catholic Church in the United States." Our bishops pointed out that the decision to belong to Jesus or to belong to the world faces all of us:

> *The emerging question for the Catholic Community in the United States may well be whether it will in the future, as in the past, derive its fundamental beliefs and attitudes from the traditional value system of Catholic Christianity, or whether its beliefs and attitudes will be drawn more and more from the secularistic, humanistic value system of the society around it.*

We live in a society where the status symbols we possess, the political clout we have, and the amount of money we can gamble away or lavishly spend are the pagan criteria used to judge success or failure. Very often we Christians have accepted these same "worldly" standards.

Thus, we must ask ourselves, "What distinguishes us as the followers of Jesus?" According to John, it is tough being a Christian. Karl Barth, the great Protestant theologian, referred to the Christian life-style as "swimming against the stream." From the prosaic philosophy of "Looking out for #1" to Stephen Decatur's so-called patriotism (" . . . my country right or wrong"), the values of contemporary society fall far short of the attitudes and values that distinguish the disciple of Christ. If we decide to be serious about following Jesus, then there will be something "different" about us in the way we relate to those with whom we live, with whom we go to school, with whom we work and with whom we seek entertainment. We should expect to receive some criticism, some mockery and some rejection because of our attitudes and behavior. We have Jesus' word on it:

If they persecuted me, they will persecute you too, . . . because you are mine'' (15:20–21).

STUDY GROUP QUESTIONS

1. Jesus' image of the grapevine and its branches was very familiar to his readers. With your group create a similar image which would be familiar to city dwellers.

2. Discuss an experience which proves the truth of Jesus' teaching that the believer cannot bear fruit apart from him.

3. How does joy (15:11) differ from happiness? from contentment?

4. We have usually understood 15:16 as applied to the religious life. How do you understand it as applied to the life of the layperson?

5. Jesus has declared, "If they persecuted me, they will persecute you too" (15:20). What are some of the ways society (the

world in the negative sense) persecutes you for striving to be a faithful disciple of Jesus? In what ways does society measure you by its standards, pressuring you to give in to its values? How can we help one another to endure society's rejection, etc., as we try to remain faithful to Jesus' teaching?

Chapter Sixteen

JESUS' TEACHING ON THE WORLD'S OPPOSITION CONCLUDED

OVERVIEW. Chapter Sixteen is basically a repetition of the themes found in 13:31–14:31. The disciples are being prepared for the events of Jesus' passion and death. By bringing in the themes of Chapter 14, with slight variation, the author gives evidence of his concern for the believing community. On one level of meaning, Jesus is preparing his disciples for his death and for the persecution they will receive as his disciples. On a second level of meaning, the Paraclete, whom Jesus promises to his disciples, is seen as already active in the Church, helping the disciples of the 80's and 90's to bear up under the persecution they are receiving and protecting them from disillusionment.

Keep in mind the two-fold content of Jesus' discourse. On the one hand Jesus speaks as he looks ahead to his death. On the other hand Jesus looks back, speaking from the perspective of his victorious return to his Father.

READ 16:1–4a

COMMENTARY. The first three verses of this chapter parallel the words Jesus spoke in Matthew's account of the missionary discourse:

Listen! I am sending you out just like sheep to a pack of wolves. . . . Watch out for there will be men who will arrest you and take you to court, and they will whip you in the synagogues. For my sake you will be brought to trial before rulers and kings, to tell the Good News to them and to the Gentiles (Matthew 10:16–18).

I have told you this, so that you will not give up your faith. You will be expelled from the synagogues, and the time will come when anyone who kills you will think that by doing this he is serving God. People will do these things because they have not known either the Father or me (16:1–3).

Notice that Matthew records a universal thrust to Jesus' words: the disciples will be witnesses in both synagogues and before "rulers and kings." But John has narrowed the extent of the persecutions. In the heat of the hostile antagonism between the Johannine community and the synagogue, the synagogue has become the symbol of the persecuting world. Even those who are good people (they want to serve God) are putting the disciples to death (16:2). According to Luke's account in Acts, Paul himself was among those who thought they were serving God by persecuting the Christian Jews:

I myself thought that I should do everything I could against the cause of Jesus of Nazareth. That is what I did in Jerusalem. I received authority from the chief priests and put many of God's people in prison; and when they were sentenced to death, I also voted against them. Many times I had them punished in the synagogues and tried to make them deny their faith. I was so furious with them that I even went to foreign cities to persecute them (Acts 26:9–11).

THE WORK OF THE HOLY SPIRIT
(READ 16:4b–15)

COMMENTARY. Not only have the disciples learned that Jesus is leaving them (13:33), now they are also told of the terrible persecutions that will come (16:4). Completely overwhelmed with sadness (16:6), they do not think of asking why or where Jesus was going (16:5). In the rest of the chapter Jesus will dispel their sadness in two ways. First, Jesus explains why he must go: so that he can send the Spirit to them (16:7–15). Then Jesus will explain where he is going: to his Father, so that he can again come back to them in his risen glory (16:16–33).

The Fourth Gospel speaks interchangeably of the Father and of Jesus sending the Holy Spirit (see 14:16, 26 and 16:7). Once the Spirit is given, he will have two roles, prosecuting the hostile world (16:8–11), and continuing the revealing work of Jesus (16:13–15). In verses 8–11 we may be facing the most difficult passage in the Fourth Gospel. To grasp John's thought, keep in mind that even though this is taking place in the Last Supper setting, Jesus speaks from the perspective of his Passion, death and Resurrection as having already happened. Thus, we can best perceive the prosecuting role of the Spirit by placing ourselves in the position of the disciples as they remember the trial, death and Resurrection of Jesus. The trial is conducted in the "courtroom" of each disciple's memory. Recalling the events of Jesus' Passion and death, the Spirit enables each disciple to understand the truth in those events. The Spirit "convicts" the people of the world by proving to the disciples how wrong the world is in three crucial areas, "sin," "what is right," and "God's judgment" (16:8).

First, the Spirit proves to the disciple that the world is in the wrong because it refuses to believe in Jesus. In John's dualistic outlook (all is either good or evil), whatever is not of salvation is sin. John has stated that the reason why people do not believe in Jesus is that they "love the darkness rather than the light" (3:19). Not only are Pilate and the chief priests convicted, but also any and all others who refuse to believe and persecute the disciples as a result of that unbelief.

Secondly, the Spirit will "convict" the world "about what is right" (16:10). The world had judged Jesus guilty and had put him to death. They wanted to stone him because "You are only a man but you are trying to make yourself God" (10:33). They cited a law "that says he ought to die because he claimed to be the Son of God" (19:6). But the world's standard of judgment is wrong. He really is divine. Therefore Jesus was innocent even though the world convicted him of crime: "they are wrong about what is right" (16:10). His going to the Father (his Resurrection) is the evidence on which the world is convicted (16:10). Jesus' reference to the fact that he will no longer be seen is another reference to his Resurrection.

From the perspective of the audience for whom the Fourth Gospel is written, the Spirit enables them to know that Jesus is risen even though they cannot physically see Jesus. Through the Spirit they (we) understand what the world will never know: Jesus is vindicated.

Thirdly, the Spirit proves that the people of the world "are wrong about judgment, because the ruler of this world has already been judged" (16:11). The Spirit clearly proves to the believer that, in sentencing Jesus to death, the people of the world sentenced themselves. Since they have allied themselves with Satan, the "ruler of this world," they are judged guilty along with him. It is as Jesus declared when he spoke of his coming death:

> Now is the time for this world to be judged; now the ruler of this world will be overthrown (12:31).

Verse 12 functions as a transition to explain the second role of the Spirit, that of teaching the disciples to understand the meaning of the words and signs of Jesus during his earthly ministry: the Spirit "will lead you into all the truth" (16:13). This is precisely what is happening as the Fourth Gospel is being written; the Spirit has been guiding the community for decades, teaching the meaning of Jesus' signs to those who believe. Thus, in every generation, those past, that of our own, as well as the generations of our children and grandchildren still to come, the Spirit glorifies

Jesus by helping us to understand the meaning of his deeds and words in our present situation (16:14).

SADNESS TURNS TO JOY
READ 16:16–33

COMMENTARY. In verses 7 through 15 Jesus responded to the sadness of his disciples by speaking about the Spirit whom he will send after his departure. Now, Jesus dispels their sadness by speaking of their seeing him again after a "little while" (16:16). On one level of meaning verse 16 refers to their seeing him after his Resurrection. However, the puzzlement of the disciples, "What does this mean?" (16:17–18), indicates that there is much more contained in this statement than a single reference to the Resurrection. On the second level of meaning we find a reference to the Second Coming of Jesus.

Thus, after Jesus is risen, he will send the Spirit so that the disciples will understand in faith the meaning of his trial, death and Resurrection (16:7–15). In verse 16, the period of Jesus' absence and the time of his appearance have two meanings. First, Jesus dies and is buried; then the disciples see him in his risen self. Secondly, after his Resurrection appearances, Jesus returns to his Father. No one sees him for a time. Then he will appear again in glory. At this Second Coming the visible demonstration of Jesus' victory will be seen by both the disciples and the whole of humankind. However, in between the time of his death and the time of his Second Coming, there will be persecution: "you will cry and weep, but the world will be glad" (16:20). However, in the final hour, the sadness of the believers "will turn into gladness" because "I will see you again" (16:20, 23).

In sum, to see Jesus "a little while later" is to see him in two different sets of circumstances. First, the disciples will momentarily "see" Jesus in the post-resurrection appearances and after that they will see the risen Jesus with the eyes of faith. We also "see" the risen Jesus in this way. Secondly, the disciples as well as the whole world will see Jesus in his Second Coming.

With the second sentence in verse 23, "I am telling you the

truth . . . ," Jesus is once more referring to the events that will take place in the immediate future: his death and Resurrection. Thus, when Jesus states that they have not asked for anything *in his name* (16:24, 26), John is probably indicating that they have yet to understand his complete identity. Only after he has been lifted up will they "know that 'I Am Who I Am' " (8:28). Only after the resurrection will Thomas be able to utter the complete profession of faith: "My Lord and my God!" (20:28).

The time when Jesus will "speak plainly about the Father" is the time after his Resurrection (16:25). Then Jesus will speak to them in the Holy Spirit. Since Jesus is the one who reveals the Father, the Spirit will particularly enable them to understand Jesus' teaching about the Father (16:25). Thus, Jesus declares that once the Spirit has come, the disciples will find themselves in direct and immediate communion with the Father (16:27). They will know that the Father loves each of them as he loves his own Son:

> *Righteous Father! . . . I made you known to them, and I will*
> *continue to do so, in order that the love you have for me may be in*
> *them . . .* (17:25–26).

Jesus concludes with a restatement of what he has said earlier: he came from the Father and is now returning to the Father (14:28; 16:28).

In response, the disciples appear overconfident, almost boastful, about understanding the words of Jesus (16:29–30). While they recognize Jesus as the one who "came from God" (16:30), their faith is still incomplete. That is why Jesus first questions the depth of their faith (16:31) and then foretells that soon his Passion will begin and they will scatter to their own homes (16:32). Nevertheless, Jesus is not alone, for he is always in union with his Father.

The chapter ends with Jesus claiming the victory that will give his disciples of every age the courage they need to face persecution. United in his victory, they too will overcome the world. Notice the similarity in the endings of both chapter 14 and 16:

I cannot talk with you much longer, because the ruler of this world is coming. He has no power over me, but the world must know that I love the Father (14:30–31).

But I am not really alone because the Father is with me. I have told you this so that you will have peace by being united to me. The world will make you suffer. But be brave! I have defeated the world! (16:32–33).

REFLECTION. Jesus declared, "But be brave! I have defeated the world!" (16:33) Yet, when we look around at our planet, we see wars, soaring crime rates, people hungry and starving, repression, racism, abortion, obliteration of basic human rights and meaninglessness. We are tempted to think that the death of Jesus on the cross has not defeated Satan (12:31–32). Looking back over the Fourth Gospel, we have seen that John has spoken in terms of the paradox of the already-and-not-yet. He constantly switches back and forth between the present and the future. On the one hand, eternal life begins now; on the other hand it will begin on the last day. On the one hand we are judged now; on the other hand we will be judged at the end of time. On the one hand Jesus is the Lamb who takes away the sin of the world; on the other hand people continue to sin by persecuting his disciples. On the one hand Satan is overthrown; on the other hand Satan still seems to rule.

John tells us that Jesus has won the victory, but there is still work to be done by the community of believers. We are the ones who manifest his victory to the world. As disciples, we carry on the work of Jesus. It is as Jesus said, "whoever believes in me will do what I do—yes, he will do even greater things, because I am going to the Father" (14:12). Jesus is saying that the impact he has had on the world is limited. He preached for several years, gained some followers, met resistance, and was betrayed by some of the religious leaders of his own people and was crucified. But his disciples will do greater things in his name. Through them the teaching and the example of Jesus have spread through the world. Where there is healing, ministering, reconciling, witnessing and suffering for one's faith in Jesus, the "greater things" are being done. When he raised Lazarus, Jesus commanded his friends, "Untie him and let him go free." That is what the Christian community continues to do until the day of the Second Coming of Jesus.

STUDY GROUP QUESTIONS

1. Verses 7 through 15 speak of the Holy Spirit in two ways. First, the Spirit is viewed as a prosecuting attorney (16:8–11), winning the case against the world (which has persecuted Jesus and his followers). Secondly, the Spirit continues the revealing work of Jesus (16:13–15). Share with one another the events of your life in which you have experienced the presence of the Spirit in one role or the other.

2. There seems to be a two-fold reference to the return of Jesus in 16:19–23. Share with your group how these words of Jesus are thus addressed both to the original disciples in the first century and to us in the twentieth.

3. How can we reconcile Jesus' promise in 16:23 with the fact that sometimes what we pray for is not given?

4. Discuss the significance of Jesus' statement, "But be brave! I have defeated the world!" (16:33).

Chapter Seventeen

THE PRAYER OF JESUS FOR HIS DISCIPLES

OVERVIEW. With the prayer of Jesus we reach the most solemn moment of the Last Supper Discourse. Until this moment we have heard only brief prayers of Jesus (11:41–42 and 12:27–28). Now we are privileged to enter deeply into the relationship of Jesus as Intercessor (Priest) with the Father. Thus, this chapter is often called the high priestly prayer of Jesus.

The prayer of Jesus is saturated with the desire to glorify his Father and to intercede on behalf of his disciples, both those present at the Supper as well as all those who will become his disciples in the future. Jesus prayerfully refers to his followers forty-nine times, as he asks his Father to give them his love and protection. As do all the discourses, this priestly prayer of Jesus reveals his true identity to his disciples: he is the one sent by the Father to reveal to all how much the Father loves them.

READ 17:1–26

COMMENTARY. At the completion of his long conversation with his disciples (13:31–16:33) Jesus begins to speak with his Father (17:1). The prayer powerfully witnesses to Jesus' unity with the Father. (As we saw in 11:41–42, Jesus lives in the certainty of his intimacy with the Father.) Note how often during the prayer he uses the title, Father.

Having declared that he has already defeated the world (16:33), Jesus prays, "Father, the hour has come" (17:1). The fourth evangelist envisions the hour as a process which extends from the arrival of the Greeks (12:23) until his return to the Father's side. The glorification of Jesus, anticipated during the ministry by his powerful signs, has already begun (13:31–32).

Jesus' prayer reflects his constant filial attitude: he seeks his Father's glory, not his own interest. Jesus prays that all might recognize the glory of the Father.

Such recognition of the Father takes place through the gift of eternal life (17:2). Remember that glory in the Fourth Gospel involves the experience of God's loving presence. The Son has authority over all people so that he can grant eternal life to those who have been given to him (see 6:44). In receiving eternal life believers become aware of the Father's presence.

This is exactly what eternal life means: knowing the Father, and knowing the Son whom he has sent (17:3). (Remember that "knowing" in Hebrew thought expresses an intimate, loving union.) To know God involves both acceptance of the Covenant relationship he offers and obedience to his will. Note again the evidence that for John eternal life is not delayed until the end of time, or even until the personal death of the disciple. It begins in our present life through faith in Jesus Christ.

In verses 4 and 5 Jesus speaks as if his death and Resurrection have already been completed. Jesus' "work" was to give eternal life. This life-giving work is accomplished by his redemptive death (17:4). Now he asks to regain the glory that was his before the Incarnation. Note how clearly Jesus' request is linked with the prologue:

Before the world was created, the Word already existed; he was with God, and he was the same as God. From the very beginning the Word was with God (1:1–2).	Father! Give me glory in your presence now, the same glory I had with you before the world was made (17:5).

In verse 6 the evangelist summarizes two important themes: (1) the disciples are given to Jesus by the Father; (2) Jesus reveals the Father to those whom the Father has given him. The first theme began in the discourse on the bread of life. There Jesus taught that believers must be drawn to him by the Father (6:44). Now he explains why this is so. Every human person belongs to the Father. But because of sin, every person also "belongs" to the world ("world" as hostile to God, not "world" as the locus of human life). The giving of the disciples to Jesus is a specific act of the Father; it is the Father's deliberate choice, a special grace. The mystery of the Father's choosing transcends our ability to comprehend. Why does he give you and me to Jesus, rather than others? Such reflections should fill us with gratitude and with humility.

Verse 6 also affirms that Jesus reveals the Father to those whom the Father has given him. Jesus' prayer in 17:1–8 teaches us that we can speak of his mission in two ways. First, Jesus comes to give the gift of eternal life; second, Jesus comes to reveal the Father. That these are two sides of the same coin is clearly stated in verse 3: coming to know the Father *is* eternal life. Jesus reveals the Father not only by telling the disciples about him but also by making him "visible" and "knowable" (see 14:7–10). Thus the disciples know/believe that Jesus has been sent from the Father. Jesus will emphasize this theme in the final part of his prayer. (Verses 6 through 8 are spoken from the perspective of the risen Jesus. The disciples have already been strengthened by the completion of the Passion and Resurrection.)

With verse 9 Jesus begins to pray for the disciples. But he is not indifferent to the salvation of the world (those under the power of the Evil One); in verses 21 and 23 Jesus prays that someday the world will also believe that he has been sent by the Father. However, after Jesus' departure, the salvation of the world depends on the mission of his disciples. As Jesus revealed the glory of the Father, so now the glory of Jesus is manifested in the ministry of the disciples (17:10).

Verses 13 and 14 repeat themes which have already been developed in the Last Supper Discourse: although the disciples are

granted the joy of Jesus (15:11 and 16:24), they will also receive the hatred of the world (15:18–25). They cannot leave the world, since Jesus is sending them to continue his own mission of offering eternal life to the world. Therefore, Jesus asks his Father to protect his disciples from the malice of the Evil One (17:15).

Jesus reaches the climax of his prayer for the disciples in verses 17–19. The Father has consecrated Jesus and sent him into the world (10:36). Now Jesus prays that the disciples be consecrated (made holy, sanctified, set apart) so that they can complete his work on earth. (We will see that this "work" was given not only to the original disciples but also to the disciples of every generation.) The word of Jesus both cleanses the disciples (15:3) and sets them free (8:32). Now Jesus prays that his Father will sanctify them in his own word (17:17). God's word always achieves what it expresses; from that moment on the disciples are those dedicated, those set apart for their mission in the world (17:18).

Looking ahead to his death, the sacrifice of himself for the sake of his disciples, Jesus consecrates himself to the Father (17:19). Jesus' prayer in chapter 17 has many parallels with the early eucharistic prayers of the Church. Some commentators see in 17:19 a clear parallel with the Eucharistic Preface: Jesus offers himself to the Father as both priest and sacrificial offering.

With verse 20 Jesus begins the final part of his prayer. Until now he has been praying specifically for the original disciples (although the believers of subsequent generations have been included indirectly). Now he turns his attention specifically toward those who will come to belief through the preaching of the original disciples and their successors.

The theme of unity has already been raised in 10:16 (one sheep herd around the one shepherd) and 11:52 (gathering into one body all the scattered children of God). Now unity becomes the dominant focus of Jesus' prayer for the Church (17:21,23). Although unity was not even mentioned in his prayer for the original disciples (17:9–19), Jesus urgently prays that this gift will be given to later generations of believers (17:20–23). This indicates how crucial the problem of unity has become in the evangelist's own day. From the opening chapter of Paul's First Epistle to the Corinthian community we can see that divisions arose very quickly within the young Christian churches. Whether based on loyalty to a particular person/group or on differing understandings of the teaching of Jesus, these divisions became one of the most difficult problems that pastoral leaders had to face. The fourth evangelist's response to this problem is to appeal to Jesus' passionate desire for unity among his followers.

As we have seen so frequently in the Last Supper Discourse, the model for the unity of the disciples is the unity of the Father and his Beloved Son (17:21). Believers are to be one just as the Father dwells in Jesus and Jesus in the Father. In 17:21 John makes three affirmations: (1) Christian unity is a gift of God and not the result of human efforts; (2) Christian unity is a two-fold relationship: it is both horizontal (the fellowship of believers) and vertical (the believer's dwelling in the Father and Son); (3) Christian unity must be visible to the world, or else it cannot serve to bring the world to believe in Jesus.

Verses 24–26 conclude the Last Supper prayer. Because his will is in perfect harmony with the Father, Jesus expresses his final request as a desire: "I want them to be with me where I am, so that they may see my glory" (17:29). Although the disciples have seen the glory of the ministry (1:14, 2:11) and of the Resurrection (17:10 and 22), they will see Jesus' eternal glory (17:5) only when they reach heaven (17:24). Until that time they will remain distinct from the world, since they know who Jesus really is (17:25). In the very last sentence of his prayer Jesus solemnly sums up what he has done out of love for his Father and his disciples: he has revealed his Father so that both the love of the Father and the presence of the Son can forever abide in the disciples (17:26). In the Covenant with Israel God dwelt in the Tabernacle; during the ministry he dwelt in the body of Jesus; now the Father dwells in the disciples of Jesus.

REFLECTION. Throughout the Supper Discourse Jesus has been teaching the disciples—and us!—about the parallels between his relationship to the Father and the disciples' relationship to him. A diagram may help us:

Jesus and the Father	Jesus and the Disciples
As I live because of the Father	So who eats my flesh will live because of me (6:57).
As the Father knows me and I know the Father	So I know my sheep and they know me (10:14–15).
As the Father loves me	So I love you (15:9).
As you gave me glory	So I have given them glory, that they may be one as we are one: and I in them (17:22–23).
You in me	
As the Father has sent me	So I send you (17:18).

In one of her talks Mother Teresa of India applied these parallel relationships to prayer. As Jesus felt both the need and the desire to spend hours in silent communication with the Father, so we should experience both the need and the desire to spend time in the company of Jesus.

In prayer we become aware of what Jesus means to us: that he is our life; that he knows us completely; that he loves us totally; that he has shared with us his own glory! Then we hear his word of mission: "Go forth. I send you into the world as the Father sent me." As our "interior" life in Jesus is modeled on the union of the Son with the Father, so also is our "exterior" life (our apostolic ministry) based on that same union. We are sent out with the authority and power of Christ himself. We are sent out to continue his own work of bringing the message of eternal life to all people. We are sent out to do "even greater things" (14:12). In this life we will not fully comprehend the mystery of our insertion into the divine life. Yet reflection, prayer and, above all, living out this mystery can enable the heart to "understand" what surpasses our intelligence.

STUDY GROUP QUESTIONS

1. Discuss with your group what it means "to know Jesus Christ" (17:3). How does this involve eternal life?

2. How could Jesus say "I have finished the work you gave me to do" (17:4) before his death?

3. Why does Jesus refuse to pray for the world? (17:9). How is his glory shown through the disciples? (17:10).

4. What are some of the practical implications of Jesus' statement, "I do not ask you to take them out of the world"? (17:15).

5. What does it mean to be "truly dedicated" to the Father? (17:19).

6. How can we cooperate today with Jesus' prayer for the unity of believers (17:20–23): on a neighborhood level? on a parish level? on a diocesan level?

Chapter Eighteen

THE ARREST OF JESUS AND PETER'S DENIALS

OVERVIEW. Having completed his account of the Discourse at the Last Supper, John begins his account of the Passion and death of Jesus (chapters 18 and 19). On the one hand there is much in common between the Fourth Gospel and the Synoptic versions of the last events in the life of Jesus. The reason why there is great agreement between these accounts is obvious: the death of Jesus was the most public act of his life. The religious leaders, the ordinary people, the Roman governor, the soldiers, and some of Jesus' disciples either took part in or witnessed the crucifixion. The oral traditions recounting Jesus' Passion and death were probably the first to be fashioned into an ordered narrative.

On the other hand, the Fourth Gospel presents the events surrounding the death of Jesus in a broader, more cosmic perspective. John reworks certain episodes in order to give them a greater symbolic significance. For example, John plays down the trial of Jesus before the Jewish authorities (18:19–24) so that he can dramatically highlight the exchange between Jesus and Pilate (18:23–38). In this encounter, Pilate is presented as a man who is both an individual and a symbol of the Roman Empire.

READ 18:1–27

COMMENTARY. In examining verses 2 and 3 we notice that John has greatly reduced the role of Judas. He simply leads a group of men to the place where Jesus can be found. Note that among this group of men are Roman soldiers, a detail found only in the Fourth Gospel. The crowd symbolizes the conspiracy against Jesus. Religious authorities have sent armed men, temple guards and Roman soldiers, to arrest Jesus during the night. They are led by Judas, the man whom Satan had incited to betray Jesus. Thus, at the instigation of Satan, the various forces of the world form an alliance against Jesus.

Unafraid, Jesus takes the initiative. Stepping forward he asks, "Whom are you looking for?" (18:4). As Jesus identified himself, the whole crowd "moved back and fell to the ground" (18:6). In the Greek text the words which are translated "I am he" are the same words used in 8:24, 28 and 58 to indicate that Jesus bears the name which belongs to Yahweh. This explains the strange reaction of the crowd. They fall on their faces before Jesus' divine majesty. In interpreting the Passion narrative it is important to remember that John sees the Passion as the climactic moment in the manifestation of Jesus' glory. Thus, in spite of the combined power and might of the world, John asserts that Jesus is taken captive only because he wills it. Nobody drags Jesus to trial and cross. He goes freely. Perfectly in command, Jesus instructs his captors to allow his disciples to leave (18:8–9). For the fourth evangelist this physical protection which Jesus provides (at the very moment of his own capture) symbolizes the way in which

Jesus protects his disciples from the power of evil (18:9; see 6:39 and 17:12).

When Peter uses his sword to defend himself and his Master, Jesus rebukes him (18:11). Human power, whether political (power of the state, i.e., kingship, 6:14–15, and 18:36) or physical (armaments, symbolized by Peter's sword) cannot accomplish what Jesus has come to do. The food of Jesus has been the doing of his Father's will (see 4:34); Jesus will "drink the cup of suffering which my Father has given" (18:11).

Jesus is first brought to Annas, the man who had been High Priest from 6 to 15 A.D. John then reminds us of the prophecy of Caiaphas (the current High Priest): Jesus was the one man who "should die for all the people" (see 11:50–52, 18:14). By interweaving the interrogations of Jesus by the Jewish officials with the questioning of Peter by their servants, John contrasts Jesus with Peter. Verse 15 mentions that Peter and "another disciple" followed Jesus to the house of Annas. The unnamed disciple (possibly John) is described as one "well known to the High Priest." Thus, he gains access to the courtyard of the high priest and then instructs the girl to open the gate for Peter. From this point on, the Fourth Gospel contrasts Jesus with Peter in terms of their responses to those who question them. When Jesus is questioned (even physically abused by the Jewish officials) he retains his dignity (18:19–24). When Peter is questioned by the servants of the Jewish officials, he fails miserably. Although he is the representative disciple, he is intimidated first by the girl keeping the gate (18:17), then by the servants warming themselves by the fire (18:25), and finally by one of the High Priest's slaves (18:26). Although Peter is the rock (1:42) and the spokesperson for the disciples (6:67–68), he denies three times that he has any relationship with Jesus.

While John has recorded a semi-official interrogation of Jesus in verses 19–24, the Fourth Gospel does not mention the trial before the Sanhedrin as we find in Mark 14:53–65. John tells us nothing of what took place after Jesus was brought to Caiaphas (18:24). No witnesses are brought out and no charges are directed against Jesus. John seems to have deliberately downplayed the trial and the role of the Jewish officials in order to develop the exchange between Jesus and the Roman Governor.

JESUS AND PILATE

OVERVIEW. Between the time when Jesus is brought to the governor's palace (18:28) and the moment when Pilate delivers Jesus up to be crucified (19:16), John dramatically narrates seven scenes. The setting for Jesus' dramatic "trial" before Pilate alternates between scenes which take place outside the governor's palace (centering on the dialogue between Pilate and the crowd, 18:28–32; 18:38b–40; 19:4–8; and 19:12–16) and scenes within the palace which focus on the dialogue between Jesus and Pilate (18:33–38a; 19:1–3; and 19:9–11).

READ 18:28–40

COMMENTARY. Scene one opens in the courtyard of the governor's palace. It is now early Friday morning, half-way through Passover Eve according to the Jewish calendar (18:28). John is the only evangelist who notes that the Jewish officials stayed outside in order to avoid ritual uncleanness (which would have been caused by entering a Gentile house). According to the other Synoptic writers, Pilate speaks with both the people and Jesus outside the palace.

Although history records that Pilate was a corrupt tyrant whose brutal cruelty eventually caused Rome to remove him from his position in Israel, none of the four evangelists explicitly records this facet of his character. In John's account, Pilate first appears (18:29) as an efficient governor, asking the Jewish officials for the charge being brought against Jesus. (But, as John develops his characterization of Pilate, we will see that Pilate himself is challenged to decide for or against Jesus. In the end, Pilate is himself judged as an accomplice in the betrayal and death of Jesus.) In reply to Pilate's question about the charges against Jesus, the Jewish authorities evasively reply, "We would not have brought him to you if he had not committed a crime" (18:30). Pilate tells them to "try him according to your own law" (18:30).

Pilate's response seems to indicate that he recognized the religious nature of the accusations being made against Jesus. Mark's account contains a similar awareness: Pilate "knew very well that the chief priests had handed Jesus over to him because they were jealous" (Mark 15:10). Since the Passion narratives are a blend of historical events and theological explanations of the profound meaning of Jesus' death, it is difficult to give a precise account of exactly what took place on that first Good Friday; the same may be said about the motivations of Pilate, the Jewish authorities, and the courtyard full of people crying out for the death of Jesus.

When the leaders respond that they cannot impose capital punishment (18:31), Pilate decides to investigate the matter more thoroughly. The second scene takes place inside the palace. Pilate's opening question, "Are you the King of the Jews?" indicates that the Jewish leaders have accused Jesus of being a political revolutionary (see 18:30 and 19:12).

Pilate's question contains both a political and religious dimension. From the religious perspective of the messianic expectations of Israel, the people were hoping for a descendant of David to rule over Israel as God's anointed one. From the perspective of Roman domination, the title, "King of the Jews," was the equivalent of sedition, i.e., rebellion against Roman rule. All four accounts of the Gospel record Pilate's question, "Are you the King of the Jews?" In Matthew, Mark and Luke, the reply of Jesus is the same: "So you say" (see Matthew 27:11–14; Mark 15:2–5; Luke 23:2–5). According to the Synoptic accounts, Jesus says nothing else to Pilate. For John, however, the trial of Jesus before Pilate is the climax of all the "trial" themes in the Fourth Gospel (i.e., the various interrogations, the references to judgment, the calling of witnesses, and the language of prosecution and defense). In John's dramatic account of the confrontation between Jesus and Pilate, it is not really Jesus who is on trial; it is Pilate. Thus, in response to Pilate's question, Jesus interrogates Pilate (18:34), asking him to specify which notion of kingship he is referring to—the religious or the political.

Pilate's response in verse 35 indicates that he is not interested in the religious dimension; he wants to know the secular implications of the phrase, "the King of the Jews." Only then does Jesus respond: "My kingdom does not belong to this world" (18:36). Jesus' kingship transcends not only the Roman concept of kingship but the Jewish concept as well. Jesus states that his reign exceeds all human experience and goes beyond all previous religious expectations. It is as Jesus had taught: only through water and the Spirit could one "see the Kingdom of God" (3:3, 5).

Pointing to the absence of fighting at the moment when he was arrested, Jesus tells Pilate that he is no threat to Roman rule (18:36). However, as Jesus concludes his statement with a second reference to the fact that his kingdom "does not belong here," Pilate presses Jesus for an admission that he is a king (18:37). Jesus does not deny the title: "You say that I am a king." But Jesus prefers to be identified in terms of the mission his Father has given him:

> *I was born and came into the world for this one purpose, to speak about the truth* (18:37).

Jesus is the revealer. He has come to bring to the world the truth about God. He is the way to the Father (see 14:6–10).

When Jesus declares that whoever belongs to the truth listens to him, he and Pilate change places. In terms of John's theology, the reader sees that it is Pilate who is now on trial. He is at the point of crisis:

> *Whoever believes in the Son is not judged; but whoever does not believe has already been judged, because he has not believed in God's only Son. This is how the judgment works: the light has come into the world. . . . But whoever does what is true comes to the light in order that the light may show that what he did was in obedience to God* (3:18–21).

When Pilate responds "And what is truth?" we can see two levels of meaning. In terms of what is happening in the interrogation, Pilate seems to be unable to grasp all the distinctions Jesus is making with regard to religious expectations, secular rule, and kingship which is not of this world. But in terms of theological meaning, Pilate refuses to accept the invitation to hear the voice of Jesus and belong to the truth. As an individual, Pilate becomes a symbol of those who bring judgment upon themselves. As a representative of the Roman Empire, Pilate symbolizes the world which refuses to acknowledge its creator (1:10).

The third scene opens with Pilate's return to the courtyard. Although he declares that Jesus is innocent, Pilate will not acquit Jesus outright. As a compromise, Pilate offers to "pardon" the guiltless Jesus according to a Passover custom. The unjust scheme fails when the crowd shouts for the release of the bandit Barabbas instead of Jesus (18:40). While John says little about Barabbas, the Synoptic tradition speaks of him as having incited riot and committed murder (see Mark 15:7 and Luke 21:19). It is likely that Barabbas was a Zealot, a guerrilla soldier fighting against the Roman occupation. If so, the crowd seized the opportunity to free the man who was a hero in their eyes. The irony of the situation is dramatic. Pilate must free a man who is guilty of the very crime Jesus has falsely been accused of committing: sedition against the Empire.

On the symbolic level, the crowd's choice of Jesus over Barabbas indicates how the world prefers deceitful appearance to the truth, liberation by the sword rather than deliverance by God.

Thus, the Jewish authorities in the courtyard of the governor's palace take on the characteristics of the world. Preferring the darkness of violence to the light of truth revealed by Jesus, the Jewish leaders merge with the Roman Empire. Together they symbolize "the world" in its rejection of the Word of God:

> *The Word was in the world, . . . yet the world did not recognize him. He came to his own country, but his own people did not receive him* (1:10–11).

REFLECTION. Who brought Jesus to Pilate? What was their motivation? A review of the life of Jesus will help us answer these questions. Jesus began a ministry of public preaching in which he tried to bring to his people a new appreciation of God and what God wants of his people. Jesus interpreted the Law and the Prophets in ways that gained the support of many. Thus, Jesus was recognized by some as teacher (rabbi) and by others as a prophet.

But others regarded him as a threat to the religious and political status quo. While his radical interpretations of the Law brought opposition (as well as support) from the Pharisees, Jesus seems to have been a far greater threat to the Sadducees. They were an aristocratic group of established Jewish families from whose ranks the temple priests were chosen. Since the Sadducees exercised power chiefly by permission of the Roman rulers, it was in their own best interests to rid themselves of the teacher, reformer, and prophet known as Jesus of Nazareth:

> *If we let him go on in this way, everyone will believe in him, and the Roman authorities will take action and destroy our Temple and our nation!* (11:49).

The plot of a few men in high places, aided by Judas Iscariot, succeeded in bringing Jesus before Pilate. Note that the High Priests, Annas and Caiaphas, the chief priests and the temple guards are the principal authorities involved (18:13–14; 19:6, 15, 21). Historically, the Sadducees had the most to fear with regard to what Jesus could set in motion. In point of fact, the uprising which they feared did take place in 66 A.D. Jerusalem was put to the torch, the Temple destroyed, and the Sadducees annihilated. The motivation of the men who plotted against Jesus seems to have been that of self-preservation.

STUDY GROUP QUESTIONS

1. In what ways does the portrayal of Jesus' arrest in the garden (18:1–11) reflect John's understanding of the full identity of Jesus?

2. Compare Jesus' words to Peter in 18:11 with Jesus' words to one of the disciples in Luke 22:51 and Matthew 26:52–54.

3. How does John turn around the trial of Jesus before Pilate (18:28–40) so that the trial reflects the theme of judgment? (see 3:18–21).

4. Christians have sometimes used Jesus' statement in 18:26 as a justification for avoiding involvement in the political process. Do you think Jesus intended this?

5. In what ways do we cry out today for the release of Barabbas?

Chapter Nineteen

JESUS IS SCOURGED AND HANDED OVER TO BE CRUCIFIED

OVERVIEW. Chapter 19 continues the Passion account begun in the eighteenth chapter. John continues to portray Jesus as the one in command of everything as he accomplishes the purpose for which he has come into the world.

READ 19:1–16

COMMENTARY. Inside the palace, the fourth scene opens with Pilate's decision to have Jesus whipped (19:1). While Mark and Matthew mention that Jesus was first condemned and then scourged, John reverses that sequence. The fourth verse indicates that Pilate ordered the beating as an attempt to save Jesus' life. Perhaps Pilate is being represented as one seeking to gain the crowd's compassion for Jesus. Luke's account of Pilate's words supports this view: "I cannot find he has done anything to deserve death! I will have him whipped and set him free" (Luke 23:22).

During the scourging, the soldiers mock Jesus with crown and purple robe, the symbols of kingship. The soldiers taunt Jesus with the title, "the King of the Jews." Again we confront the irony of the fourth evangelist: Jesus is a king, but he is not the kind of king they are mocking. Long before, Jesus had rejected the people's attempts to make him king (see 6:14–15). During the encounter with Pilate Jesus had declared, "My kingdom does not belong to this world" (18:36).

The fifth scene opens with Pilate's second declaration of the innocence of Jesus (19:4). Pilate displays Jesus before the crowd: "Look! Here is the man!" (19:5) It is difficult to determine precisely what this description of Jesus as "the man" is intended to convey. Pilate is obviously referring to Jesus as the man whom they had accused (see 18:30). Yet, on another level, we hear echoes of the High Priest's prophecy, "Don't you realize that it is better for you to have *one man* die for the people . . . " (11:50). On still another level the words might refer to Jesus as the "Son of Man," a title often related to the crucifixion-exaltation of Jesus.

If it was Pilate's intention to gain pity for "the man," the plan failed. Seeing Jesus, the chief priests and guards demand his crucifixion. Pilate's response, "You take him, then, and crucify him," is more a groan of exasperation than an abdication of his power to sentence Jesus to death (see 19:10). For the third time Pilate refers to the lack of evidence against Jesus (19:6). But the "crowd" objects to Pilate's attestation of Jesus' innocence: "We have a law that says he ought to die, because he claimed to be the Son of God" (19:7). The religious authorities are referring to a passage from the Torah:

> . . . *whoever blasphemes the name of the Lord shall be put to death. The whole community shall stone him* (Leviticus 24:16).

When Pilate hears that the authorities want Jesus dead because he claimed to be the Son of God, he becomes "even more afraid" (19:8). Perhaps his fear is related to his own superstition, but it seems more likely that Pilate is alarmed by the turn of events. Pilate himself lived in fear of a Jewish revolt against the cruel Roman occupation. Jerusalem is filled with Jewish pilgrims, and now the case concerning Jesus has been further complicated by the religious laws of the Jewish people.

Back inside the palace, the sixth scene begins with Pilate asking Jesus, "Where do you come from?" (19:9). Since it is likely that Pilate's political future was insecure, this question indicates that he is trying to avoid an explosive political situation by turning Jesus over to another's jurisdiction. Luke tells us that upon learning that Jesus was from Galilee, Pilate sent Jesus to Herod, who had jurisdiction over Galilee (see Luke 23:4–7). However, on the level of theological meaning, "Where do you come from?" is the most crucial question a person can ask of Jesus. To know where Jesus is from is to believe, for the believer knows that Jesus comes from God. But the unbeliever does not know the ultimate origin of Jesus. That is why those who reject Jesus do so either because they do not know where he is from (see 9:29–30), or because they mistakenly assume that their knowledge of the human origins of Jesus is sufficient (see 6:42 and 7:41–42).

Jesus does not answer Pilate's question. Pilate is annoyed; he reminds Jesus of his power as governor to decide who lives and who dies. Jesus replies that all power ultimately belongs to God, including that very power Pilate is temporarily permitted to exercise over Jesus (19:11). The full meaning of Jesus' words to Pi-

late is found in the context of the Good Shepherd's willingness
to die for his sheep:

> *No one takes my life away from me. I give it up of my own free*
> *will. I have the right to give it up, and I have the right to take it*
> *back. This is what my Father has commanded me to do* (10:17–
> 18).

Jesus' statement regarding the greater guilt of "the man who
handed me over" refers not only to Judas or Caiaphas, but also
to every one of those authorities who had participated in the betrayal of Jesus. The implication is that Pilate bears his own share
of guilt for his role in the perversion of justice for the sake of political expediency (19:11b). Because he did not initiate the betrayal, his guilt is less.

The seventh scene begins as Pilate makes one last effort to
avoid condemning Jesus to death (19:12). However, when the
crowd threatens to denounce him to the Emperor, Pilate yields to
its demands. Although Pilate positions himself on the judge's
seat, he, ironically, is the one who is being judged (19:13).

But Pilate is not the only one being judged in the presence of
Jesus. When Pilate refers to Jesus as "your king," the people
shout back, "Crucify him!" (19:15). When Pilate taunts them,
"Do you want me to crucify your king?" the chief priests respond, "The only king we have is the Emperor" (19:15). This reply is apostasy. For Israel only God or God's representative (the
Messiah) could be their true king:

> *Yahweh our God, other lords than you have ruled us, but we*
> *acknowledge no one other than you, no other name than yours*
> (Isaiah 26:13, *Jerusalem Bible*).

Throughout the Fourth Gospel the author has represented Jesus as replacing the Jewish feasts and institutions. Now, according to John, the religious leaders of the Jewish people have
renounced their covenant relationship with God. (From an historical perspective, it is unlikely that the chief priests intended to
betray the Covenant. John's interpretation of the condemnation

of Jesus reflects the bitterness that existed between the Christians and the synagogue in the late 80's and 90's.) In verse 15 the Jewish crowd has joined the world in its hostile rejection of the one whose kingdom is not of this world (18:36).

Shortly before, Jesus had told Pilate, "the man who handed me over to you is guilty of a worse sin." Now, Pilate himself is placed among the betrayers of Jesus: "Then Pilate handed Jesus over to them to be crucified" (19:16). Immediately before this, John has pointed out that it was almost noon of the day before Passover (19:14). At noon on the preparation day the temple priests began to slaughter the lambs for the Passover meal. Then three interrelated scenes swiftly take place before our mind's eye: the crowd shouts out for the crucifixion of Jesus; Pilate sentences Jesus to death; in the temple area the lambs are being slain in preparation for the Passover.

REFLECTION. Although innocent of crime, Jesus was sentenced to die by crucifixion. Fear, betrayal, and the destruction of justice in favor of political expediency were the human factors that brought Jesus to the cross. While we know in faith that the ultimate reason for the death of Jesus was his love for us, the cross is also the manifestation of human sinfulness. Thus, the cross symbolizes both the love of God for us as well as our own hateful injustice toward one another.

The night-time arrest and the unjust sentencing of Jesus serve to remind us that the same terrible proceedings are being carried out in our own day. In prisons throughout the nations of our world there are men and women who are detained without a hearing, imprisoned on false charges, and worse. Some of these people are murdered with public fanfare, while others are killed within the confines of their cells.

For the sake of our brothers and sisters the world over, and as an expression of our love for the crucified and risen Jesus, something can be done. Since 1961, through the organization of letterwriting campaigns, by the publication of bulletins and reports, and by the sending of observers, an organization known as Amnesty International has prevented the execution of hundreds of political prisoners, has stopped the mistreatment and torture of hundreds more, and has secured the outright release of more than 13,000 others. With a worldwide-membership of 50,000 people Amnesty International applies moral pressure against repressive situations. One of the principal means of protecting the victims of injustice has been the writing of letters to both prisoners and prison authorities. Prisoners learn that they are not completely at the mercy of their captors, others are interested in their welfare. The jailers know this too, as they receive concerned inquiries from someone in Hamburg, Germany, from another in Liverpool, England, and still another in Union City, Tennessee.

Perhaps we have received the gift of freedom so that we can help create it for others. In many areas, concerned Christians have the opportunity to show convicted men and women that other people really care about them and about how their families are surviving. In many instances it is just this kind of interest in a prisoner that gives him or her the motivation to become a citizen who builds up the community.

Amnesty International is located at 2112 Broadway, New York, New York 10023.

JESUS IS CRUCIFIED
READ 19:17–30

COMMENTARY. John does not mention Simon of Cyrene in order to emphasize that this is the "hour" that belongs to Jesus. Thus, Jesus carries his own cross to the place of execution. All four accounts of the Gospel tersely state that they crucified Jesus at the place of the skull; all four accounts mention that two criminals were crucified on either side of Jesus; and all four accounts refer to the inscription fastened to the cross of Jesus: "the King of the Jews." John alone, however, states that the notice was written in Hebrew, Latin, and Greek (19:20). For the fourth evangelist these are the significant sacred and secular languages of his day. Hebrew is the sacred language of the Jewish people. Latin is the language of the Roman Empire. Greek, the language in which John wrote, was the universal language of culture. Perhaps Pilate used the inscription to express his contempt for the Jewish authorities who had threatened to report him to the Emperor

(19:12). Note that Pilate arrogantly refuses to grant the chief priests' request that the inscription be changed (19:21–27).

Understood in Johannine terms, Pilate's inscription symbolizes the enthronement of Jesus upon the cross. The Gentile representative of the world's leading power bears witness that Jesus is indeed a king. The three languages imply the universality of Jesus' mission. The Father had sent his Son because he loved the whole world (3:16). Jesus foretold that on the cross he would draw everyone to himself (12:32). Perhaps too, the inscription echoes the unwitting prophecy of the High Priest:

> It was Caiaphas who had advised the Jewish authorities that it was better that one man should die for all the people (18:14; see 11:50).

While the three Synoptic accounts mention that the soldiers divided the clothes of Jesus among themselves, only John refers to the robe "made of one piece of woven cloth without any seams in it" (19:23). Since a robe of one piece was the garment worn by the High Priest, John infers that Jesus is the final High Priest, the one who is both sacrificer and sacrificed. The seamless robe may also be a symbol of the unity which Jesus so urgently prayed for at the conclusion of the Last Supper (17:20–23). John's basic concern is to show that the gambling for Jesus' clothes fulfills the Scripture. He cites Psalm 22:18 and declares, "This is exactly what the soldiers did" (19:24, *Jerusalem Bible*).

Near the cross are five of Jesus' disciples, four of whom are women (19:25). Of the twelve apostles only John is present. Nevertheless, in spite of all appearances, this is the time and the place where the Church begins. At first the setting appears bleak and inappropriate, particularly when we are more famliar with Luke's portrayal of the birth of the Church on Pentecost. However, when we recall that Jesus is now reigning from the cross, that Jesus has longed for this hour since the very beginning of his public ministry (2:4, 11), that this moment glorifies his Father's name (12:27) and that the cross is the expression of his redeeming love for his disciples (13:1), we realize how appropriate is John's understanding that the Church begins at the foot of the cross.

Mary and the beloved disciple stand near the crucified Jesus. On the historical level Jesus makes provision for his mother's well-being by committing her to the beloved disciple's care: "He is your son. . . . She is your mother" (19:26–27).

On the theological level, Mary has a very special place. Recall that Mary appears only twice in the entire Fourth Gospel, first at Cana and now at Calvary. On both occasions Jesus addressed his mother with the symbolic title, "Woman":

"Woman, how does this concern of yours involve me? My hour has not yet come" (2:4, New American Bible).	Jesus said to his mother, "Woman, there is your son." . . . From that hour onward, the disciple took her into his care (19:26–27, New American Bible).

In giving his mother to be the mother of his disciple, Jesus makes the disciple his own brother. As the Genesis story portrayed Eve as "the Mother of all the living" (Genesis 3:20, *New American Bible*), the Fourth Gospel portrays Mary as the mother of the New Israel, the believing community known as "the Church." The beloved disciple becomes a symbol of the believer. He represents every person born into the Church. Having provided for both his mother and the Church, Jesus knew that by now everything had been completed (19:28).

To fulfill the Scriptures (Psalm 22:15; Psalm 69:21), Jesus says, "I am thirsty" (19:28). We may understand Jesus' thirst in relation to the arrest of Jesus in the garden. When Peter tried to prevent the arrest of his Master, Jesus rebuked, "Do you think that I will not drink the cup of suffering which my Father has given me?" (18:11). The thirst of Jesus is both physical and filial: out of loving obedience to his Father, Jesus longs to drink the cup of suffering completely, for his death will be the source of life for his disciples. Having taken the common wine offered him, Jesus declares: "It is finished!" (19:30). While Matthew and Mark describe Jesus as dying "with a loud cry" (Matthew 27:50 and Mark 15:37), John emphasizes that Jesus' death is his own action: "Then he bowed his head, and delivered over his spirit" (19:30, *New American Bible*). In this we probably have another example of two-fold meaning. On the one hand, the delivering up of his spirit is his dying breath; on the other hand, John may be anticipating the act in which Jesus gives the Spirit, the second Paraclete, to his disciples after he rises from the dead (20:22).

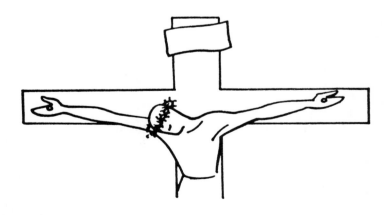

THE SIDE OF JESUS OPENED; HIS BURIAL
READ 19:31–42

COMMENTARY. In deference to religious custom, Pilate allows his soldiers to break the legs of the crucified men. This action hastened death by suffocation. But Jesus was already dead. To make certain this was so, a soldier "plunged his spear into Jesus' side, and at once blood and water poured out" (19:34). This pouring out of blood and water from the side of the crucified Jesus is such a significant event that the author exclaims, "The one who saw this happen has spoken of it, so that you also may believe" (19:35). The water and the blood are related to the very act of believing in Jesus! Verse 34 summarizes the most central themes in the Fourth Gospel. The blood symbolizes the death of Jesus, his hour, the very purpose for which he had been sent into the world. The water symbolizes the Spirit, who could only be given after Jesus passed through death and entered his glory (see 7:39).

By citing Moses' directive in Exodus 12:46, "Not one of his bones will be broken," John accomplishes three purposes. First, he links the fact that the soldiers did not break Jesus' legs with his understanding of Jesus as *the* Paschal Lamb (see 19:14). Secondly, John reminds us of another lamb, the image used by Israel to describe the Suffering Servant:

> *Like a lamb about to be slaughtered,*
> *like a sheep about to be sheared,*
> * he never said a word.*
> *He was arrested and sentenced. . .*
> *He was put to death for the*
> * sins of our people* (Isaiah 53:7–8).

Thirdly, the witness of John the Baptist is recalled to our attention: "There is the Lamb of God who takes away the sin of the world" (1:29).

Jesus hangs upon the cross. He had changed water to wine, healed a dying boy by his powerful word, cured a man who was sick for thirty-eight years, multiplied bread, walked on water,

given sight to a man born blind, and raised a dead man to life. But the cross is the greatest sign of all. The signs Jesus worked were sometimes misunderstood; sometimes they caused division among those who saw them. It is the same with the cross, the crux of faith. For those who will not believe, the cross is merely the inglorious death of a disgraced criminal. For those who believe, the cross is Jesus' passover to the glory he had with the Father before the world was created (see 17:5). For those who refused to believe, the cross was the end of Jesus of Nazareth. For those who believed, the cross revealed the identity of the Son of Man: he is the incarnate Son of God, the one who has revealed himself as "I Am Who I Am." Notice how beautifully the Fourth Gospel has interwoven the cross with the themes of believing, eternal life, and the real identity of Jesus:

> *As Moses lifted up the bronze snake on a pole in the desert, in the same way the Son of Man must be lifted up, so that everyone who believes in him may have eternal life* (3:14–15).

> *So he said to them, "When you lift up the Son of Man, you will know that 'I Am Who I Am'"* (8:28).

> *When I am lifted up from the earth, I will draw everyone to me* (12:32).

> *And there is another Scripture that says, "People will look at him whom they pierced"* (19:37).

While there is a basic difference between the Synoptic and the Johannine traditions regarding the burial of Jesus (according to the Synoptic writers Jesus is buried without being anointed), all four Gospel accounts report that it was Joseph of Arimathea who went to Pilate to request permission to take the body of Jesus. According to Mark, "Joseph went boldly into the presence of Pilate" (15:43). John notes that Joseph was one of the secret followers of Jesus because he had feared the Jewish authorities (19:38). Now he publicly commits himself. Since Jesus had been crucified on the charge of sedition, Joseph was not merely in danger of being ejected from the synagogue, he was also risking his life by identifying himself with a convicted insurrectionist. Nicodemus, who had originally visited Jesus under cover of darkness, accompanies Joseph in anointing and burying the body of Jesus in a nearby tomb. The amount of spices (100 pounds) befits the burial of a royal person. Jesus is buried in haste, with the solemn Passover Sabbath about to begin (19:42).

REFLECTION. The one whom the people have pierced (Zechariah 12:10; John 19:37) is none other than the Father's only Son given in both the Incarnation and in the crucifixion. The Father's motive is one of love for us. It is the privilege of Christian believers to know the true identity of the God-man raised up upon the cross. On the one hand, Jesus is divine. He is of God and has been sent by God. If this were not so, then we would not know the vastness of our Father's love. If Jesus were only a prophet, if he were only a holy and innocent person chosen by God and instructed to deliver a message, then God would remain in his transcendence. While we could know and praise God for his loving deeds done on our behalf, and while we could thank him for Moses and the prophets, we would still only know God through the events of history and through those human beings sent as his prophets.

That is why John insists that the one whom they pierced was Jesus, the Word made flesh, the beloved Son of God and the divine "I Am Who I Am." Jesus, because he is divine, is the manifestation of the Father's love in the most personal way. The Father loved us so much that he gave his only Son. Through Jesus we know the Father intimately. We know him as his children (1:12–13), because in gazing upon the face of the pierced Jesus, we gaze upon the face of our Father: "Whoever has seen me has seen the Father" (14:9).

On the other hand, the one whom they pierced is also like us, a human being. He is like us in all ways (except sin), even down to the dread of the death which each of us will inevitably experience: "Now my heart is troubled. . . . But that is why I came— so that I might go through this hour of suffering" (12:27). Because Jesus is God, he brings the Father close to us. Because Jesus is man, he is close to us. That is why he can be our model for living our ordinary human lives, lives filled with everyday joys and frustrations, friendships and betrayals, achievement and aging, and, in the end, the breathing of our dying breath (19:30). He died loving his friends and keeping faith in his Father's life-giving power.

Among those gazing upon the one "whom they pierced" was Mary, the mother of Jesus. Beneath the cross she has become the mother of the believing community. She is our mother. We relate her with both his death and ours: "Holy Mary, mother of God, pray for us sinners, now, and at the hour of our death. Amen."

STUDY GROUP QUESTIONS

1. Discuss the following statements: (a) From the point of view of Rome, Jesus was guilty of the crime of sedition (19:12, 19–22). (b) From the point of view of the Jewish leaders, Jesus deserved death because he was guilty of blasphemy (10:33; 19:6). (c) From the point of view of the Fourth Gospel, when the hour of Jesus

came, he freely gave himself in death in order to draw all people to himself (3:16; 12:32; 19:30).

2. What significance does the fourth evangelist see in the hour of Jesus' crucifixion (19:14)?

3. According to John's outlook, when does the Church begin? Why?

4. How does the piercing of Jesus' side relate to some of the important themes found in the Fourth Gospel?

5. In the Fourth Gospel, to glorify is to manifest God's presence. How are Cana (see 2:11) and Calvary related as signs? (See 19:37.)

Chapter Twenty

VISITS TO THE EMPTY TOMB

OVERVIEW. By the time that John writes, the traditions of the discovery of the empty tomb by the woman and of the appearances of the risen Jesus to Magdalene and to the apostles are well known. As we have seen so often in our study of the Fourth Gospel, John's primary concern is not to announce "the facts" to those who don't know them. Rather he wants to give his readers that all-important insight into the events of redemption. The meaning of those events can be only perceived in faith, and it is faith that makes possible life in Jesus' name (20:31). In chapter 20, then, the fourth evangelist completes his teaching on what it means to believe that Jesus is the eternal Son of God.

John links the life of the Church in the 90's closely to the Resurrection of Jesus. All the promises which Jesus made in the Last Supper Discourse begin to be fulfilled after his Resurrection. He returns to dwell with the disciples, bringing the gifts of his peace, his joy, his Spirit. Now that the hour has been completed, Jesus becomes the source of eternal life for those who believe in him. The risen Lord sends forth the disciples to continue his redemptive work.

We have seen (particularly in chapters 4, 5, 9 and 11) how the author "dramatizes" the tradition in order to emphasize its deeper significance. In chapter 20 John has structured the resurrection traditions into a drama in two acts, each act being composed of two scenes. The reader should be alert to the similarity between the scenes. Both of the initial scenes focus on the disciples and their coming to faith in the Resurrection. And in the second scene of both acts the evangelist turns his attention to a single disciple and the struggles of that disciple to recognize/believe in the risen Lord.

READ 20:1–18

COMMENTARY. With the conclusion of the Sabbath, Mary Magdalene comes to the tomb to mourn the death of Jesus. Magdalene has a privileged place in the traditions of the Resurrection, being named first in all four Gospel accounts. (The Synoptic evangelists agree that Mary Magdalene was accompanied by other women. We catch a glimpse of that fact in verse 2: *"we* don't know where they have put him!" Because of his catechetical purpose, however, John mentions only Magdalene.) Seeing the stone rolled away, Magdalene concludes that Jesus' body has been stolen and runs to tell Peter and the beloved disciple (20:1–2). Peter holds a special place in all the Resurrection accounts. The fourth evangelist focuses attention also on the beloved disciple (see 13:23 and 19:26), since he has become for the Johannine community the model of the faithful and loving disciple.

The events of verses 3–8 seem to be full of subtle contrasts. Peter's special role among the disciples is acknowledged (he is allowed to enter the tomb first). However, the beloved disciple both arrives first at the tomb (possibly symbolic of his greater love for Jesus) and is the first to come to faith. Both Peter and the other disciple see the same evidence—the cloths in which Jesus' body had been wrapped (20:6–7). The fourth evangelist places a special emphasis on these cloths and their position. Something about their position provided the stimulus for the believing of the beloved disciple. Peter sees them but seemingly does not yet believe in the Resurrection. Luke 24:12 (a verse which is not contained in all manuscripts) indicates that Peter was confused by the evidence.

As is evident, the fact of the empty tomb could be interpreted in a negative way, that Jesus' body had been stolen. John points out that faith in the Resurrection was required even of those who saw the empty tomb! The fourth evangelist is writing for those who were not witnesses of the appearances of the risen Lord. Thus he is concerned about believing without seeing (20:29). In his account of 20:3–8 John is not trying to diminish the important role of Peter (see 21:17). However he does want to highlight the response of the beloved disciple as a model of faith. The beloved disciple is the more perceptive in "reading" the evidence. Even though he has not yet seen the risen Lord, he believes. In verse 9 the evangelist notes that only later did the disciples understand that Jesus' death and Resurrection fulfilled the teaching of the Hebrew Scriptures (see Luke 24:25–27).

Scene two of the first act begins with Mary Magdalene weeping outside the tomb. Grief-stricken by Jesus' death, her sorrow is increased by the thought that his body has been taken away. The evangelist draws our attention to the failure of Magdalene to recognize the risen Jesus. All of the Resurrection accounts give evidence of the difficulty of the disciples in recognizing Jesus. This is important for several reasons. In the first place it answers the argument of those who contended that the disciples had "made up" the story of Jesus' Resurrection. The disciple's failure to recognize the Lord demonstrates that they were as surprised by the Resurrection as everyone else. Secondly, the difficulty in recognizing Jesus emphasizes that in his risen body he is somehow different. His humanity has been transformed.

Without any recognition, Mary sees Jesus and hears him speak (20:14–15). Jesus had been buried in a garden (19:41), and Mary concludes that the man she meets must be the gardener. Only when he calls her by name does she realize that this is the Teacher (20:16). In this meeting of Magdalene and Jesus we have a beautiful fulfillment of Jesus' teaching in 10:3–4:

> . . . *the sheep hear his voice as he calls his own sheep by name,*
> *and he leads them out . . . and the sheep follow him, because they*
> *know his voice.*

Jesus' command to Mary Magdalene, "Do not hold on to me" (20:17), has been interpreted in many different ways. It should be understood in terms of the new relationship to the disciples which Jesus had promised during the Last Supper Discourse. Mary mistakes Jesus' Resurrection appearance for the abiding presence of his promised return (14:18–21). She wants to cling to the "old" presence of his earthly existence. However, Jesus' abiding presence with the disciples after the Resurrection will be different from his dwelling with them during the ministry. He will return in the gift of the Spirit to the Church. He will "touch" the disciples now through the sacraments.

Thus he tells Magdalene that he is even now returning to the Father. She is wrong in clinging to Jesus' (even risen) humanity, since he does not become the life-giving source of the Spirit until he has ascended.

Instead of clinging to Jesus, Magdalene is sent to prepare the disciples to receive the gift of the Spirit. It is the coming of the Spirit that will complete the transformation of the disciples into children of the Father. Since they will have the same Father, Jesus now calls the disciples "my brothers" (20:17).

JESUS APPEARS TO THE DISCIPLES
READ 20:19–31

COMMENTARY. Jesus appears to the disciples on "that Sunday evening" (20:19). The evangelist has a two-fold purpose in using this phrase: (1) he informs us that it is still Easter Sunday. Thus in John's perspective Jesus' Resurrection, return to the Father and giving of the Spirit all take place on the same day. (2) Secondly, he indicates that the end-time begins with the coming of Jesus into the midst of his disciples. (The phrase "that day" is frequently used in the Jewish Scriptures to refer to the end-time. See also its use during the Last Supper, 14:20 and 16:23.)

By noting the locked doors the evangelist emphasizes the spiritual qualities of Jesus' risen body. We should not imagine a ghostly body, however, since Jesus continues to bear the marks of the Passion (20:20) and will later invite Thomas to touch them (20:27). Jesus' presence quickly dispels the fear which had gripped the disciples. His greeting of peace carries the creative power of the divine word: it brings into being that peace which Jesus had promised (14:27). In a similar way Jesus' risen presence fills the disciples with the joy he promised (16:22). Peace, joy and the Holy Spirit (20:22) are all gifts of the end-time.

Jesus comes to the disciples in order to send them out to continue his own mission from the Father (20:21). An apostle (that is, one who has seen the risen Lord) is by definition a missionary, one sent out. The gifts of peace, joy and the Spirit are not to be hoarded for personal gain or enjoyment. They are intended also for the world which God so loves. It is not clear in the text whether the risen Lord appears only to the twelve apostles (minus Judas and Thomas) or to a wider group of disciples. In either case the fourth evangelist intends Jesus' words of commission for all believers. The entire Church continues the work of redemption which Jesus' death has accomplished.

In verse 22 the evangelist summarizes the entire Gospel. At the very beginning of the ministry John the Baptist testified that the Spirit had come to dwell with Jesus; thus Jesus was empowered to baptize with the Holy Spirit (1:32–33). Although the Father gave the fullness of his Spirit to his Son (3:34), Jesus was not to become a source of the Spirit for the disciples until the Resurrection. Frequently during his last conversation with the disciples Jesus spoke of the Spirit he would send from the Father (e.g., 14:26 and 15:26). Now Jesus' "work" is finished and he has handed over his breath/spirit (19:30). Jesus pours out the Spirit upon the disciples by breathing on them, saying, "Receive the Holy Spirit" (20:22). By his choice of the Greek verb for "breathe" John reminds the reader of the original moment of creation:

> *Then the Lord God took some soil from the ground and formed a man out of it; he breathed life-giving breath into his nostrils and the man began to live* (Genesis 2:7).

In the beginning the breath of Yahweh transformed the clay of the earth into a living being. Now the breath of Jesus transforms life-from-below into life-from-above, earthly life into eternal life (see 3:3, 5). John understands this moment in terms of a re-creation of humanity. The vision of Ezekiel finds its fulfillment (Ezekiel 37:1–14).

During the Last Supper Jesus spoke of the many roles of the Holy Spirit: abiding with the disciples (14:16), teaching and bringing them to remembrance (14:26), speaking about Jesus (15:26), proving the world wrong about sin and judgment (16:8) and leading the disciples into all truth (16:13). The gift of the Spirit will also enable the disciples to continue Jesus' work of forgiving sins (20:23). There is a strong similarity between 20:23 and the words of Jesus about binding and loosing in Matthew 16:19 to Peter and 18:18 to the disciples, *Jerusalem Bible.* In both Jesus promises that God will ratify the decisions of the Church as she exercises the power of forgiveness.

Regarding 20:23b, the disciples do not arbitrarily withhold forgiveness from a repentant sinner. This verse should be understood in light of Jesus' sayings about judgment. He does not condemn anyone; yet the person who deliberately refuses to believe condemns himself/herself. Those who refuse to respond to the preaching of the disciples are not forgiven. In the early tradition of the Church 20:23 was related to baptismal forgiveness. Later generations came to understand that it is the foundation for the sacrament of Reconciliation.

In 20:24–29, John highlights the struggle of an individual disciple to come to faith in the risen Lord. Thomas refuses to accept the testimony of the other disciples. He demands a tangible proof that the one they have seen is the same Jesus of Nazareth who was crucified (20:25). The evangelist wants to contrast the joyful enthusiasm of the disciples ("We have seen the Lord!") with Thomas' stubborn doubt ("Unless I see . . . ").

Verses 26–28 describe Thomas' growth in faith. Appearing to the disciples for a second time, Jesus challenges Thomas to change his attitude and to put aside his hesitation to believe. Thomas responds with the clearest and most complete profession of faith found in the Fourth Gospel: "My Lord and my God!" (20:28). Encountering the risen Lord in person, Thomas no longer needs to probe the wounds of Jesus (20:25). Thomas penetrates the "sign" of the cross in his encounter with the risen Jesus. Now

Thomas knows the meaning of Jesus' death-resurrection-return to the Father. Thomas addresses Jesus with the same titles which Israel used for Yahweh. Thus the last words of a disciple in the Gospel demonstrate that the desire of the Father is accomplished: "That all will honor the Son in the same way as they honor the Father" (5:23).

Jesus' final words in the Fourth Gospel are directed to us—believers who have not seen the risen Lord with our own eyes. As the Gospel concludes, Jesus envisions the new type of faith which will characterize all those who will believe on the basis of the preaching of the apostles. Jesus contrasts the disciples who have both seen and believed with us, his future disciples who will believe because of the testimony of the apostles:

> *Blest are they who have not seen and have believed* (20:29, *New American Bible*).

This is the second and final "beatitude" found in the Fourth Gospel. The first accompanied Jesus' action of washing the feet of his disciples. Having given them an example of the way they should serve one another Jesus declared:

> *Once you know all these things, blest will you be if you put them into practice* (13:17, *New American Bible*).

Thus, loving and believing are the fundamental responses of the disciple of Jesus.

There is no nostalgia in the Fourth Gospel for "the good old days." New disciples will not be regarded as second-class Christians because they have not seen the Lord. Jesus remains in the midst of his disciples through his Spirit. He continues to speak to them a word which gives life. He continues to work his powerful miracles through the sacraments of the Church.

It is exactly for this reason, the evangelist concludes, that he has written this book (20:30–31). The believers of John's own community will "see" the risen Lord both in the sacraments and in the written account of his miracles. John has written primarily for those who already believe that Jesus is Messiah and Son of God. He is concerned that they continue in belief, for that faith opens the door to eternal life.

REFLECTION. In his *Spiritual Exercises* St. Ignatius Loyola recommends the beautiful prayer "Anima Christi." Several of the verses of this prayer reflect the devotion of the Church to the wounds of Jesus: "blood of Christ fill all my veins; water from Christ's side wash out my stains . . . in your wounds I wish to hide. . . ." The wounds of Jesus have an important role in the Johannine community. In addition to proving that the risen Lord is the same Jesus who had been crucified, the wounds are the "badge" of Jesus' victory. They testify eloquently to the costliness of our redemption and therefore to the great love of the crucified Lord for his disciples.

The wounds of Jesus in chapter 20 also teach us that Jesus retained his humanity when he returned to the Father. Remember that in the Johannine perspective Jesus pours out the Holy Spirit only after his return to the Father (16:7). In 20:17 he tells Mary Magdalene that he is in the act of ascending to the Father. When Jesus appears to the disciples on Easter evening (20:19–23) his body is glorified, but it remains a human body. The wounds of the Passion are still present. A parallel text in the book of Revelation contains the same teaching: "I saw a Lamb standing, a Lamb that had been slain" (Revelation 5:6).

Sometimes believers assume that the Second Person of the

Trinity took on our human nature for a time and then discarded it when his earthly mission was completed. Catholic devotion to the wounds of Jesus leads us to a more adequate understanding (theology). Jesus intercedes for the disciples before the Father by the witness of his wounds. The wounds of Jesus are a living reminder (1) to the Father that his Son has given his life for his disciples, and (2) to us that our humanity has been taken up into heaven, to the right hand of the Father. Believing in Jesus as the Son of God is at the same time believing that our humanity has been exalted to a participation in the divine life.

STUDY GROUP QUESTIONS

1. Why was Mary Magdalene given the privilege of discovering the empty tomb and being the first to see the risen Lord?

2. Why did the beloved disciple believe (20:8) while Peter seemingly did not?

3. Relate the statement, "there was no nostalgia in the early Church," to Jesus' saying in 20:17.

4. Role-play the scene in 20:19–23 in two ways: (1) Jesus chides the disciples for their loss of faith on Good Friday and for their present-fearful attitude; (2) as it actually occurred. Relate the two "scenes" just role-played to people's experience of the sacrament of Reconciliation.

5. In what ways are we like doubting Thomas?

6. In what ways has your study of the Fourth Gospel increased your faith (20:31)?

Chapter Twenty-One

JESUS APPEARS IN GALILEE

OVERVIEW. The assertion that "these have been written in order that you may believe that Jesus is the Messiah, the Son of God" (20:31) probably concluded the "first edition" of the Fourth Gospel. It is likely that both the prologue (1:1–18) and the epilogue (chapter 21) were added to the original edition by the final editor. The fact that all of the early manuscripts of the Fourth Gospel contain both the prologue and chapter 21 indicates that these verses were added not long after the first edition had been completed for circulation. The epilogue contains material from the Johannine tradition that was not included in the earlier account. Nevertheless, the authority of John stands behind the entire tradition. Furthermore, from the beginning the Church has accepted the material in this chapter as inspired by God.

Chapter 21 provides us with a fascinating glimpse of life in the Church around the year 100 A.D. These verses focus particularly on issues that deal with the relation of the Johannine community to the Church at large: the primacy of Peter as shepherd of the sheep; the martyrdom of Peter; and the relationship of the death of the beloved disciple to the second coming of Jesus.

READ 21:1–14

COMMENTARY. The phrase, "after this" (21:1) has the general meaning of "at another time." It may well be that some of the events narrated in chapter 21 actually took place before the material found in chapter 20. Thus, the Resurrection appearance of Jesus recounted in 21:1–13 could well be an account of the first appearance of Jesus to his disciples. In order to harmonize this incident with the preceding two appearances of the risen Jesus to the eleven (20:19–23 and 20:26–29), the writer of the epilogue refers to this Galilean appearance as "the third time Jesus appeared to the disciples after he was raised from death" (21:14).

If this Galilean appearance actually occurred first, even though it is listed as the third appearance of Jesus, then several details are more easily understood. First, the very fact that Peter and some of the disciples are back in Galilee (on Lake Tiberias) fulfills the prophecy of Jesus:

> *The time is coming, and is already here, when all of you will be scattered, each one* to his own home . . . (16:32).

Verse 3 seems to indicate that Peter has gone back to his old way of making a living as a fisherman. Several others have joined him. Secondly, when Jesus appears at the water's edge, the disciples do not recognize him. This is a characteristic of each of the first appearances of the risen Jesus. If this account were the third time Jesus had appeared to them, it would be unlikely that they would fail to recognize a risen Jesus by now familiar. Yet, even after they are on the shore, there is hesitation about his identity: "None of the disciples dared ask him, 'Who are you?' because they knew it was the Lord" (21:12).

Although they had caught nothing all night, by following the stranger's directions they net a huge number of fish. Again we see Peter side-by-side with the disciple whom Jesus loved. Both of them had been together during the Last Supper (13:23–24), and both of them had raced to the empty tomb (20:3–10). The beloved disciple "saw and believed" there at the tomb (20:9). Now, the beloved disciple tells Peter, "It is the Lord!" (21:7)

The relationship of Peter and the beloved disciple seems to tell us much about the relationship between the Johannine community and the larger Church. Throughout the Fourth Gospel we have seen instances in which John is in dialogue with other Christian communities, telling them that the understanding of Jesus found in the Johannine Church was the full truth. As the disciple whom Jesus loved declares to Peter, "It is the Lord!" we can read between the lines an assertion that the followers of John are the ones who possess an adequate understanding of Jesus. Their founder, the beloved disciple, perceived the true identity of Jesus sooner than all the others—even Peter, the one chosen by Jesus to lead the community. Through their teacher, the disciple whom

Jesus loved, they came to understand Jesus as the divine Son of God, while the other Christian communities were still talking about Jesus as the Messiah and the Prophet foretold by Moses.

Nevertheless, the Johannine community is in communion with the other Christian communities through their acceptance of the role of Peter. While John recognizes Jesus as the Lord, Peter immediately dives into the water and comes to Jesus before the others. It is Peter who takes the initiative in hauling the fish net to shore after Jesus requests that some fish be brought to him (21:10–11). The net that Peter drags ashore is filled with 153 large fish.

The observation that the net did not tear despite a large number of fish (19:11) probably refers to the unity of the Church, sustained in spite of the vast number of converts entering the community. Recall that the author had also taken care to point out that the seamless robe of Jesus had not been torn by the soldiers who crucified Jesus (19:23–24).

Some commentators think that originally the catch of fish was an incident separate from the account of the meal Jesus shares with his disciples. Arriving at the shore, the fishermen see a charcoal fire, fish and some bread (21:9). Notice the similarity between verse 13 and the account of Jesus' multiplication of the bread and fish in chapter six:

Jesus took the bread, gave thanks to God, and distributed it to the people who were sitting there. He did the same with the fish. . . . (6:11).	So Jesus went over, took the bread, and gave it to them; he did the same with the fish (21:13).

It is clearly a eucharistic meal. As the reader comes to the end of the Gospel, he or she realizes that the signs Jesus worked during his ministry continue in the "signs" that are now the sacramental rituals of the community. On Easter night the risen Jesus gave his disciples the gift of the Spirit (20:22). Now, on the shores of Lake Tiberias, the risen Jesus reveals himself and gives them the gift of life he had promised them and us: "The bread I will give is my flesh, for the life of the world" (6:51b, *New American Bible*). Over nineteen centuries later, we the descendants of the second and third generation Christians for whom John wrote the Fourth Gospel, continue to encounter Jesus in the breaking of the bread.

JESUS AND PETER

OVERVIEW. The first section of chapter 21 emphasized a missionary theme: the disciples were presented as fishers of men with Peter as their leader. Verses 15 through 19 have a pastoral theme: Peter is the disciple who is entrusted with the care of the faithful. The author continues to show that the Johannine community acknowledges the primacy of Peter along with the other believing communities. Jesus chose Peter to lead those who come to life through faith.

READ 21:15–19

COMMENTARY. Three times Jesus asks, "Simon son of John, do you love me?" At the heart of the issue is the scope and depth of Peter's love for Jesus. We are accustomed to relate this passage to Peter's three denials of Jesus in the courtyard of the High Priest (18:15–27). However, while the questions may be read as an opportunity for Peter to repent publicly and be reinstated as a disciple, there is a more basic significance in this exchange between Jesus and Peter. Each time Peter declares his love, Jesus replies, "Take care of my lambs/sheep." Thus, Jesus is drawing a total commitment from Peter in view of the awesome responsibility he is receiving as the shepherd of the believing community.

In verse 18 Jesus explains to Peter what taking care of the flock will mean. The basic point of the comparison between Peter as a young man and an old man is this: the youth followed his own inclinations and went in any direction he chose to go; but the old man can no longer move about. He can only go where another will carry him. Jesus is telling Peter that from this point on his life can have only one direction. The responsibility for the community demands total dedication. No longer will Peter have the choice of loving Jesus up to a point, and then returning to the old way of life (as hinted at in 21:2–3).

Verse 19 points out that following Jesus in the role of the Good Shepherd is to follow Jesus to death itself. The lamp of God's glory will burn with the oil of Peter's life. Tradition tells us that Peter died a martyr's death in Rome during Nero's persecution (64 A.D.).

JESUS AND THE OTHER DISCIPLE, THE SECOND CONCLUSION
READ 21:20–25

COMMENTARY. Even though Jesus is risen, the evangelist still envisions his disciples walking with their Master (21:20). Having been told, "Follow me!" (21:10), Peter is doing exactly that when he observes John following too. Peter, now knowing what his own future holds, seems to be curious about what will happen to the beloved disciple. Jesus does not satisfy Peter's curiosity. Jesus' gentle rebuke in verse 22 reminds Peter that John's future is not his concern. Peter's responsibility is following Jesus (21:22).

Verse 23 tells us that some people had interpreted the words of Jesus to mean that the beloved disciple would not die before the second coming. This was coupled with the expectation of the early Christians that Jesus would soon return. We may suppose that, when John did die before the return of Jesus (perhaps shortly before the Fourth Gospel was circulated), his death was an embarrassing disappointment for the Johannine community. With great pastoral sensitivity, the final editor of the Gospel gives an account of how "a report spread among the followers of Jesus that this disciple would not die" (21:23).

The second conclusion (21:24–25) is modeled after the original conclusion of 20:30–31. The editor points to the beloved disciple, the witness whose authority stands behind the Fourth Gospel: "He is the disciple who spoke of these things, the one who also wrote them down (caused them to be written down); and we know that what he said is true" (21:24).

Verse 25 refers to the literary plan of the Fourth Gospel. Only a small number of Jesus' signs were selected, so that their meaning could be explored in the light of the understanding given by the Spirit. Books that would contain an exhaustive treatment of all that Jesus did are unnecessary. Believing on the basis of the community's faith is sufficient. Every believer of every generation encounters the risen Jesus in the preaching and in the sacramental signs celebrated by the believing community.

REFLECTION. Referring to the spiritual roots of the Johannine community, the author of the epilogue stated: "We know that what John said is true." At the end of this long and searching ascent to the place that the Eagle (the traditional symbol for the fourth evangelist) has led us, we recognize that the faith of John and the faith of his community is our faith. The opening words of John's First Letter sum up where we have been and where we now find ourselves:

We write to you about the Word of life, which has existed from the very beginning. We have heard it, and we have seen it with our eyes; yes, we have seen it, and our hands have touched it. When this life became visible, we saw it; so we speak of it and tell you about the eternal life which was with the Father and was made known to us. What we have seen and heard we announce to you also, so that you will join with us in the fellowship that we have with the Father and with his Son Jesus Christ. We write this in order that our joy may be complete (1 John 1:1–4).

Our journey through John has brought us to the mountain top of faith:

No one has ever seen God. The only Son, who is the same as God and is at the Father's side, he has made him known (1:18).

STUDY GROUP QUESTIONS

1. Why is the author so interested in the relation between Peter and the disciple whom Jesus loved? How are 20:8 and 21:7 related?

2. Jesus breaks bread and shares it with his disciples (21:13). Discuss this statement: "In 21:13 we find another Johannine assertion that Jesus continues to act in the sacramental liturgy of the believing community."

3. According to the Gospel of Matthew, the faith of Peter (in the risen Jesus) is the rock upon which the Church is built (see

Matthew 16:13–19). What is the Fourth Gospel's view of the basis of Peter's leadership of the Church?

4. In light of 21:25, compare the Fourth Gospel with the Synoptic Gospels.

5. Your ascent up the mountain of faith now finds you at the summit of faith. From the mountain peak of the Fourth Gospel, look back over the trails you have climbed. Share with each other some of the views you have enjoyed.